Beat Your Depression For Good
Move from Rats' Den Misery to Palace Happiness

DEMI SCHNEIDER

Copyright © 2013–2014 Demi Schneider.

All rights reserved. No part of this book may be used or reproduced by any means, graphic, electronic, or mechanical, including photocopying, recording, taping or by any information storage retrieval system without the written permission of the publisher except in the case of brief quotations embodied in critical articles and reviews.

Balboa Press books may be ordered through booksellers or by contacting:

Balboa Press
A Division of Hay House
1663 Liberty Drive
Bloomington, IN 47403
www.balboapress.com
1 (877) 407-4847

Because of the dynamic nature of the Internet, any web addresses or links contained in this book may have changed since publication and may no longer be valid. The views expressed in this work are solely those of the author and do not necessarily reflect the views of the publisher, and the publisher hereby disclaims any responsibility for them.

The author of this book does not dispense medical advice or prescribe the use of any technique as a form of treatment for physical, emotional, or medical problems without the advice of a physician, either directly or indirectly. The intent of the author is only to offer information of a general nature to help you in your quest for emotional and spiritual well-being. In the event you use any of the information in this book for yourself, which is your constitutional right, the author and the publisher assume no responsibility for your actions.

Printed in the United States of America.

ISBN: 978-1-4525-9635-8 (sc)
ISBN: 978-1-4525-9637-2 (hc)
ISBN: 978-1-4525-9636-5 (e)

Library of Congress Control Number: 2014907222

Balboa Press rev. date: 9/10/2014

PLEASE NOTE:

There are 2 free audio downloads or, if you prefer, 2 purchasable CDs that accompany this book which will greatly assist your journey out of depression for good.

Please visit www.demischneider.com

Experience the benefit of them as you read through this book.

With love and blessings.

Contents

Foreword ix
Acknowledgements xi
Introduction xiii

Chapter One   *The Palace Or The Rats' Den?* 1
Chapter Two   *What's Stopping Us Packing Our Bags?* . . . 11
Chapter Three   *Dealing With The Rats* 25
Chapter Four   *The King Rats* 39
Chapter Five   *Forgiveness* 61
Chapter Six   *Learning To Live In The Palace* 65
Chapter Seven   *Palace Protocol And Etiquette* 89
Chapter Eight   *Boarding Up The Rats' Den - Part One* 95
                       - Part Two . . . 113
Chapter Nine   *Staying In The Palace* 123
Chapter Ten   *The Palace Regime* 127
Chapter Eleven   *Relationships* 131
Chapter Twelve   *The Way To Lasting Happiness* 147
Chapter Thirteen   *My Life Ambition* 167
Chapter Fourteen   *Time For Action* 171
Chapter Fifteen   *Real Life Scenarios* 193

Recommended Resources 210
Recommended Listening 211
Recommended Reading 215

Foreword

"Beat your Depression for Good" is an elegant and enjoyable book.

It combines all the best aspects of well-researched modern psychotherapy with sound metaphysical principles and good old common sense. Demi uses her knowledge of neuroscience to give us a real insight into how our brains work and she does it in a beautifully creative metaphorical way.

It is essentially a 'doing' book. It is so easy, as many of us know, to suffer as a result of the stresses and strains of modern living. Sadly this can sometimes manifest itself in the clinical illnesses of Depression and Anxiety and the multitude of symptoms that can be associated with them. Depression and Anxiety are essentially primitive negative 'clamps'. "Beat your Depression for Good" will show you how to break the bonds, leave them behind and move successfully, and happily, into the future.

We can choose to take control of our lives when wise people give us the facts on which to safely base decisions and harness the inner strengths which all of us possess. "Beat your Depression for Good" is a wise book.

David Newton
Fellow of The Association for Professional Hypnosis and Psychotherapy
Senior Lecturer Clifton Practise Hypnotherapy Training
Trustee and Chair of the Association for Solution Focused Hypnotherapy

Acknowledgements

It is with great joy and immense gratitude I thank all the wonderful teachers I have had over the years: Louise Hay, Patricia Crane, Janeen Detrick, Bronwyn Carson, Sacha Knop and David Newton, all of whom have contributed so much to helping me become the person I am today; a far happier and more fulfilled soul than I could ever have imagined. I would also like to acknowledge the numerous others from whom I have learned, through their books and other media.

Enormous gratitude goes to those who have given their services so willingly to enable me to teach my courses: my good friend Sandy Gliddon for the photo shoot for my Depression Busting Courses website, Mark Harper for his beautiful compositions for the CD tracks 'Relaxation for Sleep' and 'White Light Treatment', Richard Clatworthy for my computer lessons (and his incredible patience!) and my brilliant brother, Derek Kitchener, for creating and maintaining my websites and for being my computer oracle and rescuer.

I want to thank each and every one of my clients, from whom I have learned so much. I have grown through all my experiences and bless you all with love and appreciation.

I send love and big cuddles to my beautiful daughter for her enthusiasm and awesome ability to remind me of things I've taught *her* and what's important in life!

Finally, I'd like to thank my dear friends: Carolyn Palmer and Jane Bennett for their constant support and valuable help and a very, very special thank you to Dawn Harrison for all her indispensible editing input often till the wee hours, her support, belief, energy and technical assistance!

I love you all and dedicate this book to you in joy, pleasure and gratitude.

Introduction

If you're looking for a genuine and practical way to Beat Your Depression for Good you have just found it.

In this book I guide you through a unique and powerful process based on the Depression Busting Course I founded and teach in my online courses and retreats, which I developed from some twenty years of personal experience and much professional training. I know that if you really work with what is here, assimilate it, integrate it and LIVE it your life will change forever.

I've had many challenges in my own life and, in the past known depression and despair myself, so I do know how you feel. I also know, first hand, the incredible benefit of what I teach. I have learned to live well and feel good about myself and my life just because I am alive, regardless of what is going on around me. I have a happy, rich and fulfilling life through living exactly what I am sharing here. I know I will never experience depression ever again.

It gives me great joy to have helped so many people as clients and even greater joy to now reach people globally with this book, including you. With a unique and simple approach to take back command of your own mind, I give new understanding and insight to enable swift progress out of the mire and back into the sunshine again – for good.

This goes way beyond 'head therapies' as I call them. It is true that if we're thinking good thoughts we feel good, and if we're thinking bad thoughts we feel bad. However, "Beat Your Depression For Good" is about achieving what we *really* want: to feel good about ourselves, our life and our future and know we have the power to stay this way; to be able to overcome our issues, handle life's challenges, to have good relationships, a satisfying career, financial security - and most of all to have inner peace, joy, good health, wonderful experiences and love.

Feel the relief and the sense of taking back your own power as you once again walk your own self-honouring path, aligned with your true integrity. Each step becomes easier and more rewarding as the landscapes along your life's journey become increasingly rich and vibrant, so that walking this path is a pleasure all in itself.

Enjoy the journey now back to the 'real you' and a great life ahead!

Chapter One
The Palace Or The Rats' Den?

So, you're feeling depressed, or at least not as good as you'd like to feel.

There are all the reasons that we know or can think of, or sometimes even for no apparent reason, why we're in this miserable space yet there seems no real answer. It's like we're living in a Dark Den full of Rats and Big Spiders and can't get out. We just know we feel bad and stuck.

We yearn to have the relief of feeling good, feeling able to participate in life fully, feeling confident and motivated, able to live well, embrace joy and feel it for real, deep within, don't we?

This is the exciting journey I guide people through when they come on my courses and that I'm going to share with you in this book. You need never know depression again! Instead you can learn to live well and 'come home to yourself' so you feel good just because you're alive.

If it seems a little overwhelming, take heart. Once you understand the straightforward process and concepts laid out here and follow the simple exercises, the small Cut-Out section towards the back of this book is all you'll need to work with to assimilate everything here and create a life of lasting happiness.

How Your Mind Works

To begin our journey out of depression for good and into the dynamic place where we want to be, (and stay!) let's first understand what's going on in our brain, our own mind, which of course is where the depression is living. We can then understand how it is created and what we can do to rectify it.

The brain is an incredibly complex organ, in fact the most complex thing in the known universe, with immense power! The images of the brain shown below are purely for illustrative purposes and do not represent the scientific positioning of the parts of the brain mentioned; we don't need to get that technical to understand or overcome our problem. For our purposes simplicity is sufficient and, no doubt, preferable.

Figure 1 shows an oval representing your brain. You can see the grey oval inside it representing your *prefrontal cortex.* This is your consciousness, the part that you know as 'you', your perceptions, interactions, awareness and so on. This conscious part can be positive, in the left prefrontal cortex, or negative, in the right prefrontal cortex. It makes up only about 10% of your brain. About 90% is subconscious!

FIG. 1

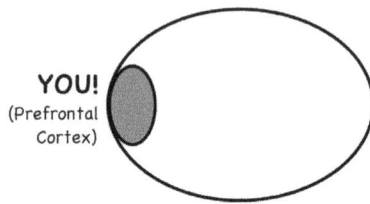

The subconscious part of the brain on the left side has evolved since our caveman days, some 1.7 million years ago. This part of our mind is phenomenal! It has the incredible ability to think for itself and is called our *intellectual mind;* see Figure 2. It is very positive and, instead of freaking out or throwing our hands up in despair, we can make sensible assessments of things and be rational. It has a vast resource with all our answers and solutions and we naturally perform well and achieve meaningful results. We live well. It's like living in a splendid Palace, feeling good about our selves and our world, even if sometimes our world isn't quite how we'd prefer. We can cope with life's challenges and unexpected 'lemons' without slipping into depression.

It's never 'what happens' that is the problem, it's what we *think* about the problem that makes the difference between finding ways forward or being overwhelmed with misery. In the Palace part of our brain we can always make positive choices for ourselves.

FIG. 2

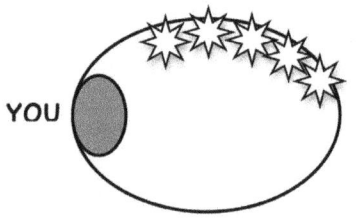

PALACE MIND
(Intellectual Mind)
*An intellect; can think for itself
*Positive
*Makes sensible assessments
*Rational
*Vast resource of answers & solutions
*Performs well & lives well
*Achieves

The problem is that we also have the original caveman part of our brain, called our primitive mind, which is a very different story; see Figure 3. Imagine a caveman coming out of his cave in the morning. He has to be immediately on the alert for the potential danger out there, which is hardly a calm and relaxed feeling to start his day! If he sees a woolly mammoth he can't possibly relax his guard and think "I'll be ok - that woolly mammoth has probably already had his breakfast"; he must immediately anticipate the worst and run back in his cave for safety. His primitive mind then continuously needs to remind him the woolly mammoth is out there so he keeps guard and doesn't wander out ten minutes later to get snaffled up.

Essentially this part is all about our survival so is always very negative, looking for the worst possible scenario in everything and then constantly reminding us of any perceived threat, lest our survival be put at risk.

The worst thing, from our depression perspective, is that this primitive mind is not an intellect so it can't find ways forward; it can only use the negative data it's stored over the years (in your *hippocampus*) to remember how you've 'survived' before and encourage you to do the same again. It can't work out that you have beliefs and patterns and behaviours that don't serve you; it just records what you've done before and encourages you to repeat these patterns and behaviours, because as you've 'survived' before they must be good! This primitive part would be our Rats' Den.

Let's take the example of smoking. Everyone now knows that smoking can kill you and it says so on all the packets. The Palace intellectual part of your mind knows the sensible thing to do is to give up smoking because of all the reasons, including health, that would benefit you, yet your Rats' Den primitive part knows you smoked 20 cigarettes yesterday and survived, so encourages you to smoke another 20 cigarettes today - even though it's killing you! It doesn't have the intellect to realise that this is to your detriment, even though it wants you to survive.

FIG 3

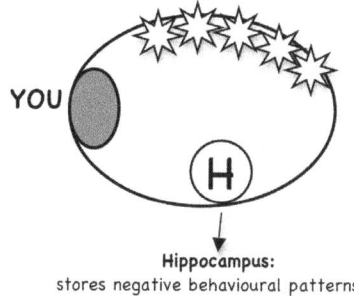

Hippocampus:
stores negative behavioural patterns

PALACE MIND ☺

RATS' DEN MIND
(Primitive Mind)
*All about Survival
*Negative
*Only sees worst case scenarios
*NOT an intellect; just stores data and encourages you to repeat it even if detrimental

This applies to all the negative programming and beliefs that we took on board right from birth. We are each made up of our mother's DNA and our father's DNA, thus we can look like them and have certain similar traits. Fundamentally however, we learn about our selves and our world from our environment and the people surrounding us. By the time we're just five years old we have developed a firmly ensconced 'blueprint' from which we live. If we've had a difficult background it's easy to see where our negative data has come from. Yet even when we've had a very happy childhood it is likely we still received messages such as "When you're good you're approved of and when you're naughty you're disapproved of" or "You must always put other people first" or "Look at that terrible thing those other people did" or "You're only good enough if you get good grades in school" and so on. These lead us to believe our worth is dependent on external approval, to feel we're not as deserving as others, to be judgmental, or feel 'not good enough'. None of these serve us yet are faithfully stored in the hippocampus without evaluation (the primitive mind not being an intellect) and we live by them and then experience the frustration of living by them!

To add to the misery further, this part of the mind, having only the capacity of a small child or an animal, is very good at 'upping the ante' or even 'throwing tantrums' to drag you back to where its stored data says you need to be in order to survive. Hence when you try to change habits or behaviours or do things differently, it is very good at pulling you back to your old ways - like giving you a big craving when you're trying to give up cigarettes or talking you out of doing something positive for yourself. Then you give in and get to beat yourself up all over again, all of this being stored in your hippocampus to then encourage you to repeat again! (Is this sounding familiar?) And, just like a small child who seeks comfort from 'bad feelings' by hugging a teddy or sucking their thumb, as adults we seek comfort from this misery in the form of cigarettes, alcohol, drugs, comfort eating, chocolate, OCD, over-spending, self-harming, crying, staying in bed, or whatever else you've chosen. And we know these things only bring us temporary relief because it's not long before we need another cigarette, drink, etc.

What happens is that when we have a genuine positive experience we produce certain brain waves that trigger the production of serotonin (the chemical that makes us feel good). When you choose your 'comfort' or 'relief' option, your mind has the belief pattern this will make you feel better and that you'll survive (false positive experience), so the same brain waves are produced. However the brain is then fooled into accepting the substitute chemicals in the 'relief' option instead of producing serotonin. Hence a genuine good experience can keep you feeling satisfied for a long time while the 'comfort' choices only keep you satisfied for a very short time before you need another fix.

Beat Your Depression For Good

No wonder being in this part of the brain feels like living in that Dark Den with all the Rats and Big Spiders. You may be realising already just how many Rats you've been nurturing!

Often anxiety is associated with depression. The awful feelings of breathlessness, churning tummy, sweaty palms - right up to a full panic attack - are all the result of your *amygdala* stepping in. In the quest for survival the amygdala triggers a rush of adrenalin to enable you to react quickly in the event of threat. This is useful if you are in a burning building or in some other potentially life threatening situation to make good your speedy escape. However, when you're living in the Rats' Den, where you're constantly on the alert for the danger and assuming the worst possible scenarios, your anxiety levels rise. The amygdala consequently responds to this risen level of threat and triggers the 'fight or flight' response, as it's known, in less and less serious situations; see Figure 4. Effectively, instead of the 'threat alarm' being triggered by a real fire it gets triggered because you've burnt the toast! It's not a pleasant way to live.

FIG 4

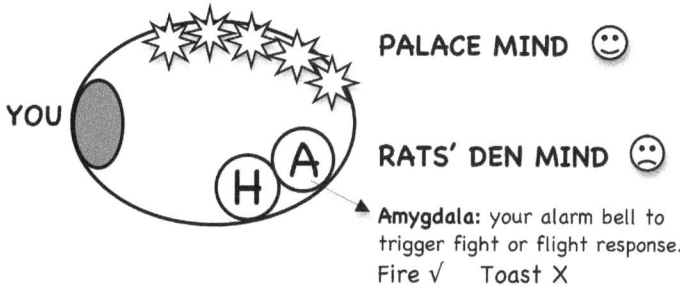

Amygdala: your alarm bell to trigger fight or flight response.
Fire √   Toast X

Another relevant part of the brain for our purpose is the *hypothalamus* because it produces our chemicals. As noted, the chemical we want to be producing is serotonin. (When we're really happy we can produce chemicals all the way up to dopamine). When we're producing lots of serotonin we're very brave, coping, happy little souls. When we're in the Rats' Den we only produce anxiety chemicals such as noradrenaline and cortisol (which is very damaging to our health) or, in the case of depression, we don't produce any chemicals at all - and then we wonder why we're miserable! See Figure 5. (N.B. Many anti-depressants just keep any serotonin you are producing in your system a bit longer - they don't change anything).

Demi Schneider

FIG 5

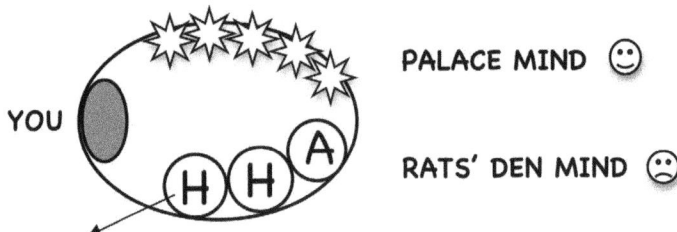

Hypothalamus: produces chemicals; we want Serotonin. In our Rats' Den we only produce anxiety chemicals, or in depression, none at all!

With this new understanding, it is very evident the desirable place to live is in your Palace mind. So the question is, how did you instead come to be in your Rats' Den feeling low and depressed?

The simple answer is this: *by having negative thoughts.*

Every single time you have a negative thought you slip out of your Palace into your Rats' Den to a greater or lesser extent. The Palace is positive so you can't be in there with a negative thought!

We have some 60,000 - 90,000 thoughts a day. The question is, typically, how many of yours are negative? This can often be quite a revelation in itself.

I find many people think they're positive but actually are *not* as they're being positive about their *problems*. If we spend our lives fixing problems it's like being in the Rats' Den trying to exterminate all the Rats. We're still in the Rats' Den. Even if we were able to get rid of them for a while, we'd just be stood looking at a dark empty Den. Where's the joy in that? And more Rats (problems) will soon arrive because life is full of challenges. In the Palace we don't give the power to the problem. In the Palace we engage our wonderful *anterior cingulate gyrus* to enable us to move forward.

If you're feeling anything less than good, let alone depressed, your thoughts are clearly on the negative side to a greater or lesser extent and you will no doubt be experiencing at least some of the unpleasant consequences.

All our negative thoughts go into what I will call our 'stress bucket'. If you have so many negative thoughts your bucket overflows, you may experience a panic attack or irritable bowel syndrome or various other unpleasant manifestations. It's a very unpleasant place, that Rats' Den!

We have a marvellous way of emptying our bucket each night in the part of our sleep known as REM (Rapid Eye Movement) which makes up about 20% of our sleep pattern.

During this time the Rats' Den primitive mind and the Palace intellectual mind come together and the negatives and problems in the Rats' Den are transferred to the Palace where they can be dealt with, thus releasing them from our bucket. You may recall the old adage: 'if you've got a problem sleep on it - you'll feel better in the morning' which is the result of this process.

Ideally we have just a little (healthy) stress in our bucket at the end of our day, we are able to go to sleep easily and sleep pleasantly through till morning, any negatives in our bucket being transferred in REM time. We awake feeling refreshed with a nice empty bucket to start the new day.

However, when we've had lots of negative thoughts and been languishing in our Rats' Den our stress bucket can be rather full. We go to sleep, sometimes with difficulty and then either wake up in the early hours and have a hard time getting back to sleep, or we go into a deep 'comatosed' sleep from which it is difficult to wake and we struggle to get up. Sometimes we might experience a combination of both.

In the first case, once we've had our 20% quota of REM sleep, our mind has awoken us to avoid overdoing this quota. We often find our thoughts racing around as they were literally still in transfer at this point. We then have the remaining negatives left in our bucket before we even start the new day. This would be an anxiety pattern.

In the second case, we've stayed in REM sleep way beyond our 20% quota, desperately trying to empty our bucket, which is very hard work. We consequently awake feeling exhausted! This would be a depression pattern. The longer we sleep the more we exacerbate the problem in overdoing our REM quota, which is why even after sleeping 10 or 12 hours we can awake feeling more tired than when we went to bed. If you can relate to this limit yourself now to a maximum of 8 hours a night. You may be feeling tired all the time yet too much sleep is not the way to help yourself. It is making the problem worse.

To help you 'empty your bucket', experience a healthier sleep pattern and awaken feeling more refreshed I recommend you play the 'Relaxation for Sleep' track on the free audio download (or purchasable CD) that accompanies this book, available through www.demischneider.com Play it *every night* when you go to bed and allow it to send you to sleep. Clients often report significant improvement in just a few days or perhaps a week or two. If you are still awake at the end (it's about half an hour long) or if you wake in the night, play it again. You are re-training your mind. Keep using it for several months after you feel better and then periodically in times of challenge or when you have lots going on. I still do!

Given that your negative thoughts have put you in your Rats' Den with the miserable consequences, consider this:

Who is the only one who thinks in your mind? *You are!*

Therefore, who is 100% responsible for what goes on in your mind? *You are!*

Referring back to Figure 1, the good news is that the conscious part of your brain that you identify with as 'you' is truly in charge! You have *the choice* to be in the left positive side or the right negative side of your prefrontal cortex. See Figure 6.

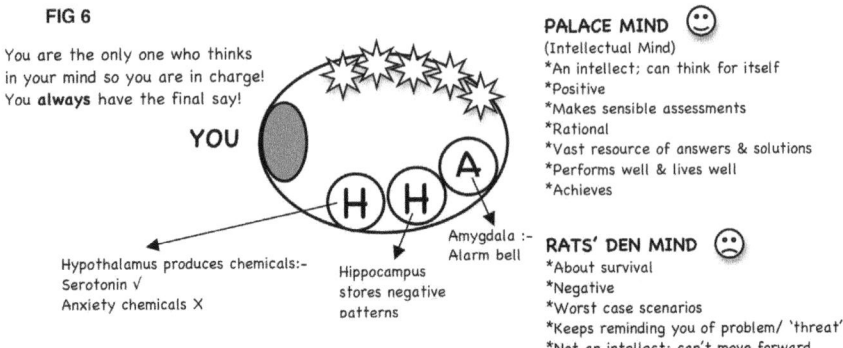

If you don't want to be in your Rats' Den any longer, there really is a simple solution: *pack your bags and move into your Palace, which is waiting for you just next door in your own mind!* And know that in your Palace there's a throne waiting for you. Isn't that where you truly belong? Isn't it your rightful place to be King or Queen of your own Life?

You are the only one who thinks in your mind and you absolutely have the power to choose thoughts that enable you to live well and put you in your Palace mind and on your throne. It is just a case of learning what to do and taking those steps, however slowly and tentatively, to get there.

Clearly your thoughts need to be positive to be in your Palace. We've established that anything less takes you into your Rats' Den to a greater or lesser extent. However, 'Living in Your Palace' and being 'Ruler of Your Own Life' is so much more than just positive thinking. We all know how hard it is to keep positive when we feel the opposite! Even now, you may be having negative thoughts about how you can possibly be positive in your current circumstances. We'll come onto this later. Positive thinking alone is hard work and only as good as our ability to handle 'what comes at us' in any given moment. As soon as something 'bigger' comes along, or we're having a 'bad day' we're back to square one. It is also unrealistic to stay positive if we're coming from the space of "when things go right I feel good and when things don't go as I want them to, I feel bad". Inevitably as soon as things don't go the way we want we're back with our Rats. This just gives away our power! Even if something doesn't go the way we want we don't have to feel 'bad' or negative. Our Palace mind knows exactly how to handle everything and we can stay in good space while we handle or come to terms with the life challenge.

The truth is *it is impossible to move into positive space authentically if you are still coming from a negative 'blueprint' ingrained deeper down in your subconscious that holds you back in that negative space.* To really live in your Palace it is necessary to shift any 'blueprint' negatives to new positive beliefs about yourself and your world. If you had been fed this different data when you were very small and growing up, you would be living a different existence today. Reprogramming your 'blueprint' with all that is positive and that serves you, just as though that is what you'd learned in the first place, means your changes are both authentic and permanent.

We need to clear out all the old Rats' Den baggage that doesn't serve you and keeps 'pulling you back' to the negativity and depression when you're trying to move forward. This is absolutely *not* about revisiting painful times in your past - that kind of therapy puts you in the very Rats' Den part of your mind you're wanting to escape from. We'll do it differently and very effectively.

You'll need to learn *how* to live in your Palace authentically. In order to live there instead of your Rats' Den, besides learning and assimilating new ways of thinking, feeling, speaking and behaving, you'll need to cultivate self-belief and self-worth to *allow* yourself to live there. When your focus is direct and clear, your wonderful anterior cingulate gyrus steps in to help you achieve what it perceives you want to achieve. For our metaphorical purposes, we can imagine it summoning up or creating an appropriately handy 'neural gang' of Palace mentors to come up with your best options at any given point, to enable you to live well. Your Palace is a very special place to be!

Yet, even this is still only 'head stuff'. **To feel good permanently**, instead of living from the pulled off space that 'life has caused us to become', we really need to connect with that core part of us deep within, the part of us that is 'who we really are', our source and soul. Thoughts are in our head; feelings are *inside* and it's when we connect with *good feelings about our self deep down inside* that we're able to take our rightful place on our throne in our Palace and live there effortlessly.

When you come home to yourself in that inner space, aligned with the magnificence of your true self, *you feel good every day,* regardless of what is going on around you - and being automatically in your Palace, you have all the capacity and ability to handle what life throws at you with aplomb!

From this space you can never feel depressed ever again!

To get started right now you can begin to familiarise yourself with your Palace mind so that you can move there. Don't be surprised if this very simple exercise actually proves to be slightly more challenging than you might expect; it's just your Rats putting up resistance to this strange language they don't recognise! Just know you are more than your Rats and can do it.

EXERCISE:

Learn off by heart the key aspects of your Palace mind as shown again below, ingraining them as well as you know your own date of birth. Focus on them all day, every day, so you can start living there.

Your Palace mind:

*is an intellect – has the ability to think for itself
*is positive
*makes sensible assessments of things
*is rational
*has ALL your answers and solutions (like having Google in your head!)
*knows how to perform well and live life well
*achieves

With clients on my courses it's the first thing on their homework sheet!

N.B. To further assist positive change, (as well as the 2 free audio downloads/ purchasable CDs that accompany this book, available on www.demischneider. com) my CDs/downloads 'Stress Relief & Self Recognition' and 'Self Feelings & New Direction' are especially effective in helping to directly 're-educate' your 90% subconscious mind to positive space, whilst also being very soothing, relaxing and supportive. You can see a description of each track at the end of this book on the Recommended Listening page.

Chapter Two
What's Stopping Us Packing Our Bags?

It might come as a surprise to learn that the biggest block we have to our own good is *our own resistance!* We literally get in the way of our own good every time we have a thought that does not align with our good. When we're aligned with our good we're in the Palace and when we're not, we're in our Rats' Den. This inadvertent resistance to our own good comes from our negative subconscious patterning and beliefs, which we hold onto even though they aren't serving us. We need to dissolve these if we're going to get to our Palace.

Hard as it might be to swallow, the truth is we can often sabotage ourselves from even starting our journey because we *think* we want to get out of depression but actually, in our all-important 90% subconscious, we don't. This deeply held resistance prevents us from packing our bags to enable us to move, despite our conscious mind wanting us to be in our Palace.

Here are some examples:

Some people really just want someone else to wave a magic wand for them so they can have what they want to feel happy without any effort on their part. This can never happen. They have to accept their own accountability - it's *their* life! These people have to be willing to pick up their own magic wand and learn to use it.

Some people feel they are not worthy and deserving of good things happening to them or of even *owning* true happiness, or are so full of self-loathing they can't allow themselves to be anywhere other than their Rats' Den. They don't feel worthy or deserving enough to climb out or they feel they need permission to do so. They have to be willing to accept this is *just what they've learned* and instead, recognise their truths.

Some people feel they don't have the right to live well when others in the world are suffering. This is again based on unworthiness, perhaps with deeply held beliefs that they're not important and don't matter. The truth is no one gains because someone diminishes their own capacity. When someone is at their best they feel good, have more to give and everybody gains.

Some people have lived from such a dysfunctional 'blueprint' they have never had the opportunity to engage with their own power or to authentically live their own life. Whilst this is very sad, they can realise they can go beyond the limitations of their past and re-engage with the truth of their birthrights. They weren't born powerless. They need to recognise they do have all the ability and capability to gently recreate their 'blueprint' both mentally and emotionally and be willing to find their own power on which to build.

Some people have been so battered and broken they feel they have no resources left to help themselves. They can still choose to reach out to the many available external resources for help if they really want to get out of their Rats' Den, even if their progress is slower and they need more support. It is still their life and the truth is that they are the only ones with accountability for it.

Some people have just 'given out' so much for so long they are burnt out and don't feel they have any energy left to get out of their Den. They have to realise this too is their choice - it doesn't take any more *effort* to live well when that becomes habitual, than to live poorly; the difference is to choose to spend life happy or miserable. They firstly need to learn to nourish and nurture themselves, to sustain their wellbeing. If spending life happy seems too much effort that is choice and choice alone.

Some people are full of excuses as to why they need to stay in their Rats' Den, for example, "I'd like to live in my Palace but I can't change now - I'm too old", or "I'm too depressed!" (This is an excellent way to *stay* depressed!) They need to be willing to 'stop complaining and start creating' if they want to experience joy.

Some people are just too afraid to venture out of the familiarity of their Rats' Den. They fear they wont be able to live in their Palace, or the journey will be too hard or there's too big a mountain to climb, or that they'll make the effort and just end up disappointed. This keeps them trapped in the very space they don't want to be! Sometimes it might be through a sense of worthlessness, or lack of self-belief in questioning "Who am I without my depression?" (Or excess weight, alcohol, drugs, etc). They have a choice of giving in to the fear and staying stuck or 'feeling the fear and doing it anyway'.

Some people are caught in their Rats' Den because they're intent on analysing how they got there. If you were stuck in a dungeon and someone came to rescue you, would you just want to get out or would you want to stay there discussing how it happened? These people make it an unnecessarily tough journey for themselves.

Some people want validation for their plight. They want to keep focused on how difficult it is for them, either to avoid something, or to draw in sympathy, or have acknowledgement to justify they are right. They are totally giving their power away. This often leads to increased health problems as they 'need' more and more reinforcement.

Some people insist "but that's how it is - my situation *is* this awful" and get quite upset if someone tells them it's a choice and they could get out of that horrible place. "It's not a choice - no one would choose to be like this!" These people can only see the negative in everything, which is why they are stuck in their Rats' Den. "It *is* like this - you tell me how anyone can *not* be depressed faced with this!" The truth is there are always people 'worse off' who aren't depressed, yet these 'wilfully stuck' people just choose to nurture the negativity, though they'd even argue at that and take umbrage, feeling misunderstood. Really they are only fooling themselves.

Some people are game players. They might genuinely believe they want to move forward and find happiness yet will continuously put up irrational obstacles whilst believing them to be valid. They focus on excuses why they can't do things and cannot see how they are blocking themselves. These people can have excellent therapy yet stay stuck in the same place, still searching for a breakthrough that can never come because they throw back any help that is given to them, giving the power to their irrational responses rather than taking accountability and just doing what they need to do to help themselves.

Some people feel their lives would be great if their loved ones, their surroundings, their job, their boss, their finances etc were different. They essentially believe it is outside circumstances or other people who are responsible for *their* happiness. They have to realise they are 100% responsible their own happiness.

Some people live a life totally revolving around their relationship, their job, their children, or some other external source. However much they feel it is 'loving them' they actually are very dependent on that source matching their hopes and expectations. This again gives their power away and indeed puts a great burden on that source. What would happen if their relationship was to end, or they retire or get made redundant, or their children grow up and leave the nest, or disappoint them in some way? These are often times when people fall into depression, feeling they've given so much yet are left bereft. They too have to realise they need to look to themselves and create happiness from within.

If you have recognised yourself in the above, acknowledge yourself for this and say at least 100 times a day, out loud if possible, "I am willing to leave that negative pattern behind". As you go through this book you'll find many tools and techniques to help. I love the expression "If it is to be, it's up to me" because ultimately that's just it - we always have the final say. Or as Jim Rohn says, "If you really want to do something you will find a way. If you don't, you'll find an excuse."

Some people feel self-pity and hold or nurture pain because deep down they know they are 'good souls' yet no matter what they do or how hard they strive, they can't seem to quite manifest the life they see others living, that they want. These people invariably have never learned to *live well* and once shown, grab the new ways with both hands and never look back!

The fact remains you are the only person who thinks in your mind so are 100% responsible for what goes on in it. You can *choose* whether to live in your Palace or to live in your Rats' Den.

If you choose to lay down your resistance you can move forward. If you choose to find or take back your own power, pack your bags and take that short journey over to your Palace with 100% intent and commitment, success is inevitable!

The lower your self-worth or the further away you are from where you want to be, the more times you may have to go over things to get them to stick, yet the truth is, constant repetition is all it takes to learn anything.

If you use the information in this book and *live it* you will transform your life. All you need is the willingness to do so. Let's move forward.

Resistance To Our Own Good

EXERCISE:

Let's look at some other ways we block our own good. Find a pen and as you read through the following statements underline each individual one that applies to you, or add anything that comes up for you that you know is in your way. We'll be coming back to work on these so do take the time to do this now.

1) Having a sense of not feeling worthy enough with beliefs such as: "I'm not good enough" or "Who am I to be in my Palace?"

2) Making sweeping judgments such as: "That wouldn't help me" "My case is different" "Other people don't do this" "It will work itself out" "No one understands me".

3) Denying the problem: "There's nothing wrong with me" "I was all right last time" "Everyone's like that" "It's no big deal".

4) Believing things like: "I'm not that kind of person" "That's just life" "I have to work hard to have things" "Life is hard" "Life is lonely" "Life doesn't support me" "Life is passing me by" "I need outside validation before I can approve of

myself or accept myself" "I can't live without my coffee/cigarettes/relationship/work/etc".

5) Having concepts such as: "I am too old/young to do that" "I'm too fat/thin to be acceptable" "I'm too strong-minded to fit in" "I'm not loved" "I'm not lovable" "I'm a burden" "I don't have/ I can't have" "I don't matter" "I'm not important" "I'm not safe" "I'm not wanted" "I'm too serious".

6) Staying stuck by blaming others, such as: "It's my parents' fault I'm like this" "My family wouldn't approve if I did that" "My boss would never let me have that time off" "My doctor says.........." "My partner would never let me do that".

7) Putting things off, such as: "I'll do it later" "I don't have the time right now" "As soon as I get through with..........".

8) Buying into that old enemy, *fear*: "It might not work" "I might be worse off" "I don't want to open *that* can of worms" "It's too hard" "I don't want anyone to know I have a problem" "I'm afraid I can't handle this" "I'm not good enough" "I don't believe it will help" "I'm only safe if I look from a sceptical view point to avoid the risk of embracing something I might regret".

9) Having the burden of self-consciousness and the consequent paradox of self-importance! (It is strange how the more self-doubt we have the more 'self-important' we become, convinced that everyone is looking at, or having an opinion about, *us!*)

10) Procrastinating or getting easily distracted, finding ways to avoid doing the things you know would benefit you. Or repeating what you've done before and hoping for a different result.

11) Letting impatience get in your way. Does that really bring things to you more quickly? Or does it lock you into a feeling of frustration? (Rats' Den).

12) Having a 'fixed agenda'. Life is only a disappointment if you have fixed ideas about how it 'should be'! It is one thing to have goals, yet quite another to be emotionally attached to the outcome. (My own motto for years used to be "Bright hopes, shattered dreams" because I always had such rigid narrow views about the way things had to be for me to be happy! Needless to say I was often disappointed. It is not a prudent way to live).

13) Using strategies to hide behind, for example, you might have adopted certain expressions such as "I'm probably wrong but.........." to cover the fear of

looking silly, or laugh loudly to cover up a lack of confidence, or use aggression to hide your sense of powerlessness, or say 'sorry' too readily.

14) Perfectionism: believing that only doing something *perfectly* is good enough and therefore either constantly holding yourself back because you don't believe you can achieve this, or else striving beyond all reason to feel acceptable.

15) Feeling guilty if you enjoy yourself, have pleasure, get to do what *you* want, have things others don't have, have things when others are suffering etc.

16) Being stuck in self-righteousness. When you decide how someone else needs to change or behave this is ultimately about making *you* happy. As soon as you judge another you are being self-righteous, putting *your* perspective on them.

(For example, "I can't believe the way he/she behaved today - who does he/she think they are?" is just *your* opinion. Or "Mother would be so much happier if she went out more". That may be true, but if she doesn't want to, that's *her* prerogative. Simmering on the fact she's not taken your advice just keeps *you* in negative space. It's her life and her choice. We all just want to be accepted the way *we* are, which means to be authentic, you have to accept others as they are too)!

17) Avoiding doing exercise, and/or eating healthily, even though you know it would benefit you.

18) Using your abilities to constantly 'fix' what you perceive as wrong, despite it being hard work and never lasting very long before there's something else to fix.

Look over these and be honest with yourself. Whether you've underlined several statements or just a few, choose to feel pleased that you've now identified reasons for feeling stuck and unfulfilled. All these ways just give away your own power and are blocking your way to happiness. They keep you in the Rats' Den.

There are some powerful exercises coming up to change all this! For now, know you have all the ability and capability you need to change these to move forward and that it is much easier than you might think.

Beliefs

Whilst we're delving into the blocks that are preventing us from packing our bags to move to that glorious Palace next door in our brain, let's look at some more. It is sad how our Beliefs about our selves and our world can be so incredibly destructive to our wellbeing.

Let's first be clear about the word *belief*. We give so much power to our words - as we shall see over and over. What *is* a belief? What do we mean by a belief? I get several different answers from clients but they're generally centred round the concept that a belief is something that is true.

Yet let's consider this again. Isn't a belief just a *thought we gave attention to* and consequently collected more data to support, until eventually it became *our* 'truth'?

Doesn't it stand to reason that if instead we'd had a *different* thought and given that different thought our attention and collected the corresponding supporting data, we would have ended up with a different belief?

All our beliefs are based on what we took on board in our 'blueprint'. When we have positive beliefs they serve us yet those that are negative can severely hamper us. Given that our 'blueprint' is formed by the time we're five years old, it is not surprising things seem so deeply entrenched and 'true' for us. Yet our beliefs are just what we've learned to believe from the influences we had from birth. That doesn't make them true at all. We just live out what we've learned, gathering the supportive data, forming our increasingly deep-seated beliefs that either support our wellbeing or damage it.

For example, take two little children going to school. One is shy and timid and the other is confident and cocky. Which one is most likely to be bullied? The shy timid one. Which is the one most likely to be given the lead part in the school play? The confident one. Even if the shy one secretly yearns to have that part in the play the chances are they'll be overlooked or they'll sabotage themselves in some way, even though they may have a good deal of ability. They'll each experience the manifestation of their thoughts and beliefs about themselves and their world, ultimately resulting in different paths through life.

The point is this: all the damaging negative beliefs you have about yourself and your world were only installed from the data you took in a long time ago and *are not true*. If they were, *everyone* would believe them, which is not the case. If you'd had different influences you would believe different things today so you really *can* let go of beliefs that are unhelpful and change them to those that do serve you - to the beliefs from which you would have lived if you'd learned those positive messages from the start.

This is not to blame our parents or any other influential person in our lives. That just gives our power away again and keeps us stuck. Parents and carers

Demi Schneider

can only do the best they can coming from their own backgrounds and what *they* learned. You might have suffered neglect because your mother didn't know any different or you might have a wonderful mother who happens to be shy and timid so you've learned to be that way. Your mum would have learned that too! She's just doing the best she can - just as *we* are. This is where stopping our judgmentalism and just accepting things as they are, because that's how they are, makes life a whole lot easier! We'll come onto that in later chapters too.

EXERCISE:

Have a look at the following list and write down the first things that come up for you for each subject. What do you really believe about each of them? Be honest. Write 3 or 4 different things for each if you can.

Depression - Black hole, lost, despair

Health - Illness, ageing

Yourself - Old, grey, not attractive, no standing

Men - Self-centred, Closed, Trust issues, Protective

Women - Open, sharing, talk, feelings, listening, advice

Friends - Not many, Uplifting

Love - Fickle, Hope, Warmth/Cold

Work - Retired, Important

Money - Open up opportunities/dreams. Not enough - not managed earlier enough. Savings

Success - *Relationships, Work, Children,*

Failure - *Life, Relationships*✕, *Sex*✕. *Need* ✕*Approval*

What have you written? Realise that anything negative is the resistance you need to dissolve before you can *receive your good.* For example, how can you have a wonderful relationship if you believe "Men/women let me down" or allow yourself to enjoy money if you believe "Only bad people have money"?

Sometimes it is very clear what is 'negative' and what is 'positive'. If you are not sure, say your belief and *tune into the feeling* that you get. If it feels good, it's a positive. If it feels 'less than good' it is a negative. We'll work more with your beliefs in chapter eight but for now just be aware of the negativity you have in your 'blueprint' that isn't serving you. It needs reprogramming to allow meaningful permanent change.

Our feelings are always our guide to whether our thoughts serve us. Notice when you are feeling anything on the 'less than' side. That thought is not serving you. You might like to spend a moment to consider what belief is underlying that thought. Some beliefs we can turn around easily. Others take more dedicated effort. Whatever it takes is worth it to let it go and move into a space where you are free to move forward.

Worthiness and Deservability

Of all the blocks in our way of truly living in our Palace, I have often found the most challenging is our sense of Worthiness and Deservability. This affects most of us on one level or another.

Put simply, how are you going to 'let good things in' (which can include joy and inner peace and comfort as well as good jobs, relationships, fun experiences or material things) if, on your deepest levels, you don't feel worthy and deserving enough to have them - or keep them?

Again, it is from what we have had installed in our 'blueprint' that determines our feelings of Worthiness and Deservability. Of course our conscious mind can tell us we're as deserving as anyone else, yet our subconscious can have a very different view.

How can you 'be' and 'do' and 'have' all you would want if you have an inner self-loathing because you feel useless? Or if you feel you don't matter and don't count, or that you're wrong or inferior? Or maybe you came from a poor family and believe you 'can't have' abundance, however much you might yearn and work for it. You may even feel unworthy of being loved. If you believe you can't trust good things to happen, you will inevitably sabotage yourself from having good things happen. These are huge false blocks in the way of your good! If you will just be brave enough to trust the deeper truth that you *are* worthy and deserving of all your good, even if you're way off believing it fully yet and trust it is safe to allow yourself to learn to believe this, you will allow the space to move forward.

You can see what you *really* feel you're worthy and deserving of by what you are witnessing in your life. *Your current life is reflecting what you've allowed yourself to have.* In some areas you may be doing well - acknowledge yourself for that. As you grow and change your 'blueprint' you'll be able to let in more of what you want, including sustained happiness.

You may have created a wonderful life yet can't feel the joy of it. Guilt or "Who am I to have all this good?" are definite indicators of an inner belief you are not worthy or deserving of your good, or that you're 'not allowed to have it'.

The pattern of negativity surrounding our Worthiness and Deservability often continues as we grow up. We are often rewarded with treats when 'we're good' and are punished when 'we're naughty'. Learning the difference between appropriate and inappropriate behaviour has nothing to do with how deserving we are of having our good in life. Yet many of us grow up with this concept and then continue to live this out, not feeling worthy of our good unless we perform as we perceive we ought. If we'd learned we're deserving of all good and, as a separate issue, learned to discern what behaviour is appropriate or inappropriate, we would not have that damaging association today.

We learn that *we* are not good enough if we don't get good grades at school rather than the *grades* not being good enough; we learn that we need to *have* certain things or *be* a certain way in order to be good enough. If we don't feel 'good enough' how can we have a positive sense of self-worth and self-esteem? How can we believe we are worthy and deserving of all our good?

The absolute truth is this: you were born on the planet Earth. *That makes you as worthy and deserving as anyone else!* Even in very poor countries or challenged countries, those who feel a greater sense of Worthiness and Deservability generally do better. Know that if you had received more positive messages you would have a more positive image of your Worthiness and Deservability today. If you feel less than '10 out of 10' you need to reprogramme the truth into your mind.

Imagine a line of twenty little children. Which one does not deserve a good life? They *all* do, don't they? Now put *yourself* as a little child in that line of twenty children. *Now* who does not deserve a good life? *Of course you do too!* It's just that some of those little children, including you, learned to believe differently. This can now be changed. Choose to re-connect with the truth and choose to take it on board - you *are* worthy and deserving of *all* the good life has to offer.

Realise you would not be who you are today, at this point of your growth, if you had not experienced all you have. Choose to embrace all that has been, however painful, because it is all part of the magnificence that is 'you' now. Allow yourself to now recognise your true self, letting go of whatever does not serve you and cultivate instead nourishing things that support you in what you *do* want to be and do and have. You deserve it!

The most ardent feelings of self-loathing have only come from the thoughts you have had and thoughts can always be changed. The lowest self-worth and self-esteem are just false beliefs that deny your own good and cause you to be detached from your true self. Your inner beauty becomes more and more shrouded; now is the time to let it shine! If someone else was to swap places with you they may very well perceive you and your life as something to feel very proud of. They may feel completely different about a sense of self-worth, esteem, confidence and so on, standing in your shoes.

You can begin to change your negative beliefs today. Tell yourself you deserve the very best, because you do! And there is enough on this incredible planet for you to have *all* your good without denying anyone else so much as a bean. We don't all want the same things anyway.

You may have heard of the word 'affirmations'. These are phrases or sentences that reinforce what you do want to focus on. Constant repetition retrains your mind. Let your affirmations become your mantras as you go through your day, to firmly entrench the positive changes you want to make.

Let your new mantra be "I am worthy and deserving of all my good and I am open to receiving it". If this feels too big a leap from where you are right now, start with something that feels more realistic and then gradually work up to this. It doesn't matter how far back you have to go; just make it feel 'doable' for yourself.

Some examples of 'stepping stones' you could choose are:

"I am willing to accept the concept of being worthy and deserving of my own good"

"I am willing to learn to feel worthy and deserving of all my good and to learn to be open to receiving it"

"I allow myself to be willing to be open and receptive to all my good"

"I give myself permission to feel worthy and deserving of all my own good and to receive it readily"

"I now choose (to be willing) to feel worthy and deserving and let all my good in"

"I am willing to believe deep in my soul I am fully worthy and deserving and can have all my good"

Write down whatever feels right for you and repeat your chosen mantra over and over. Go through your day appreciating all the little things which demonstrate to you that you *are* worthy and deserving. If someone smiles at you, say to yourself "I'm worthy and deserving of that!" If someone holds a door open for you, thank them, smile and say to yourself "I'm worthy and deserving of that" or if the supermarket checkout operator is friendly, say "I'm worthy and deserving of that!" The Universe doesn't measure big and small in the way we have learned to. If you keep saying "I am worthy and deserving" and focus on feeling good about even the smallest things, you'll be reprogramming your 'blueprint' to *believe* you are worthy and deserving! And you'll be in your Palace each time you do so, producing serotonin, the chemical that makes you feel good! Win Win.

Notice this is very different from anticipating something you want and then seeing if it shows up to prove your Worthiness and Deservability. This is the wrong way round, which will become clear in the course of this book. Work on yourself to increase your Worthiness and Deservability and then notice it manifesting in delightful little ways at first and then in bigger ways as you grow.

From my background I've had to focus a great deal on my Worthiness and Deservability to *let in* the good I always strove so hard for. Indeed, I have had to realise that 'striving for' is the very opposite of 'allowing in', which is what makes the shift in deservability! I was good at the striving - it was the manifestation that always lacked because I had no template in my 'blueprint' for 'allowing in' my rewards. Once I understood this, I could work on myself to release my blocks and focus on 'striving less' and 'allowing in' more.

From time to time, you may well reach a 'plateau' and need to choose a different mantra, or work on your growth some more, to move forward and expand further. Allow yourself to keep growing until, on a scale of 1 to 10, you are a 10!

One time in my life I found myself regularly telling people, in unexpected circumstances, "I'm happier now than I've ever been". Then all sorts of things happened; I lost things, dropped things, broke things - which is a sure sign I was not feeling worthy and deserving of something. It was easy to work out what that was. I'd never been so content and happy *in myself*, so this was new territory! I immediately started saying "I am worthy and deserving of my happiness and I embrace it". Very soon, I stopped losing, dropping and breaking things and could feel how much more I'd taken ownership of allowing myself to have this happiness.

You may need to repeat your chosen mantra many hundreds of times before your mind is willing to let go of the old Rats' Den negative belief and change to the truthful Palace belief that you *are* worthy and deserving of all your good. Yet even if you have to say it 1000 times before it becomes your new template, starting today at just 10 times a day means you'll have changed your old pattern around in less than three and a half months. If you compare that to the length of time you've been holding the negative belief, it's a very short time. And you may get away with considerably less than 1000 times if you really give your full commitment, or achieve it more quickly with more than 10 repetitions in a day. Out of 60 – 90,000 thoughts a day there is plenty of opportunity for you to choose to focus on your life-changing mantra instead of a negative thought. Know that every time you make the new statement you've made a step towards your Palace and saved yourself being in the Rats' Den for that time, avoiding putting more negativity into your stress bucket too! You will realise even greater value of positive self-talk as we go on.

Question yourself to help you move forward. "If I felt a bit more worthy and deserving what would I allow myself to have that I didn't have yesterday?" "On a scale of 1 – 10 ('1' being low and '10' high) where am I now?" If the answer is, say, '2', ask yourself "If I was a '3' what would be different?" (This is Miracle Questioning, explained in the next chapter). Paint the pictures in your mind of what your next step of Worthiness and Deservability looks like; your anterior cingulate gyrus and neural gangs (Palace mentors) will help you get there. There is more on this subject coming up, including a script for what a 10 looks like on page 82, so you'll know in detail what you're aiming for. When you've reached there, that 10 just expands and gets bigger and better!

To help us make this shift in our 'blueprint' belief, it is worth realising it's *us* that measures our deservability, *the Universe doesn't!* If it did, all the 'good' people would be wealthy and healthy and the 'mean' people would be poor and sick! It doesn't work that way. Deservability is something *we've* invented. If someone is comfortable having money they will get it regardless of whether they are a 'good' person or a 'bad' person! Some of the richest people in the world aren't necessarily the sweetest! There are plenty of successful 'stars' who have nowhere near the talent of others who are less successful. It's not about what they deserve; it's what they allow themselves to have, from their deepest beliefs.

To get past your conditioning, another mantra you could choose to use is *"It doesn't matter whether I deserve (this) or not I allow myself to have (this) anyway".* (Substitute your desire).

Be willing to open yourself fully to the joy of manifesting a rewarding and fulfilling life. Allow yourself to receive it and keep it. "I am willing to *receive and keep* all that I know I am worthy and deserving of" can be a helpful mantra too. Often times, we lament things we're lacking that we want, yet we can't even receive a compliment comfortably!

Demi Schneider

In order to authentically be able to pack your bags ready to move to your Palace we need to turn around all those Resistances you underlined earlier, establish a set of good strong positive Beliefs and cultivate your sense of Worthiness and Deservability. We'll come back to this later in chapter eight, when we've covered the ways to make these changes. You'll then be able to 'board up' these areas of your Rats' Den for good with some strong wood and large nails and focus on the path to your Palace. It's only next door in your own head. Meantime, you can start working now on your sense of Worthiness and Deservability by consciously repeating your chosen mantra as many times as possible each day, to start installing your new desired data.

Besides dissolving these blocks to packing our bags, we need to stop feeding our Rats with our constant negative focus. This happens automatically when we live in our positive Palace. However, to take back our own power we need to know we can deal with our Rats and, if we were to get a new influx anytime from a life challenge, know how to never let them rule us again. Read on.

Chapter Three
Dealing With The Rats

There are four ways that allow us to handle all general negativity. It really is incredible the difference it makes between feeling the overwhelm and misery of letting our Rats rule and realising that we can actually be in charge of them with these simple techniques! You need never again let another negative thought (Rat) drag you down. The more you use these the more automatic they will become for you, until they are your natural way of living. That's taking back your power!

The four ways are (in no particular order):
1) "Stop It"
2) Use a Letting Go exercise
3) Switch the thought
4) Use the Miracle Questioning technique

Do remember though, the goal is to live in your Palace, not to spend all your time exterminating your Rats. It is not helpful to put your focus on your negative thoughts and live life 'releasing them'. Where is the joy and peace in that? When you live in your Palace you automatically stop feeding your Rats so they wither and die anyway! It can be very satisfying to find how many of your issues just disappear when you are living in your Palace mind. However, if you catch yourself having a negative thought, or you're caught up in negative emotion, using one of these four ways will ensure you have a quick and effective way to take back your command.

Stop It

This is somewhat self-explanatory. There are so many self-destructive, harmful, unhelpful, untrue, out-dated, irrelevant, unnecessary, demeaning, antagonistic, unkind, negative thoughts you could choose to just *stop* - right here and now! They are not serving you! Why allow such ugly thoughts to live in your mind?

For many thoughts you can just say "Stop it" firmly to yourself and then choose a thought that makes you feel a little bit better rather than a little bit worse. You are the only one who thinks in your mind and you do have control. You always have the final say.

The potential trap is to catch yourself having a negative thought and then berate yourself because you *had* the negative thought! "Stop it" then becomes a bit like a stuck gramophone record: you catch the negative thought - *"Stop it"* - berate yourself for having had the thought - *"Stop it'* - berate yourself some more for now going in a downward spiral - *"Stop it"* - and so on.

I have found the best antidote is to be able to say "Stop it" and have a comic attachment so that as soon as you say "Stop it" you find yourself smiling. This puts you in your Palace mind ready for choosing your next thought towards something more constructive.

To this end I recommend you go to YouTube and watch American comic Bob Newhart's sketch, called 'Stop It', about a woman who visits a therapist for help with her issues. It is only about six minutes long and the vast majority of my clients find it very beneficial in putting a smile on their face when they say "Stop it" to themselves. Do watch it a few times over to really imprint it on your mind. It's also worth watching it periodically for reinforcement.

At the very least, this sketch demonstrates the resistance this lady has to her own good. If she instead chose to 'get out of the way of herself' most of her problems would disappear very quickly.

Letting Go Exercises

When we have a negative thought that is charged with negative *feeling*, such as an angry thought, or a disappointment thought, we need to release all that negative energy before we can authentically be free to move forward. If we try to resist the thought and feeling, or 'not think about it', we are actually still giving that thought a lot of power. It's still got our attention *because* we're trying not to think about it. We usually also still feel the negative feeling even though we're 'not thinking about it'. It's easy to recognise this because invariably we don't feel much relief or freedom as a result. The solution is to release the negative feeling so it no longer exists for us.

To do this I have collated a number of simple visualisations listed in the exercise below that I have found to be the most effective. Some have come from the Joe Vitale programme I did with my coach Janeen DeTrick, others from Louise Hay and some are my own. It doesn't matter if you're not an expert 'visualiser', just do the best you can; it's always good enough.

Visualisation is an incredibly powerful tool! Our minds cannot tell the difference between 'real' and 'imaginary' so when we visualise something, effectively it's 'real'. We can do authentic deep clearing, healing and reprogramming work on our deepest levels, just by using the power of our mind and visualising relevant scenarios!

For Letting Go exercises, I ask clients to think of a recent situation where they had a high degree of negative feeling. (Yes, I know I'm taking them into their Rats' Den but only very temporarily.) I then ask them to visualise the following images in turn, getting them back to the high degree of negativity in between (by having them focus intently on the negative feeling again), so we can see which ones work best for them. It gets harder and harder to feel the original negativity because these really work! You might like to do this for yourself to see which suit you best, or just select the ones you feel the most resonance with as you read through and then put them into practise. You can always try others as necessary.

To start with, these visualisations will take some effort and concentration and a little time to do. After a very short while, with practise, you will be able to turn to the ones that suit you best in an instant and very quickly find the negative feeling has gone, or at least reduced enough not to bother you anymore.

You can also use them if you have some random unwanted thought from the past 'pop up' in your mind anytime. Know this means it's ready to be released! Instead of feeling the attached emotion of embarrassment or angst and burying it again, you can choose to let it go with one of these Letting Go exercises and be free of it.

EXERCISE:

1) Imagine picking up a mallet and just 'Splat That Rat' as if you were in an amusement arcade bashing the moles that pop up in the holes! This is an easy one to teach children too if they have an unnecessary worry or angst. 'Splat that Rat' and be done with it!

2) Really feel the negative feeling and then just say "Thank you" to it. Say "Thank you... I know you're trying to protect me... I'm now choosing new positive ways to deal with this." You cannot be 'blessed' and 'stressed' in the same moment so the positive replaces the negative. Being back in your Palace mind, you can choose your next thought to further benefit you.

Demi Schneider

3) Imagine your negative feeling as a snowball that you are pushing up a mountain, getting bigger and bigger and bigger until you push it off the top with all your might. See it falling on the rocks below, smashing up into little bits, falling further and further away from you till there is just a scattering somewhere in the valley below that blows away in the wind. Feel the relief.

4) See the negative feeling as a firework shooting up high in the sky and exploding with full force, coming down into little sparks that then just die out till nothing is left. Gone.

5) Imagine the thought and feeling as a pool - maybe even a muddy pool - and from a very high diving board dive down into the middle of it, smashing through it, seeing it splash out and sprinkle down in insignificant little droplets. There's nothing holding the feeling together now, so it can no longer exist.

6) Imagine having a large pair of cymbals in your hands and as you clash them together the negative thought/feeling crushes and turns into a cloud of dust!

7) Grasp a pen tightly to your chest or stomach, gripping it till it matches the intensity of the negative feeling. Then extend your arm out, still gripping the pen, palm toward the floor, and *let go!* The negativity will drop with the pen. Gone. This is a really quick one to do and is especially good in the office if you are feeling stressed. *Feelings never hold us, we hold them.*

8) Imagine you are standing beside a wide rushing river, or on a bridge over the river, and hurl that negative feeling into the water and see it being swept away, off into the distance, breaking up, going off out of sight, off to the sea where the last of it dissolves into its vastness like salt. Gone. (This one is very popular).

9) Feel the negative feeling and instead of resisting it, welcome it in like you would welcome a friend into your home. (It may come in as a caricature or a symbol, or even a sound; that's fine). As you continue to just observe it, giving it no power, notice how powerless it becomes and actually *is*, until it is all gone. No thought or feeling has power unless we give it power!

10) Feel the negative feeling and then notice the negativity you have towards it. Make a decision to feel love for it! Say "I love you" to the feeling. Feel love for it. Love yourself as you feel the feeling. Enough love heals anything.

11) Imagine you are looking up at the expanse of the sky, a beautiful blue sky with a few fluffy white clouds. Notice how the sky neither holds onto the clouds nor rejects them; equally the birds and planes and the satellites. It simply lets them be and *is* as it is; open space. Now put your negative feeling on a cloud, or on the back of a bird, or on a plane, or on the satellite and see it being taken away; the cloud floating away, the bird flying off, the plane zooming into the distance, or the satellite drifting off into space. Then return to the feeling of expansiveness within you that is the same as the expansiveness of the sky. You cannot see outside of yourself that which is not within; the limitlessness of the sky is in you as well. Feel the new sense of peace and calm.

You can always make up your own visualisation if you prefer. One client, a keen golfer, mentally puts his negative thoughts on the end of his golf club and whacks them far into the distance out of sight. Another client puts it in a catapult and twangs it away. You can use whatever works for you as long as it means the negative thought/feeling is *released.* One client told me every time he caught a negative thought he changed it to colours. I explained this was not getting rid of it and encouraged him to find something that enabled him to expel it, as in the suggestions above.

Switching Thoughts

When your negative thought is focused on what you *don't* want, Switch it to the opposite positive (from Rats' Den to Palace) to directly focus on what you *do* want and give your power to that instead.

Some examples are:

Instead of "I can't" Switch it to *"I can"*

Instead of "I have panic symptoms" Switch it to *"I choose to feel calm and relaxed"*

Instead of "I'm worried about money" Switch it to *"I choose to put my energy into attracting money"*

Instead of "I feel tired and lethargic" Switch it to *"I focus on now feeling energised and alert"*

Instead of "I really hate my body" Switch it to *"I'm blessed that I've got legs, or features that function"* etc.

Instead of "It's really difficult" Switch it to *"I choose to find this easier than I supposed"*

You can see the immediate difference it makes to change a thought that isn't serving you and is holding you back, to the opposite positive. When you focus on the Switched thought you are in your Palace with all your answers and solutions. Your neural gangs (Palace mentors) can come on board to help you achieve your positive desired state. This is much more helpful than buying into the original Rats' Den statement with it going straight into your stress bucket and keeping you stuck!

We have all been brought up hearing "Don't run", "Don't talk", - don't do this, that and the other. There are so many examples of the unhelpful language patterning we learn! Why *don't* we focus on what we *do* want? To say "Walk steadily" or "Listen respectfully" gives a much clearer and more direct picture. All those 'don'ts' automatically make us feel we're *wrong*, which is exactly what creates negative beliefs about our selves and our world in the first place! With a little practise you'll find you can Switch your negative thoughts and speech easily and naturally and feel proud of yourself for taking back your own power.

Miracle Questioning

Miracle Questioning is an incredibly valuable technique. In order for clients to experience the full benefit of it for themselves I prefer to share it with them rather than just use it myself to help them move forward in that moment.

Used appropriately, Miracle Questioning immediately puts us in our Palace mind to access its vast resource of answers and solutions. It is also hugely beneficial to use with other people, to assist them to access their own Palace resources helping them far more than by just offering advice, or to address something non-confrontationally.

This technique was initiated by a therapist named Insoo Kim Berg. One day she was with a client who was in an extremely stuck place and out of desperation asked "If there was a Miracle, what would be different?" The client started to open up with all sorts of answers, giving the way forward. The concept of Miracle Questioning had been created.

There is just one tiny thing to note - *initially it takes some concentrated practise to learn and perfect.* However, it is absolutely worth whatever commitment it takes.

I remember, only too well, sitting in the training centre at The Clifton Practise Centre of Excellence in Bristol, under the austere eye of the highly regarded and well respected Senior Lecturer, David Newton, practising this technique with my colleagues and constantly finding ourselves completely tongue-tied! Yet, once you have mastered the technique it seems so obvious you can't remember why it ever seemed difficult. It's only asking a question or series of questions using everyday language.

Sometimes a client will respond with "I don't know" as their answer to my Miracle Question. This can never be true. Sometimes we may need a little time but our Palace mind *always* has a positive answer. If a client says "I don't know" I smile at them and say "I'll wait". It is amazing how they come up with a response from which we can move forward.

It is my life ambition to have the essence of this book taught in schools because it would help avoid so many problems for our children and transform so many lives. To learn the art of Miracle Questioning early in life would have inestimable benefits!

The Miracle Questioning Technique

The Miracle Question is made up of 3 parts. The first part is the word 'if', so that's simple. The second part is about what we want to achieve, which is again fairly straightforward as we know what we're wanting, whether it's to lose weight, tidy up, stop anxiety, etc. The third part (and where the practise is needed) is how to end the sentence to give positive direction.

Here are some examples showing these 3 parts:
(This is another reason it's a good idea to learn the key aspects of the Palace mind from chapter one; they make excellent words to form a Miracle Question, as these first examples show).

"If..... I were being more positive..... what would be different?"

"If..... I were making a sensible assessment here..... what would it be?"

"If..... I were being rational..... how would I respond?"

"If..... I were taking one small step towards a solution..... what could that be?"

"If..... I were performing well..... what would I be doing?"

"If..... I were achieving what I want to be/do/have..... what's the first step I'd need to take?"

"If..... I felt worthy and deserving of all my good..... what might I allow myself to have?"

"If..... I believed I was worthy and deserving of my good..... what difference would that make?"

"If..... I were feeling more confident..... how would I know? What's the first thing that would show me I was more confident?"

"If..... I were taking better charge of my finances..... what's the first change I could make?"

"If..... I were applying for that new job..... when would I be applying for it?" Or "..... what preparation would I need to be doing?"

"If..... I were being more tolerant..... what's the first thing I'd notice that would be beneficial?"

"If..... I was to allow myself to feel good..... what could I feel good about?"

"If..... there was a miracle.....what would my life look like?"

You can see the difference that engaging your solution oriented Palace mind makes. You cannot possibly be in your Rats' Den using this technique!

When appropriate, you can then continue to build more questions until you've painted the picture clearly enough to be able to move forward to a positive conclusion. The trick here is to use the answer from the previous question to form the next question.

For example: "I'm fed up sitting on the couch, watching TV, feeling miserable".

"If I wasn't fed up sitting on the couch, watching TV, feeling miserable, what could I be doing?" *"Clearing out the shed."*

"If I was clearing out the shed, where would I start?" *"I'd empty it out."*

"If I was emptying it out where would I start?" *"I'd start by throwing out the rubbish and then cleaning where needed."*

Beat Your Depression For Good

"If I'd thrown out the rubbish and cleaned, what would be next?" *"Putting stuff back in neatly."*

"If I did this how would it make me feel?" *"Like I was achieving something."*

"If I was to achieve this, when could I start?" Etc.

Now that you have the picture clearly in your mind of what *would* serve you, the plan of action and how it would make you feel, you are in your Palace mind and can achieve it!

Second example: "I'm always procrastinating"

"If I wasn't procrastinating what would I be doing?" *"I'd be tidying my papers."*

"If I were tidying my papers, where would I start?" *"I'd sort them into different piles of 'types'."*

"If I sorted them into different piles, which pile would I start with?" *"The urgent bills."*

"If I paid those bills and cleared that pile, how would I feel?" *"Relieved and happy."*

"Who else might feel that way too?" *"My wife."*

"If my wife felt happy and relieved, what difference would that make?" Etc.

Again, you have now given your focus to your Palace mind where you can follow through and achieve something beneficial. If we're focused on the problem we can never move forward. Miracle Questioning *guarantees* us a way forward.

You can also use this technique to build on thoughts you have Switched. If you have Switched a thought of "It's really difficult" to "I choose to find this easier than I am anticipating" you could use Miracle Questioning to help build the picture of what that would look like and help make it reality:

"If..... I were to find this easier than I am anticipating..... how would I feel?" *"Relieved".*

"If..... I was feeling relieved what difference would that make?" *"I'd be more relaxed about getting on with it"*

"If.....I was more relaxed about getting on with it.....where would I start?"
"Gathering together what I need"

"If.....I was gathering together what I need.....what specific things would that be?"

When you have in mind the specific list of things you would need, you could continue with questions such as "If I was to do this job, when would I start?" "How would I feel when I've finished?" And so on until you are in action.

Similarly if you've Switched "I feel tired and lethargic" to "I want to feel energised and alert" you could ask one of the following Miracle Questions to inspire this:

"If..... I felt more energised and alert..... how would that show?

"If..... I felt more energised and alert..... what would be different?"

"If..... I felt more energised and alert..... what would that enable me to then do?"

When you have an answer, use it to form another question, as above, until you feel energised and alert.

Once you have 'painted the pictures' in your mind clearly enough, your anterior cingulate gyrus and Palace mentors will go to work to help you achieve the desired outcome.

Miracle Questioning always moves us forward. We can further appreciate this by using the example of the very common thought "I'm not good enough" and applying each of the four ways of dissolving negativity, Stop it, Switch It, Let it Go, and Miracle Questioning, in turn.

Our Example: "I'm not good enough."

You decide to Stop it. Then you find yourself thinking "I've stopped it - but I still don't feel good enough!" That clearly wasn't the best technique to use for this example.

You use a Letting Go exercise. "I'll hurl that thought in the river and see it being swept away. It's gone! Oh..... I still don't feel good enough". Whilst being a very useful tool, this approach wasn't right for this case either.

You move to Switch it. Instead of "I'm not good enough" you say "I *am* good enough. I *am* good enough..... I *am* good enough". Then that little voice on your shoulder says "No you're not!" It just becomes a ping-pong match in your head! That again didn't work for this situation.

That leaves Miracle Questioning:

"If I *did* feel good enough, what would be different?" *"I'd stand up for myself."*

"If I was standing up for myself, what action would I take?" *"I'd refuse to do………."*

"If I refused to do………. how would I feel?" *"I'd feel empowered."*

"If I felt empowered, how else would that show?" *"I'd apply for that new job."*

"If I was applying for that new job, when would I be doing that?" *"Tonight after dinner."*

Or

"If I felt empowered, how else would that show?" *"I'd be more confident."*

"If I was more confident, what else would I do?" "How else would it show?" Etc.

You have your light. Notice how different this is from being stuck in "I'm not good enough". As you follow through on your answers and feel the benefit of doing so, you will also witness your self-esteem growing.

An excellent addition to your questions is to ask, even repeatedly, "What else?" You may be very surprised at how much you can keep stretching yourself to find all those answers and solutions in your Palace mind!

Using Miracle Questioning to Help Others

It can often be far more helpful to someone to Miracle Question them so they can find their own answers that feel right for them instead of jumping in with our opinions or advice. This also enables them to feel more self-empowered, more confident to take ownership of their conclusions and gives other indirect beneficial messages about their ability to handle things, as the following stories show:

My young daughter came out of school one day with a tale of woe about a minor issue in the playground. Rather than tell her how to react, I used Miracle Questioning. I asked "So, if that happened again tomorrow how could you deal with it differently?" She was able to come up with some suggestions (which I added to as she was only 7) and I could see the difference in her stance and her walk and her face as we were talking. She not only felt empowered to now handle *that* situation, she had also taken into her subconscious other beneficial messages such as confirmation of her ability to make a sensible assessment

Demi Schneider

of things, self-confidence, self-trust in being able to handle things and her capacity to stand up for herself. She came home happy.

A group of friends were out one night discussing the poor relationship one of them was in. Everyone was putting forward their opinions and giving advice. The poor recipient was evidently becoming distressed trying to filter the information and even defend her position. My colleague who was with them used Miracle Questioning. She asked questions such as "If you were really valuing yourself, what would be the main things you would find unacceptable?" "If you were to decide to leave him, what would be your biggest fear?" "If you were to decide to leave him, what would be the biggest gain?" "If you were prioritising your own needs, what outcome would you prefer?"

Notice how this gave the recipient the opportunity to examine and process her own thoughts and feelings, gain her own clarity and take responsibility with her own answers. Instead of going home with a head full of her friends' opinions, she went home feeling supported and with a sense of direction.

Many times this approach also helps forge much better relationships with our loved ones. Rather than forcing our perspective on them, nagging, controlling, moaning, or inadvertently disempowering them, we can use Miracle Questioning. This can more easily achieve happy agreement, help them to access their own Palace mind to find their own ways forward, help them to feel supported, give them indirect beneficial messages for their own self-respect and wellbeing and makes us feel a whole lot more in positive command of ourselves.

For example, a frustrated mother was unhappy with her son's choice of subjects for college. She told him "It's your life but you know what I think you ought to do". That is a very loaded statement. The son has the choice of pleasing his mother and displeasing himself or vice versa. Perhaps it's not the best scenario to inspire a bonded relationship. Instead, I encouraged her to ask "If you were taking the subjects you wanted what opportunities would that give you once you've left?" "Where do you see yourself in the next 5 years?" This way she is allowing him to assess his choices himself. She may even be surprised at his answers! She could then ask the same questions about her preferred choice of subjects. She could ask *herself* "If I was willing to allow my son to live his own life what difference would that make?"

Whether it be with our children, teenagers, partners or families, in any number of given situations, some appropriate questions can help them on their own path as well as promote much peace and harmony in the relationship.

There are so many opportunities to use this technique with everyone: doctor/patient, teacher/pupil, loved ones, friends, neighbours, work scenarios and so on as well as for use on yourself. If it were taught in schools from a young age we'd all be doing it automatically and it would be easy!

Handling Situations Non-Confrontationally

When using Miracle Questioning in difficult circumstances with other people, we always retain our own power without compromising or diminishing theirs, leading to very much more positive outcomes. The following examples demonstrate this:

One day I bumped into an acquaintance who'd had a bad day at work. She is a supervisor at her firm and was called to a management meeting to be told that the following week there would a big staff meeting where every member of staff would be asked to come up with a way to cut costs or to expand business.

This lady wanted to help her team by giving them advance notice in order for them to be prepared so she called them together and explained the situation. One lad then called out "I could hand in my notice - that will save them twelve grand a year." Frustrated, she said to him *"Well - if you're not going to take this seriously....."* only to hear someone else then pipe up with "One of the Management could hand in their notice and that would save twenty grand!" My friend was in a big hole! It ended up with her being hauled into the manager's office and being reprimanded for having stirred up the staff. No wonder she was upset!

I put it to her that a simple change to a Miracle Question would have changed that whole scenario. Had she turned to that first lad and just pleasantly said *"So if you were answering me seriously what would your answer be?"* she would have retained the control without putting him down and at the same time given a message to everyone else not to be flippant. It is very unlikely the other person would have added his quip and she would have achieved her intent of helping her team.

In another example, following a two day course with me, a client told me that she was really applying what she'd learned yet things had gone awry one day at work. She had needed to designate some work to a junior colleague she found challenging. She smiled pleasantly and asked the colleague some questions about whether she felt capable of doing certain work on her own or whether she wanted something dictated, believing she was being positive. The colleague was blatantly awkward. In the end, having tolerated things quite well for most of the day, my client had a complete overwhelm of negativity and lost the plot for a while.

I reminded her about Miracle Questioning and we re-ran the scenario just changing her questions a little, such as "if you were to do this task on your own how would you best approach it?" and "if you were to do this unassisted what would show you that you were confident to do that?" This way she is giving the colleague messages of respect and allowing her to feel valued and worthy of being heard, and in the process, getting the colleague to meet her in a space to get the tasks done amicably and efficiently. (There were other ways to improve this scenario too that will become clear in this book but this is the relevance of Miracle Questioning in this situation).

Another client had relationship issues. She had found it nearly impossible to have any meaningful conversation with her husband because it would quickly erupt into a row. We worked out some appropriate Miracle Questions for her. Instead of resorting to nagging, she could ask "If you were going to help in the house, what jobs would you be willing to do?" Or "If we were to divide the chores evenly, as we both work, what do see the fairest way would be?" Instead of being defensive when he spoke harshly, she could ask "If you were going to speak nicely to me, how would you rephrase what you just said?" Or "If you were going to take my feelings into account, how might that change things?" Instead of arguing, she could ask "If we were to get some agreement here, what compromises would you be willing to make and what compromises would you want from me?"

Of course the other person may respond with a negative comment, yet continuous well chosen Miracle Questions will lead to a point where there is nowhere to escape other than a solution.

Sometimes you don't even need an answer. If, in response to some unpleasant quip, you said something like "If you were going to be nice to me, what might you say?" *you've made your point,* in a controlled and empowered way that gives messages of self-respect and acknowledgement of their capacity to be nice, even if they don't reply.

Just know that by using one of these four methods, Stop It, Let It Go, Switch It or Miracle Questioning, you can stay empowered and feel in charge of your Rats (negatives) so that they never have the opportunity to overwhelm you again. The more you use them, the more quickly they will become habitual for you to turn to them effortlessly when you need to.

Chapter Four
The King Rats

Criticism (including self-righteousness), Fear (including jealousy and selfishness), Anger (including old buried resentment) and Guilt are guaranteed to keep us in that negative Rats' Den. Shame and Humiliation or other deeply held negative feelings keep us trapped too. These King Rats can easily seem to overwhelm and control us and certainly cause us the most harm, filling up our 'stress buckets' with extra speed and strength. They can also be the root of much ill health. To deal with these King Rats, we need to go in and evict them!

Criticism

Criticism is another *learned* language pattern and behaviour that permeates our very core, causing untold misery and destruction where it most prevails. If we've grown up in a critical family we tend to continue criticising ourselves in the same way and may extend that to others too.

Who likes being criticised? Do *you* like being criticised? Has it ever helped you make positive change? Does it ever make you feel good? Or does it make you shrivel and feel inadequate and maybe want to reach for a 'comfort' in the form of nicotine, alcohol, chocolate, self-harming etc?

If you don't like being criticised *why do it to yourself?* It is just self-abuse. It perpetuates the negativity, putting those Rats into penthouse accommodation, feeding them caviar! It blocks self-acceptance and denies your own magnificence. It is an act of sabotage on your self. You deserve more than this.

Equally, if you criticise others it not only damages *them*, it also keeps you in your Rats' Den indulging in such negativity. Sometimes people think they gain satisfaction from criticising others, adopting the strategy of putting others down in order to build them selves up. This can never work for more than a few minutes. We cannot build ourselves up through negativity.

Criticism is sometimes used as a form of humour. We say "Look at the state of her!" and laugh, or we tease someone for not being able to do something and find it amusing. Comedians often use this form of judgmentalism in their acts. Self-deprecating humour is self-criticism too. How can we feel good with all this fault finding?

Constructive 'criticism' has its place but needs to be worded to only 'paint the picture of the way forward' to be most beneficial. I prefer to call it *Constructive Encouragement* and leave out the negative word 'criticism' altogether.

We must remember that in the Palace negativity does not exist. Therefore, if we want to live there, we must be willing to eradicate all criticism and judgmentalism. This is also an act of love towards our selves and others and everyone gains.

To make this change, the simple and very effective method to use is to 'Stop it'. *Choose to stop all criticism,* from now. Stop criticising yourself and stop criticising or judging others. Life will be very much sweeter!

If you haven't yet watched the Bob Newhart sketch 'Stop It' mentioned before, I recommend you go on YouTube as soon as possible so you can 'Stop it' with a smile on your face. Know that you are leaving behind a very ugly and damaging pattern and instead, allow yourself to start being kind to yourself. How can you feel worthy and deserving of kindness if you're *un*kind to yourself? Choose to start changing this today.

Criticism From Others

We also need to handle any criticism we receive from other people effectively. To do this, firstly realise that when you stop the pattern of criticism, including self-criticism, you will no longer have that negative 'energy' in you to attract it back as a 'pattern match'. Even if it does come it will no longer bother you. You will realise it is the criticiser themselves who is in their Rats' Den.

If you are being criticised, immediately put yourself inside an imaginary big, indestructible bubble or a 'Star Trek' type force field so that it 'bounces off' before it reaches you. This enables you to block the criticism 'going in' and feeling so hurtful. Realise reading this or knowing about this powerful tool isn't enough: you'll need to practise it and use it with absolute full focus to gain the benefit. You may well be surprised by how much difference it makes.

To test this, recall some criticism that you have received or some unpleasantness from someone and relive that experience for a few moments. Then shake it out of your arms and legs and body to be rid of it. Put yourself inside your bubble or forcefield and when you have the image of this clearly in your mind, relive the experience again. If you are properly engaged with this you will find the criticism or unpleasantness has far less impact on you now that you are protected. Now that you trust it's value, practise putting your bubble or forcefield around you and feeling it protecting you in any spare moment so that you can reproduce this instantly when you need to.

Then either shrug your shoulders and say to your criticiser "I'm sorry you feel like that", realising it's their destructive pattern that they are living out, or ask a Miracle Question in response. One (divorced) client had a particularly critical son; behaviour learned from his father. I suggested that each time she was with him she put herself in her bubble and then as any criticism came (and bounced off), she smile and say to him *"So if you were going to say something nice to me what would it be?"* This is another example of where it doesn't matter if you don't get an answer. You will have retained your own integrity and made a point without undermining the other person. They are also less likely to criticise you in future if they know this will be your response.

If you are going to visit family, or anywhere else where there is a lot of criticism, put yourself in your bubble or force field before you even walk in and stay in it until you leave. You'll feel protected, much safer and more empowered. You might even choose to fill your bubble with flowers and butterflies and a beautiful fragrance.

Another powerful practise is to mentally bless the 'criticiser' with love. When you can view them with compassion because they still have this destructive pattern and genuinely feel love for them you'll know you have really set yourself free!

We so often allow other people's opinions of us, or the fear of them, to knock our confidence or prevent us fulfilling our true potential. It's time to start acknowledging our own power. The following Neuro Linguistic Programming (NLP) script encapsulates the message:

Taking Control Of One's Feelings

I used to believe that other people could make me feel bad. I believed that because there was a time when I felt hurt by what someone else said. I realise now that we build fortresses around our weaknesses and I was protecting and guarding something that I believed about myself and that they pointed out. I realise now that anytime I am inclined to feel hurt by what someone else has said it is always me that is in agreement with what they said or it would not have hurt my feelings. I realise now that it isn't always that I agree with them, it's just that it hits a nerve in me or resonates with an issue charged with lots of energy. So it is my responsibility to analyse why. No one out there

can make me feel anything. I choose to feel everything that I feel. I realise now that as I am convinced of this I need no longer think that I am responsible for how other people feel toward me. Other people's opinion of me is none of my business. I salute the divinity within all people including myself. I treat all people, including myself, with respect. Therefore I am free. I love myself and I love others. Thank you Self for realising this now. I forgive you Self for having held on to my old patterns of thinking for so long.
I am free and I love myself.
It is done.

This script is repeated in the 'Daily Rotational Reading' in the Cut-Out section later in this book so you can regularly reinforce this into your mind. The more attention you give to these words the more they will become ingrained in your brain and become your new way of living!

Self-Righteousness

Self-righteousness is really saying "I am right and you are wrong". Whilst we are all entitled to our opinion, if we vehemently hold onto ours without accepting another person's opinion is just as valid from their perspective, we start to nurture another King Rat. This "I am right and you are wrong" mentality, or even "I am more right than you" is fraught with potential negative consequences for all concerned and in particular, yourself.

Sometimes people criticise a loved one or friend genuinely believing they're helping them to 'improve'. If you have fallen into this form of self-righteousness realise it is not helpful to them or you. Judgmentalism in all its forms is negative.

Indeed, I have found judgmentalism to be one of the biggest blocks to harmonious living generally. It seems to be a 24/7 occupation for some people, constantly having an opinion on everyone and everything around. We seem to live in a culture where criticism and judgment is encouraged. With the advent of the Internet we are constantly being asked for comments, be it about topics on TV or for holidays or products. There are endless opinions expressed on Twitter and Facebook every day. It is one thing to rate something with a view to helping others make an informed choice. Yet it is quite another to waste energy on judging other people and their choices and their lives, with the negativity going into our own stress bucket!

The antidote is to 'Stop It' and instead cultivate your own self-worth so that you can be more relaxed and open. When we realise everyone is on their own path and it is not our prerogative to judge we allow the space for harmony. We can choose to accept everyone has their own values and standards and levels of expectation and lessons to learn, whether we agree with them or not. We can choose to put our energy into surrounding ourselves with those who do share our perspectives and stop wasting energy on judging those who don't. They can attract others who reflect *them*. It takes all sorts to make a world; it's only our job to be accountable for ourselves and to work towards being the best we can be. We can also know that what we choose is nobody else's business if it's right for *us*. No one has the right to criticise or judge us either.

Fear

One of our most paralysing emotions and biggest blocks to us moving out of our Rats' Den is Fear. We have so many different fears, some obvious and some more deeply buried, which can completely sabotage our wellbeing and ability to embrace life.

The primitive Rats' Den mind is concerned for our survival. Ask yourself if the fear you're experiencing is about a life threatening situation, where you want your amygdala to step in to give you the adrenalin rush to genuinely help you survive, or if it's just the smoke alarm going off because you've burnt the toast? (See page 5).

If it is the latter, realise that apart from a 'fear of loud noises' and a 'fear of falling down' (and arguably a fear of abandonment) which we are born with, *all our other fears are learned.* Again, most were taken on board by the time we were four or five years old and we just continue 'living them out'. It doesn't make them justified or true other than through our own perception.

We give so much power to the word 'fear'. Just saying it can immediately give us that feeling of heightened state of alert, tightening tummy and so on. It's just four letters, the same as 'foot' or 'fern' or 'foil' yet we automatically give it negative power. When we give power to the fear in any way, especially by trying to resist it, we cannot overcome it.

Let's begin by accepting fear will always be with us and that's ok. If we *accept* fear as part of life we immediately neutralise any negative energy attached and, from that free space, we can then authentically focus on how we're going to deal with it. Acceptance means we're utilising our Palace mind instead of nurturing our Rats.

What do we actually mean when we fear something?

Isn't 'fear' really just that we have *a doubt we are going to be able to handle something?* Or a *belief* we can't handle something?

Take these examples:

We are afraid we *can't handle* the future on our own.

We are afraid we *can't handle* not having enough money.

We are afraid we *can't handle* feelings of not being good enough.

We are afraid we *can't handle* parenthood.

We are afraid we *can't handle* old age.

We are afraid we *can't handle* the unknown.

Clients' faces are often a picture as the light dawns on them as this sinks in. When we realise fear is just a doubt or negative belief about our ability to handle something, we can address it very differently. Even feeling *stressed* is just an overwhelm of fear of either not being able to handle something in particular, or not being able to handle what we perceive as too much.

In our Palace mind we are totally capable of handling things! Given that we are the only one who thinks in our mind, our very first choice is whether to engage with the point of helplessness in our Rats' Den primitive mind or to engage with the point of power in our Palace intellectual mind. In our Rats' Den we will only be able to reproduce the same 'survival' behaviours that usually lead us to berate ourselves further, just staying stuck. In our Palace we can find answers and solutions and move forward - always.

Once we've chosen to address our fear from our Palace mind, some practical ways to achieve this include:

1) Using Palace language such as "I can handle this". Saying this several times over is often enough to override the Rats' Den negativity. If we say or believe we 'can't' our brain wont bother to expend the energy on what it perceives to be a futile effort. When we tell ourselves we 'can', with real focus and determination, our anterior cingulate gyrus comes on board to help us achieve what we want. I am reminded of the Henry Ford quote "Whether you think you can or you think you can't, you're right".

Never underestimate the power of your thoughts and words.

I love the exercise in Susan Jeffers' excellent book "Feel The Fear and Do It Anyway" to graphically demonstrate this and use it often. I ask clients to stand with their arm outstretched to the side whilst I lightly 'bounce' on it with my hand to get a 'control level' of comfortable resistance from them. I then have them put their arm down and say out loud, 10 times, whilst really buying into what they're saying, "I am weak and unworthy". When they extend their arm out again they have no resistance to me 'bouncing' on it as before. Their arm is all weak and floppy! I then have them put their arm down and say out loud, 10 times, whilst really buying into the feeling, "I am strong and powerful". When they extend their arm out again it is rock solid and I can't budge it even when pushing down hard with both hands! And that's after just 10 times! Imagine what we're doing to ourselves physically as well as mentally when we're sending down all those *thousands* of negative thoughts! Clients are always amazed at how quick and profound the effect is.

I once did this exercise with a lovely man I was visiting in prison, where his unfortunate 'crime of passion' had put him. It enabled him to realise the immediate effect of his thinking on his physical wellbeing. In his bouts of melancholy, instead of entrenching himself further in his Rats' Den mind, he could turn the corner with "I can handle this" and then put into effect other exercises that are in this book. He still had his Palace mind and engaging that rather than his Rats' Den made his prison experience far easier to endure.

There are many times I have personally found myself saying "I can handle this." When I decided to lay my own patio (being unable to find a workman in the time frame I wanted) I kept saying "I can handle this" and I did. When I've felt exhausted and still had lots to do, saying "I can handle this" has kept me calm and focused. When I've found my daughter challenging, I have reminded myself that I love her and repeated "I can handle this" to do so positively.

Given the power of our words, I also recommend adopting the phrase "Feel the fear and do it anyway" as part of your vocabulary for the same purpose. Susan Jeffers' excellent book with this same title is on my Recommended Reading list.

2) Staying in the Moment. Fear is related to something past or future. We are afraid we can't handle a previous experience happening again or we are afraid of something ahead. This leads to a feeling of overwhelm because we have no power over the past (it has gone) or the future (even 10 minutes ahead has not yet unfolded). The past and the future actually only exist in our mind; the only moment we have is *now*. We can't feel overwhelmed if we Stay in the Moment because when we connect with the power of *now* we have scope for positive action.

However much we might have to do in a day, whatever it is we have to face in a day, whatever unpleasant situation is before us, or whatever feelings of doubt and anxiety hold us back, none of this is *now!* When we allow ourselves to fill our mind with these things we are in fact giving all our power to our Rats, nullifying our ability to cope, and, saddest of all, wasting *this* precious moment of our life! For what purpose? Stressing over all we have to do in a day, or the interview, the ex husband/wife, the court case, the new job, the lack of money, the 'I'm not good enough' beliefs and so on, *doesn't ever change things*. When we choose to engage our own power and Stay in the Moment we are in our Palace mind; we're rational and have our vast resource of answers and solutions. Moment by moment we can more easily handle our fears, slow down to achieve more than by being the proverbial headless chicken, feel calmer and happier, stay in command and produce serotonin to feel good - and we save all that stress going straight into our stress bucket and wrecking our sleep (and harming our health). Win, win, win!

In order to train yourself to Stay in the Moment effortlessly, whenever you catch yourself thinking in the past or future immediately bring your attention back to the present. Look at the clothes you're wearing, the decor of the room you're in, the view out of the window or something specific about that moment. Appreciate this moment of your life - before that too becomes the past. As you move through your day put all your focus on each task in hand until it is completed. Then give 100% of your attention to the next item on your agenda. (There is more about this on page 88). Even when you are having a rest, be 100% 'in the rest' rather than allowing your thoughts to swirl around about what's coming next. It is a much nicer way to live and we become much more comfortable to be around.

As you go through this book you'll come across exercises that involve you absolutely thinking and visualising about the future. I know that sounds somewhat contradictory. How can you Stay in the Moment if you're doing the Swish exercise (explained below), or preparing for something next week, let alone be planning your business strategy for next year? The answer is that you can be living in the awareness of now whilst doing those tasks. It's very different from projecting yourself into forward space and losing touch with this moment.

Remember that the mind cannot tell the difference between a real event and an imaginary one. If you have, say, an interview next week, that is *one* experience with potentially *one* set of worries. By running it through your mind fifty times beforehand, you have effectively had fifty interviews and fifty sets of worry in your stress bucket! And wasted all that time in your Rats' Den when you could have been focusing on other positive things in your life, with all the benefits thereof. Staying in the Moment, with awareness of what is around you *now*, automatically prevents this happening.

3) Use a favourite or appropriate Letting Go exercise from the list given earlier. Release that negative fear thought and then approach things from your Palace mind.

4) Another NLP exercise is to notice the fear feeling in your body and notice where you're holding it. In your mind just gently take the feeling out of you and gradually shrink it down to the size of a postage stamp. Then mentally attach some tightly strung elastic to the back of it and see it 'ping' way out of sight, somewhere in the long lost distance. (This is a good general negative thought releasing exercise too).

5) Miracle Question yourself. For example "If I were a '10' on a 1 – 10 confidence scale, how would I be dealing with this fear?" or "If I was just a little bit more confident, what difference would that make?" Keep going with questions until you have 'painted the picture' in your mind's eye of how you want to be handling things. Remember you cannot be in your Rats' Den if you are solution focused.

6) For dealing with *upcoming events* that you are fearful or nervous about, there is a Neuro Linguistic Programming (NLP) technique called The Swish which is very effective. Fear over appointments, interviews, exams, driving tests, even your wedding and so on, can be totally wiped out with this visualisation. This is how to do it:

VISUALISATION:
THE SWISH

Sit or lie comfortably, close your eyes and focus on your breathing, in and out, letting it become slower and deeper, relaxing your body as you do so.

Imagine the fearful scenario in all its detail. Fill your mind's eye with the picture. Make it full colour and brilliantly lit. This is your anxiety picture.

Then put it to one side and create another picture of the utopia version of that scenario with it all going well, filling your mind's eye with all the detail, full colour and brilliantly lit. See yourself in the middle of the picture with a big smile on your face, with the 'pass' note in your hand or shaking hands as you hear that you've got the job, or ecstatic about achieving your goal or whatever is appropriate. See all the detail of the success. This is your achievement picture.

Now shrink the achievement picture down to a small black and white postcard and tuck it in the frame of the big anxiety picture. Then Swish them over, so the achievement one is big and colourful etc, the anxiety one small and dull. Then put them back as they were. Continue swishing them back and forth until it is easy to see the achievement picture in your mind and difficult to see the anxiety one. Then make a final effort to bring up the anxiety one as best you can (albeit fragmented or feint) and flash the *achievement* one on top, 5 times in quick succession, on and off. Hold the last picture - hold - and then let the screen go white.

Bring yourself back to the room and time you are in and open your eyes.

I have found this usually takes 6-8 times to Swish the pictures back and forth to feel ownership of the 'achievement' image, although it can vary considerably. Repeat the visualisation a few times over if necessary, preferably at bed time, until you *feel* complete connection with the achievement picture and the anxiety one has gone or doesn't bother you.

If you prefer to be guided in doing this you can find this visualisation on the free audio download (or purchasable CD) that comes with this book. If you prefer to do it on your own, to go at your own pace or to Swish more times, you could do this in silence or alternatively purchase my purely background music CD 'White Light & Relaxation' to have the benefit of relaxing music. (See the Recommended Listening page at the back of this book). You can use this for any of the visualisations in this book that you choose to do unguided.

If you have a specific phobic type fear, for example, of heights, flying, birds, closed spaces etc the best way forward is to visit a *Solution Focused* Hypnotherapist. The Association For Solution Focused Hypnotherapists has a register of properly qualified and regulated practitioners. Visit **www.afsfh.co.uk** to find one in your area. In just a few sessions you can be cured forever!

(Please note: whenever selecting a therapist to help you, *always* make sure you feel 100% comfortable with them. Don't just go to 'anyone' because they have certain qualifications or they're conveniently situated. Phone them up and make sure you feel confident in them. Beware of therapists who encourage you to talk about your problems. Your mind cannot tell the difference between 'real' and 'imaginary' so you'll just be putting another load into your stress bucket and it will be putting, or keeping you, in your Rats' Den!)

We must remember our focus has to be on living in our Palace, where fear can be handled from the point of power automatically. It is not helpful to say "Once I have got rid of these fears I can move forward to the Palace". Allow yourself to feel empowered right now knowing you can handle the fear that has blocked you from moving forward.

Fear of Death

I find a common fear is of death and dying. Many people see 'death' as the opposite to 'life'. I see it as the opposite to 'birth'. Our death is absolutely guaranteed the moment we are born: it's just a question of 'when'.

A fear of death is really a fear of the unknown, of not being in the state of what we know and feel now. We're born and we manage all those unknowns successfully and no doubt when it's our time to die we'll manage that too. No one can really imagine what it will be like. We can have our beliefs about whether there is an after-life or not and what that entails, yet even that is different from imagining the reality of the process. It's going to happen so our choice is to either give our power to the misery worrying about something we can't escape or to embrace the life we have for the time we have it and live it to the full. What is the point of doing anything else?

I knew a lady whose mother had died fairly young from breast cancer. This lady spent many years in depression worrying the same thing might happen to her and worrying about what would happen to her own children. If she'd chosen instead to embrace life and build as many happy memories as she could with her family, she and her family could have experienced the obvious beneficial difference, whatever happened for her in the future.

The key is acceptance. I talk about this in greater detail in a later chapter but for now, realise putting your attention on what you *don't* want doesn't make it 'not happen'; it just means you lose the opportunity to live more constructively.

As Susan Jeffers says, we don't get to choose how we die or when, but *we do get to choose how we live!* Let's choose to focus on what we *can* do something about! And if your first thought is "I know, but it's easier said than done" use the old faithful Miracle Question: for example "If I was to embrace living a bit more what's the first thing I could enjoy embracing today?"

Jealousy

This is a King Rat that can easily consume every vestige of our being. It is a very miserable way to live! Jealousy is really just a fear that *we wont get* or *can't have* what other people have, that we want. It comes from negative beliefs about ourselves, especially our own lack of Worthiness and Deservability. It just advertises our self-inflicted pain from focusing on the *lack* of having what we want. It's guaranteed to keep us in the Rats' Den in that repetitive stuck space.

The antidote is to realise that our energy is far better spent working on our selves to allow ourselves to have *our* good in life too! Paradoxically, when we no longer have the fear that 'we wont get what we want' we no longer have the block that's stopping it coming!

Even better, we can choose to work on 'coming home to ourselves' to feel happy regardless of outside things, which really lets our good in! Living in our Palace mind we are much happier and are in a space to be able to create our good, appreciate what we have and embrace life to the full, rather than lamenting about what's missing that we might never get anyway. The details are coming in chapter six, 'Learning to Live in The Palace'.

Selfishness

Selfish people feel they have to hold on tight to what they've got. This reflects a deep-seated belief there is not enough to go around, or a doubt about their own ability to provide enough for themselves. Some may focus completely on their own needs because they fear no one else will do this or to protect themselves from hurt. People who let these false beliefs of 'lack' dominate their way of living can never be truly happy because they are always in fear of the threat of not having enough and are consequently bound to their Rats.

The antidote is to release the false beliefs and start tuning into the abundance everywhere. Try counting the leaves on one tree, the grains of sand in one hand, or the blades of grass in a field. Abundance is everywhere! What we focus on grows. We can all choose to cultivate the space for safety and trust and expansion. Chapters six, seven and eight will explain more.

Anger

Anger is something else we can have a lot of attachment to. It again very much depends on what we've learned and 'installed' from the time we were very little.

We can fear anger, we can *be* angry (to the point of aggression), we can bury anger deep inside, we can hide anger, we can resist anger, we can hold on to anger, etc. *Anger is a Rats' Den emotion.* There is no point in giving *any* power to anger; why we get angry, or what 'pushes our buttons', or the rights and wrongs of how we deal with anger, or any other aspect, because we are just encouraging the Rats!

I have never understood the point of *anger management.* We are effectively just focusing on the Rats and attempting to tame them! We want to be boarding up the Rats' Den and moving to the Palace, not running a Rat House with more discipline!

The truth is our Palace mind knows exactly how to make sensible, rational assessments of situations, therefore, in our Palace mind *anger is simply not an issue.* That doesn't mean we are unaffected by situations or people - it just means we handle them differently. Our goal is to be at the point where nothing can push our buttons because we don't have any buttons to push. Or, to put it another way, nothing can stir us up because there is nothing in us to stir. From this Palace space we can just find solutions and move forward.

While we are learning and taking the steps towards living in our Palace mind there may be times when anger will surface. Or even when we're largely in the Palace there will be occasions when anger causes us to dip into our Rats' Den - we're human after all! I believe it is very damaging to our selves to do anything other than release this anger. For most scenarios it is enough to use one of the Letting Go exercises given earlier. If I need to, I find 'welcoming it in' an effective method as the more I let the anger thoughts in and watch them, the more powerless they become till they no longer 'stir me up'. Use any of the Letting Go images that work for you.

Sometimes they can successfully flit through your mind in seconds or other times you will need to go and sit quietly with your eyes closed and stay with the Letting Go vision for some minutes to clear your anger. If necessary, if you're really too angry to think straight at all, you can bash some pillows, make some noise, run or jump up and down on the spot, engage in some vigorous sport or dig the garden. This harmless physical release can pave the way to then use a Letting Go exercise and/or Miracle Questioning, although must not become a pattern in itself. The focus needs to be in engaging your Palace mind where anger does not exist.

Miracle Questioning of course gives us instant access to our Palace mind, with or without needing to first use a Letting Go exercise to release the emotion.

Miracle Questions to ask could be:

"If I was making a sensible assessment here what would it be?"

"If I was being rational how would I be looking at this?"

"If I was feeling calm how would I handle this?"

"If I was to find a solution here what would show me I was in the right direction?"

"If I didn't have these buttons in me to push what difference would that make?"

Having regained your equilibrium, you can choose the most harmonious route forward, using the information in the upcoming chapters.

Demi Schneider

Old Buried Anger And Resentment

The real problem is with old anger that still resides in us deeply today. Many people have resentment issues that are still with them many years later. I once knew a lady whose husband had left her with three children under the age of five. Fifteen years later she still talked about it like it happened last week! Whilst it was obviously a difficult situation, the only one perpetuating the pain all this time was *her*. Had she released her anger, resentment and bitterness she would have had a much more enjoyable life. I have had many clients who quite easily write a long list of the people they are angry with from years ago; parents, teachers at school, siblings, friends, ex-partners, work colleagues, bosses, people who have ripped them off, figures of authority etc. Carrying all this negativity inside us is hugely damaging; and for what purpose?

To truly rid our selves of old buried anger and resentment we need to get in our Rats' Den just temporarily to evict this King Rat once and for all, which otherwise keeps pulling us back and prevents us moving to the Palace.

EXERCISE:

Make your own list of all those you feel anger or resentment towards. If it's a long list choose to deal with one or two at a time, being gentle with your self, rather than dealing with them all at once.

1) Write an anger letter. This is an exercise; it's not to be sent. Write to each person who you feel anger towards, telling them exactly how you feel. Unload all your bitterness and resentment. This is a time when you can be totally self indulgent, writing purely from your own perspective, ignoring any rational thoughts about their perspective. Just say everything you want to say to this person.

Clients are often surprised that all the anger they perceived they had towards someone actually fitted onto half a sheet of paper, or less! Even if it's a whole lot more, it still looks distinctly more manageable now it's in front of them on a piece of paper rather than 'inside them'. What was the point of carrying all that negativity?

Sometimes just doing this letter is enough to feel free of the anger and we can move onto the all-important fourth stage, Forgiveness.

2) For others on your list where this doesn't feel enough, you can tip the scales to free yourself and take back your own power through a visualisation. Combining an Emmet Fox exercise and Louise Hay's 'revenge' exercise, I created my own visualisation which I now call Balancing the Power. I used

this myself some years ago for a boyfriend who left me twice for other women (in the days when my lack of self-worth and deservability only allowed me to attract such a relationship). Soon after he left the second time, I manifested health symptoms for which I needed an operation yet I knew from Louise Hay's book "You Can Heal Your Life" that my ailment was about holding on to anger and frustration. It was easy to identify the cause, *him!* (Or at least the power I was giving to him at that time). I used this visualisation and within a few weeks was completely healed and didn't need the operation! Powerful indeed!

Please note: this is a clearing exercise for old anger; it is not to be used on a regular basis.

VISUALISATION:
BALANCING THE POWER

Close your eyes and follow your breath in and out, relaxing and clearing your mind.

Now imagine you are walking into a theatre, through the back door as it's closed. You've had permission to go in. Make your way though the dimly lit corridors into the auditorium where it is just light enough to make your way around. Choose a seat to sit on, whether back stalls, front circle, wherever feels right. Look around at the theatre, noticing any detail. Then look at the stage with the curtain already drawn back, dark and empty. See a spot light beam appear and in the spot light beam see the person in question. Look at them and feel the anger and resentment rising in you. Feel the intensity whilst sitting from the safety of your seat. Decide what you need to do to them to get a sense of 'getting even' or 'paying them back' to appease your sense of anguish.

(For me it was holding a plastic type 'pistol' and shooting out a 'Dr. Who Dalek' type ray that made this ex-boyfriend expand and go white and vanish. One client pelted the person with rotten cabbages and fruit, reminiscent of the old days of the stocks; another chopped his head off with a Samurai sword. Another client whose ex-husband had 'treated her like shit' visualised a pile of manure dumped on him. If you want to punch them out, that's fine too, or you might just want to go up to them and tell them how you feel and see them humbly saying sorry. Whatever works for you).

Stay with this for as long as it takes to find an image that really feels it's hit the spot deep inside where you carried this anger. Be true to yourself. When you've bought into this image and feel you've released all your anger and resentment, see a trap door in the stage floor suddenly open and the person fall down through it; gone. Allow the spot light beam to fade and disappear until you are looking at that empty stage again. Then quietly thank the theatre for enabling you to have this experience. Get up and thank your seat. Walk back out of the auditorium, along the corridors and out of the back door into the room and time and space of your reality and open your eyes.

Demi Schneider

This visualisation is on the accompanying free audio download (or purchasable CD) if you prefer to be guided, or you can do it in silence, or you could use the purely background music CD/download 'White Light & Relaxation' as mentioned before, to do this exercise at your own pace.

Any time this person comes to mind, instead of trying to push the thoughts away or feeling the anguish about them again, or giving any other power to them, you can just have that instant image in your mind of that stage experience and be done with it. For example, the client with the manure husband found she smiled each time she thought of him with this image, instead of feeling consumed with outrage. After a while, she found she had no negative feelings left; her mind had dissolved them just by using this visualisation.

With my ex-boyfriend, out of my 60 - 90,000 thoughts each day about 99% were anguish thoughts about him! (How deep was I in my Rats' Den?) Instead of torturing myself, reliving over and over the anguish and pain, I could instead just have that image of shooting the Dalek Ray and him going white and vanishing, which took no more than a second. A much less painful way to live! It didn't take long before I didn't need to do it anymore because the feelings had all gone - along with the need for the operation.

Choose anyone on your list you feel this exercise is relevant for, sit somewhere quiet and spend the time you need to genuinely feel the sense of appeasement.

Clients often report back next day how different they feel just from having taken back their own power rather than giving it to their adversary. They can then move to the final stage below, stage 4.

3) For situations involving parents or abusers or acrimonious ex-partners I have found the most powerful and effective way to release all negative connections to them and truly set yourself free is to use the ancient technique of 'cutting the ties'. I like Phyllis Krystal's 'Figure 8' method for doing this in her book called "Cutting the Ties That Bind". When you cut the ties at this deep level you can really be free once and for all from even the deepest bonds. I have adapted it for my own clients but the principle is the same and my clients have found enormous benefit. One client put it to me "You've reached parts of my subconscious I didn't know I had". It gave her tremendous relief to be free of her long kept, deep-seated baggage and to be able to authentically move forward. I also find this exercise effective for those who are afraid of anger and need to release the connection with the cause of that fear on their deepest layers to set them selves free.

I believe this ideally needs to be done with a professional but I have known people do this very successfully just from reading Phyllis Krystal's book. It is really important to set aside a good hour or more of absolute peace and quiet and to be prepared to spend a long time to sink into as deep a relaxed 'trance' space as possible. This allows you to bypass your 'head space' and access your inner wisdom. (You could use The 'White Light Treatment' on the free audio download to help achieve this). Done properly, the results from this exercise can feel euphoric.

Alternatively, the visualisation 'Severance from Negative Self Feelings' on my CD/download 'Free to Be' (See Recommended Listening at the back of this book) can be very effective and helpful in freeing yourself from past troubles that still affect you. I developed it from my own deep meditations to clear old pain.

4) The final stage is Forgiveness, covered in the next chapter. Forgiveness sets us free. One client said she'd felt so much better after doing the first 3 stages she hadn't bothered with the forgiveness. I explained that she hadn't truly set herself free without doing this. Otherwise it's like putting all your rubbish in the bin but not putting the bin out to be collected. We need to get rid of old anger completely.

It is really important to replace released anger with positive feeling. Bless yourself with love each time you let go of an old attachment. Fill yourself up with light to replace the void where the old anger used to reside. Allow yourself to feel good!

The 'White Light Treatment' is also helpful here. I recommend you use this often for your wellbeing and especially any time you've released negativity.

Guilt

So many of us punish ourselves through Guilt. Sometimes the burden of guilt can be so overwhelming it can be the cause of depression in itself.

We need to ask ourselves "For what purpose?" "What does 'feeling guilty' actually achieve?" "Isn't it just holding onto the pain?"

Guilt is a totally useless emotion. As Louise Hay says *"How long is the sentence?"* Sometimes we are still punishing ourselves 20, 30 and 40 years later for a simple mistake or unfortunate choice we made all that time ago. Feeling guilty doesn't 'undo the wrong', it doesn't change anything, it just sits in our bodies creating immense damage to us. Again this is really putting our Rats into luxury penthouse accommodation and feeding them caviar. Champagne too. We can't live in our Palace if we're burdened with all this negativity.

Often we carry guilt and the person we feel we've wronged doesn't even know. Even if they do, our guilt doesn't heal anything. If they know and are *pleased* we feel guilty, realise this puts them in a prison of their own self-righteousness. Our continuing guilt is feeding this negative space for them. In all these scenarios there are no winners.

If we judge someone else by saying 'they ought to feel guilty' we are falling into our own prison of self-righteousness, which just adds to the negativity going into our stress bucket and keeps us trapped in our Rats' Den. It is not our prerogative to decide how someone else 'should feel'. Even if that person does feel guilty, it doesn't change what they did. Judgmentalism only harms our selves.

Sometimes it can be a situation we feel guilty about. If it is in the past it cannot be changed. There is no point in perpetuating the negative attachment. If it is about something in the present we can choose instead to serve ourselves much better than just nurturing our pain, which serves no one. For example, we might feel guilty about putting a loved one in a nursing home, or question "Did we really do enough for them?" or question whether we did enough to keep a marriage together. Feeling guilty is not going to help answer those issues. In fact, the sense of guilt can actually get in the way of what we know 'deep down' was/is best. These are the times when it can help to listen to a trusted friend for their more detached view for reassurance. Hearing others whose thoughts we value and respect is often a good way to get past our own head space, with its annoying 'ping pong match' of thoughts. We can connect with our own intuitive feelings, giving clarity. Sometimes these intuitive feelings might be in line with what we're hearing from our trusted friend or sometimes not. Either way we have found what feels right for *us* in line with our integrity, which is always the best path to follow. Alternatively, we can serve ourselves by *accepting* that difficult decisions sometimes have to be made or challenging situations have to be overcome and use the tools in this book to do so.

Perhaps you were brought up in a household where you were manipulated through guilt. If you've been consistently made to feel wrong or bad for things you've said or done, you probably say "I'm sorry" much of the time, being overly responsible for things that aren't your concern. I meet many people who don't even realise they are doing this as it is so entrenched in their language patterning. Sometimes we end up feeling almost guilty for living! The only time to say "I'm sorry" is for a genuine apology.

Apologising can sometimes be confused with occasions when we actually only need to acknowledge someone's integrity. If someone has calmly pointed out they would prefer you not to say or do something again, or shared with you that they didn't like a teasing comment you made in fun, or a habit you have that they find offensive, not only do you not need to be 'sorry', it often isn't what the other person is wanting! They often just want to feel heard and acknowledged, not for you to feel 'wrong'. It may even be they then feel they can't express themselves because it will make *them* feel bad knowing they've made *you* feel wrong and 'sorry', when all they are wanting is for you to know something. Sometimes it is more appropriate to just say "Ok, I acknowledge that" or "Thank you for sharing that" or simply "I hear you". Save "I'm sorry" for those sincere moments of regaining harmony when you know it is appropriate for you to take the accountability.

If we have apologised, we then need to let go of the situation, forgive ourselves if needs be and allow ourselves to move on. If the other person chooses not to accept our apology, that's *their* issue. We cannot be responsible for other people's choices.

Sometimes people have learned to feel guilty if they enjoy themselves. I had a client who every time he started to experience a good thing or have a good time he would have a panic attack. He had a deep-seated belief he wasn't allowed to have good things or a good time and therefore couldn't allow himself to feel gratification. This also affected him sexually. He could get aroused but would lose his erection half way through because the guilt set in over him having enjoyment. After sex, even if he'd managed to regain the moment, he felt extreme guilt because he'd had pleasure. A change in his 'blueprint' beliefs and a lot of focus on building his self-worth, self-belief and self-confidence were necessary for him to accept and feel comfortable with feeling good about himself and life and enjoy all experiences.

If you are aware you carry guilt or can recognise yourself in these sentences, realise guilt serves no positive purpose and be willing to let it go. The way forward is to set your self free.

EXERCISE:

Some practical, conscious level ways of helping with guilt, if and when relevant, are:

1) If you haven't apologised to someone and still can, consider doing so. It is tremendously freeing for *you*, as long as you then let it go. It doesn't matter how long ago it was. I remember apologising to my brother some thirty years after telling a tale on him when we were kids and getting him into trouble. I will always remember the look on his face when I apologised and told him "I want you to know I've felt guilty about that all these years". It was a very special moment for both of us.

Imagine a parent acknowledging or apologising to you for a long ago mistake. Couldn't that be music to your ears? Imagine the sense of relief and validation and healing. It can be the same for the person receiving your acknowledgment.

2) Other times, for perhaps when you feel you've 'taken' something; cheated at school, stolen a Mars Bar from a sweet shop, or taken stationary from the office, you could put some money in a charity box, or do a good deed

for someone which you feel is on a par with your error. As you do this say "I appease my guilt" and let it go, letting the new good feeling replace the guilt. Sometimes 'criminals' choose to positively help society after their sentence, which to me is a far more productive contribution than just 'doing time'.

3) To deal with guilt on a deeper subconscious level I have found the following visualisation very effective with my clients. This also works for Bitterness.

VISUALISATION: RELEASING GUILT

Sit or lie comfortably, close your eyes and let go of all tension, feeling a wave of peace and relaxation flowing down your body, down your arms and into your hands, down your legs and into your feet, feeling calm and clear in your mind.

Imagine you are standing in front of a long table with a white cloth on it. See the image as clearly as you can. Now take a deep breath and imagine reaching inside yourself and just gently pull out the first 'guilt' you find there, wherever it is in your body and hold it out in front of you. Just notice any detail about it, its size, or colour or shape (it doesn't matter if you can't). Now put it on that table in front of you. Reach back inside yourself and gently pull out the next 'guilt' you find and put it on the table. Keep repeating this until all the guilty feelings you can find are out on the table in front of you. (You may have to sit in silence for a time while other 'guilts' surface). When you feel you've unloaded all your guilt take a step back and look at it all spread out on that table. What was the point of carrying all that burden and pain? There was no benefit whatsoever. Notice how much lighter you feel!

Now gather up the four corners of the cloth to make a bundle. You might need a crane or fork-lift truck to help at this point! If it's a small bundle you can put it over your shoulder. Decide how you can best be rid of it. You may wish to take it, using whatever means necessary, down to the bank of a fast flowing wide river, hurl it in and watch it being swept away to dissolve into the sea like salt. Or, you may wish to burn it, or pour acid on it, whatever feels right for you. Just let it be destroyed.

Feel the relief, feel the lightness. It's all gone! Then, see yourself standing with bare feet on some fresh green grass, feel the beautiful earth energy coming into your feet. Let this soothing, healing, replenishing, rejuvenating energy (you might see it as a colour) fill every cell and fibre of your being as it flows slowly up from your feet into your legs, slowly into your torso, all up your back and front, filling every nook and cranny, every crevice where the guilt used to lie, slowly down your arms and into your hands and fingers and slowly up into your neck and head, filling every cell of your being. Feel soothed and healed and replenished and rejuvenated by this beautiful earth energy.

When you're ready, come back to the room and time and place you're in and open your eyes.

If you've done this properly, you will feel wonderful. If you need to practise more, that's fine too. The more practise and experience you have with visualisation the easier it will become. Go at a pace that feels comfortable for you.

This is also on the free audio download (or purchasable CD) that comes with this book if you prefer to be guided.

4) Be kind to yourself! Accept that you're not 'perfect' (whatever that means!) and that life is about learning and growing. You're not 'bad forever' because you make some mistakes. It's what you do with them that counts.

It is very telling that often we'd find it far easier to forgive someone else for doing something that we can't forgive ourselves for! This is not an act of self-worth, or self-value or self-respect. Be willing to forgive yourself. See chapter five.

Other Negative Feelings

Sometimes we may have memories and feelings of past shame, humiliation or embarrassment that get in the way of us living well. We need to be very gentle with ourselves and know we can heal this. Naturally it serves us to engage our Palace mind where we can realise what has happened is in the past and can be left there, where it belongs. We can realise we didn't know any better or acknowledge that we just 'messed up'. Yet to heal this and be authentically free we need to release the deep emotional attachment. We can still remember things; they just don't need to bother us or hold us back any longer.

We may have feelings of degradation. If this has been self-inflicted we can realise we were just acting out our negative space. Rather than perpetuate the pain, it is more helpful to forgive our selves and choose a different path ahead using all the information in the following chapters that enable you to live well.

If your sense of degradation was inflicted from another person know that it is not your fault. No one has the right to cause another to suffer. It is true your 'blueprint' beliefs may well not have best served you and by changing these you can help yourself in future. For now, what matters is freeing yourself from the resulting impediments of your experience. You deserve to feel the truth of your magnificence, whole and worthy.

The following visualisation is usually very helpful to be rid of this pain. Sometimes clients like to use this to release anger too, if the Balancing the Power visualisation didn't suit them. By releasing the old negatives you create new space for good feelings and can move forward. This visualisation can be found on the free audio download (or purchasable CD) too.

VISUALISATION:
PEELING AWAY NEGATIVE FEELINGS

Sit or lie comfortably and allow your whole body to become completely relaxed as you let go of all the muscles from the top of your head down to your toes.

Let your mind wander and imagine you are standing somewhere very beautiful, somewhere very safe, in your own space, ready to free yourself from old negative feelings that have burdened you and kept you apart from your happiness.

You might like some support in the form of a loved one, or a guardian angel or just feel the presence of protection and safety.

As you stand there, knowing you are safe - these are only thoughts about things from the past and cannot hurt you now - just become aware of the shame, the pain, the humiliation, the embarrassment, the anger or whatever else is uncomfortable for you.

As you become more and more aware of this feeling you want to be free from, allow yourself to feel this feeling as some sort of second skin, almost like a wetsuit, tight fitting and confining, as thick as the weight you feel you're carrying.

Now see yourself peeling off that negative outer skin, that wetsuit, peeling it off for however long it takes and then stepping out of it. Take off that negative feeling and notice the fresh skin beneath - new and vital. There may be other layers you need to peel before you can get to that new fresh skin; do so now until you are standing there, fresh-skinned and free. Feel the release! Feel the relief!

Now gather up all those old wetsuit type skins and do with them whatever you want to be rid of them forever; burn them, toss them off a mountain, put them at the bottom of the ocean to dissolve away, whatever feels right.

And now clothe yourself in something special, something beautiful that feels good..... and see yourself running, dancing, the wind in your hair, the sense of freedom coursing through your veins. Let it Feel Good! You are now free to move forward, unencumbered.

Stay as long as you like, feeling free in this beautiful place. Then, when you're ready, anchor this into that life force deep in your belly, bring it up through your chest into the forefront of your mind, bringing this feeling with you as you come back to the room and time you're in. Feel the difference and breathe it in. Go forth with this sense of freedom.

Up to this point, the tools I've laid out here are beneficial because they free us from the deep-seated emotional attachments we've held. They make us feel lighter. However, to truly set our selves back on our self-honouring path, unencumbered by the past and past experiences, we need to *Forgive*. Forgiveness is a gift we can give to ourselves. Forgiveness is the doorway to love and happiness. Let's move onto that now.

Chapter Five
Forgiveness

"I'll forgive but I wont forget". How forgiving does that sound?

Why do we hold on to our past grievances so tightly? For what purpose? I have found the following reasons to be the most common:

~we believe that those experiences and feelings are part of our identity
~we want to retain validation because "that really happened to me"
~we feel if we forgive somehow we've made it not matter
~we feel if we forgive we are condoning someone's bad behaviour
~we let self-righteousness cloud us; "He/she doesn't deserve to be forgiven!"
~we feel we can't forgive ourselves because we deserve the punishment

Notice how once again these keep us in our Rats' Den. Our primitive mind is mainly concerned with our survival so has stored our experiences when we've felt threatened or have been harmed to protect us from walking into them again, just like it reminds the caveman the wooly mammoth is outside. Remember, it isn't an intellect so can't re-evaluate or learn from things that happen, it just stores the data. Thus we hold onto what doesn't actually serve us.

I ask clients to write a list of all those people and situations they feel they can't forgive. Often they'll include their own name. They tell me with real conviction that they can't forgive these people and especially themselves.

I gently ask them "So who is the one in pain?" The light begins to dawn.

Whatever someone has 'done to us' or whatever terrible situations we've been in or whatever we feel *we* may have done that's unforgivable, holding onto past misery just infects *this* precious moment of our life instead of creating and living the joy in it. We are continuing to give our power to that person or situation from the past. We also do this if we continue to beat ourselves up for what *we* did in the past. Our Rats are now living in the Ritz Hotel part of our Den, with constant room service and champagne on tap!

Sometimes people say, with understandable cause, how can I forgive being raped or abused as a child or abandoned? As tough as it might be, it still follows that *that was then and this is now* and we're only perpetuating the pain. We can't change it. There is no point judging and getting stuck in self-righteousness because that doesn't change anything either.

We have the choice today whether we stop giving our power to our Rats and leave that pain in the past with the experience, or continue to take it into each day of our future.

To stop giving them our power and allow our selves to be free of this pain, the antidote is to use a releasing exercise as described in chapter four and then cultivate *acceptance* and *forgiveness*.

Acceptance has nothing to do with condoning behaviour. It's accepting 'that is what happened' or 'that's how it is'. Whilst we hold negative energy we are the one who is suffering. If we then try to be in our positive Palace that negative energy will keep pulling us back. Acceptance 'neutralises' it so we can be in free space to move forward and authentically forgive.

Forgiveness is a gift to our selves because it ends our pain. We can simply forgive someone for *not being the way we wanted them to be.* We can realise that they have their own perspective and maybe their own guilt, maybe they just messed up or maybe they were living out their own pain.

It is much more helpful to accept and forgive so *you're* free of the past and then focus on creating a 'whole and complete you' so that you can live in joy and create different experiences for yourself in the future.

In my own life I have had several 'bad' experiences with men, including a fire, infidelity, domestic violence, rejection and in particular, abandonment at a critical time, with much suffering and intense hardship and pain involved.

Sure these were all tough times! I certainly cried oceans (never mind rivers!) and spent time in my Rats' Den. It also took time to be able to forgive each of my partners but when I did I was the one who benefitted. It wasn't worth screwing up any more of my life over them. Looking back I can see all these men were totally wrong for me, as I was for them. It served me much better to realise they were perfect reflections of my self-worth and deservability on my deepest levels at that time and to focus on my own growth to attract much better experiences in future. I know now I will never again attract an abusive man because I have changed my deep 'blueprint' beliefs, to not just *know* I am worth more than that, but to authentically feel it in every nuance of my being. Moreover, I am now in a place to embrace the meeting of my true soulmate. Forgiveness really does set *us* free to move forward to our Palace and joy. Forgiveness is the doorway to inner peace, love, freedom and happiness.

Another situation where emotions can be challenging is when a loved one dies. Whilst it is natural and proper and important to grieve if bereaved, sometimes we can feel angry because a loved one has passed away. We may feel guilt because we're angry with them. We may feel fear because they've died. The way forward is again *acceptance;* acceptance that they were not here for *our* benefit; acceptance that they had their own life to lead and, whatever beliefs we have about death or after-life, acceptance they have now gone from this life. Nothing is going to change that. Any resistance to accepting this is just denial and is futile. From acceptance we create the space for forgiveness and can ease our pain. We may need to forgive them for being on *their* journey and leaving us. We may need to forgive ourselves for feeling the anger or fear. Be very gentle with yourself, use the offerings in this book to help you, or seek professional help if you need.

When my own darling sister died suddenly from an epileptic fit, aged 34, (her partner came home and found her dead on the floor) it was another tough experience. Friends who knew how much she meant to me were surprised at how well I was able to handle it. Even though I loved her and missed her so much I knew enough, even back then, to *accept* 'that's how it is', respect her journey here had ended, find my peace and allow myself to move on.

EXERCISE:

Make a list of all those people and situations you haven't forgiven or 'can't' forgive, including yourself if relevant.

1) Write an anger letter to each of them, as described in chapter four, telling them how you feel. (Remember this is an exercise, it's not to be sent). Get all your feelings down on paper, however irrational. If your own name is on the list you can write a letter to yourself too and then move to stage 5. Or if you have any negativity towards a loved one for dying, you can also write to them and tell them all you feel, moving onto stage 5.

2) Use one of the Letting Go exercises (pages 27–29) or the Balancing the Power visualisation (page 53) or use the Peeling Away the Layers visualisation (page 60) or explore the Figure 8 exercise (page 54) as you feel appropriate.

3) Ask yourself Miracle Questions to help you move into the space of Forgiveness. "If I was really willing to forgive this person, what would I need to let go of?" "What difference would it make to me?" "Who else would benefit?"

4) When you feel clear and authentically able to, write a forgiveness letter to all those on your list, forgiving them for not being the way you wanted them

to be. Realise all your experiences in life have made you who you are today, to reach this point in your life journey. Choose to accept them and be willing to forgive. When it feels right, burn, or in some other way destroy, the anger letter. You want to let go of all of that negative energy once and for all.

Acknowledge and praise yourself for having set yourself free from that Rats' Den tether of old pain for however long you've been holding onto it. Notice how much lighter and more positive you feel, ready to move forward to your Palace without that King Rat holding you back! Allow yourself to feel your good feelings!

5) I thoroughly recommend Louise Hay's Forgiveness visualisation, available on CD, to help you. I use it on my course and suggest my clients buy it and listen to it several times and then periodically after that. We need constant nourishment on all levels. We can't listen to something or read a book and have it stay fresh in our minds forever, anymore than the nourishment from one meal can last forever. This Forgiveness imagery is beautiful and comes together with an Inner Child visualisation that I'll also recommend when we get to that chapter.

Remember, forgiveness is the gift we give to ourselves. *Feel good* about letting go of the old bitterness, anguish, hurt and pain. There's no point in holding onto it. Let it go and set yourself free and be ready to truly live in your Palace!

Chapter Six
Learning To Live In The Palace

Living well is not about making what's wrong *right*. That just expends a lot of energy mending the broken path you're on. The way to live well is to walk on a completely different path through life's journey, in a different direction.

This is what happens when you live in your Palace instead of your Rats' Den. In your Palace your whole perspective is different so you *live* differently, with much more favourable experience.

There are 5 main Components to living in your Palace mind. They are very simple yet there are no short cuts. All 5 Components must be faithfully followed and embraced as a new permanent way of living to reap the maximum rewards. There are no half measures. I can promise if you do you will transform your life and truly know ongoing happiness and joy.

The 5 Main Components are:
1) Focus your thoughts on what you do want
2) Align your feelings
3) Align your speech
4) Feel worthy and deserving enough to let your good in
5) Learn to Love Yourself

Let's explore these and start living them.

Component One
Focus Your Thoughts On What You DO Want

It is imperative to constantly paint the pictures of what you *do* want so those neural gangs of Palace mentors in your brain can come up with the ways forward.

This could be in the present in any moment as you go through your day, such as choosing to Switch a thought of "I feel stressed" (which is guaranteed to keep you feeling stressed) to what you do want, for example "I want to feel calm and able to cope". You could say this ten times, buying into the feeling, to experience the 'arm effect' described on page 45 and indeed feel calm and able to cope. Or you could use a chain of Miracle Questions, perhaps starting with "If I was feeling calm and able to cope what would be different?" or "If I felt calm and able to cope how would I be tackling this?" Focusing on what you *do* want enables you to take back your own power.

This could also be in the short to medium term, such as for something happening tomorrow or next week. Changing concerns you *don't want* about a situation to focusing on what you *do want* about that situation allows you to engage your Palace mind to achieve this. For example *handling* anticipated bad news rather than being overwhelmed by it, or focusing on the positive outcome you want if you are facing something challenging. (The Swish on page 47 is very beneficial for this). Or it could be just generally focusing on how you do want things to be such as your day going well, or people you know being happy or you having a safe and easy journey somewhere.

It may be focusing on longer-term goals or moving forward in some way. You might want to learn something new, or change jobs, or decorate your home or buy a new car.

In *any* given moment or situation or in general thought we can focus on what we do want. We can do this and still Stay in the Moment. We can have awareness of this moment we are living, even if focusing on a future goal. I want the essence of this book to be taught in schools yet can be aware of living *now* whilst visualising my intention manifesting.

So often, we think if we know what we *don't* want, the opposite will magically appear. This can never be. If a genie popped up and your three wishes were "I don't want to live in this house, I don't want my current job and I don't want the troubles with my family", the genie may have very different interpretations than you had hoped for! We need to be specific about what we do want in order for our Palace mentors to be effective.

How Our Thoughts Work

If we tune a radio to a particular frequency we will hear the station that is on that frequency, for example, if we tune in to the frequency of Radio Four we get Radio Four and not Radio One. Similarly, if we are 'tuned in' to our Rats' Den negatives we can't align with Palace Positives. And if we're 'tuned in' to Palace Positives we don't get Rats' Den Negatives!

For our purposes we can imagine our positive Palace thoughts tuning in on a fast high frequency and subsequently producing a positive vibration (good vibe) and our negative Rats' Den thoughts tuning in on a slow low frequency producing a negative vibration (bad vibe). Each will have an ongoing effect as it ripples out into the Universe tuning into the respective things on that same frequency. In other words, when we put our thought energy into negatives we just create more negatives. When we put our thought energy into positives we create more positives!

This is very different to just positive thinking. We can become extremely worn out trying to be positive about our negatives. This doesn't help. *What are we being positive about?*

A very well meaning retired man who came on one of my courses had everything going for him yet felt depressed. He spent much of his time writing to newspapers and the council and other organisations complaining about various things. I'm not surprised he was depressed! All that negativity of complaining about what he didn't agree with, or what he didn't like, kept him in his Rats' Den nurturing the Rats beautifully. He genuinely believed he was doing good. I believe it came as quite a shock to him that in fact all he was doing was perpetuating what he didn't want! When we complain about our partner, job, lack of money, how wretched we feel, how ill we are, or whatever else is wrong, we just keep giving energy to the problem and stay in our Rats' Den. That will *never* create what we do want.

If we condemn terrorists or war we can realise we are only perpetuating the problem with our attention and subsequent negative vibration. *Acceptance* that terrorists and war exist stops the negative energy because with no attention to it, there is nothing feeding it. From that 'neutralised' clear space we can give authentic positive energy to what we do want.

Mother Teresa focused on what she *did* want. She said she would never go to an anti war rally yet she'd happily attend a pro peace rally. This does not amount to the same thing! Anti war gives energy to war. Pro peace gives energy and focus to the desired peace. The outcomes are very different.

Even some well-meaning charities make this mistake. They give all their energy to 'fighting' against what they don't want. I never support these. There are many wonderful charities that put their energy into creating what they *do* want and it feels great supporting them.

Sometimes clients tell me they don't know what they want. This is not true. We always do know really. If you're in this stuck space, write down what you don't want and then Switch it to the opposite.

For example:

"I don't want to feel so miserable" *"I want to feel confident and motivated"*

"I don't want to cry all the time" *"I want to be happy and have fun"*

"I don't want to live here" *"I want to live somewhere smaller/bigger / in a different area / nearer my friends etc.*

"I don't want this job" *"I want a job that is rewarding and fulfilling, that pays me well, where I am valued and respected"*

Now you've found what you *do* want. With appropriate focus you can create the opportunity to achieve these. "When you go there in the mind you go there in the body"! Or, as respected author Mike Dooley says, "Thoughts become things".

More Blocks To Our Good

Sometimes we can know exactly what we want, yet feel the frustration of never having things manifest as we'd like. This is invariably linked to our 'blueprint' beliefs. If, for example, we have a deep-seated belief that we're 'not wanted', no matter how much we might yearn to *feel* wanted, our belief will keep being reflected in our lives and prevent us attracting the people or situations to manifest this. People may even find us draining or difficult to be with coming from the needy vibrational space of 'please want me'.

Similarly, if we believe 'life is hard' we will only ever be able to attract situations and scenarios that support that belief, no matter how much effort we put in to make life good. We need to shift our 'blueprint' beliefs to align with what we do want too. We'll do this in chapter eight.

Sometimes people feel that goals they want are impossible to achieve or way out of reach. This is Rats' Den thinking. Your Palace mind knows how to get what you want or to still be happy without getting it. (We'll come onto that in chapter seven).

This has to be about *you*. Saying "I want my partner to be different" is futile. It gives all your power away! Focus on what you do want to experience. That might mean you need to split from your current partner or it might mean you need to start accepting them as they are, look for their good points, or stop expecting them to be responsible for your happiness and take ownership of this yourself. Realise your life is your accountability and that focusing on what you do want is about you painting the pictures in your mind of what *you* want to achieve, with *you* making the changes in the ways *you* need to.

Living This Component

EXERCISE:

Write half a page or so on your current life as it is now. Here are a couple of condensed examples from clients:

"I am fed up feeling depressed. I hate being on my own with few friends and no one to go places with. I don't have the financial security I want and life is bleak. I don't even enjoy my job really."

"My wife doesn't love me anymore. My kids take me for granted. I feel overwhelmed with stress at work and have high blood pressure".

What's your story? Write it down now before you read any further, otherwise you wont get the benefit of this for yourself.

~~~~~~~~~~

Notice anything negative you have written. This is the extent you are in the Rats' Den.

The reason you've been in your Rats' Den is that you've been looking at things from the point of *what's wrong*. This will always keep you in your Rats' Den because when you are looking at the problem you are giving attention to the Rats. Of course it may be true that you are faced with dire things but *that is only one perspective*. The truth is there are always other perspectives that are equally as true. In the Palace we look at the perspective that most serves us. *If it's just as true why not?* In the Palace we focus on 'what's good' not 'what's wrong' as a *way of life.*

EXERCISE:

Write half a page or so on your current life as it is now but only from the perspective of what's good about it. Here are the condensed examples from those same clients above:

"I have a lovely home where I feel safe and comfortable. I have family who care about me even though they're distant. I have a job that pays my bills and allows me to have *some* social life. I have the ability to get a different job. I have good health and enjoy walks on sunny days even on my own."

Demi Schneider

"I have a home and a family. The dog loves me. I have a job where I know I am respected. I have good health other than the blood pressure which I'm sure would improve if I felt better about myself."

What's your story only from the point of what's good? There'll be plenty of things if you choose to focus on them. If nothing else, if you can read and write you're not one of the 2 billion people who can't. Living in the UK you have relatively easy access to free medical help, you're probably not starving and you've got eyes that see. That's a whole lot of good right there! Write your story now.

~~~~~~~~~

Read over what you've written. Now what part of your brain are you in? Your Palace! Which version feels better? The second one of course. If every word of the first account is true and every word of the second account is true *why not choose to focus on the second account, which makes you feel better?* In the Rats' Den you just fill up your stress bucket and stay stuck. In the Palace you always choose the perspective which best serves you, from which you feel better and can move forward. In the Palace you can always look for 'what's good about this?'

If we really want to we can find the positives in most situations. One year I went to take my beautiful Harrods style, abundant Christmas decorations down from the loft, only to find traces of mice up there. Before hypnotherapy I had a phobia with mice so although I am much better I was none too pleased at this discovery. I got the many boxes down but didn't tell my daughter as I didn't want to spoil her excitement. It was only the next day when the full blessings hit me. There was so much good about it too! At any point a mouse could have been inside one of the boxes and jumped out as I was getting them down or as we were unpacking them, but didn't! My little girl could have opened a box and found her Christmas soft toys chewed up, but didn't! If I hadn't been doing our decorations that early (end of November!) it could have been another month before I'd been up in the loft to make the discovery with far worse consequences, so it was happy timing! Then, when my friend came over the next day to help me put them up, it transpired that her new husband worked for Rentokil pest control. Years ago I would have been consumed with the problem/damage/'don't want this'/'poor me' thoughts that would have put me in my Rats' Den and ruined Christmas! Instead I found plenty to be thankful for, looking at 'what's good about this?' I stayed in my Palace mind, coped with it, and it was only a minor inconvenience.

Even in major incidents' there are often good things that can be found. Among the tragic deaths there are people who survive or stories of great heroism. We can feel compassion and even get involved in support efforts yet we can still choose to dwell either on the negativity or think of and be thankful for all the positive aspects. Rats' Den or Palace? Both are as true. Stress bucket or solution focus?

Whilst having the utmost sympathy and time for those who suffer or die in tragic situations and for their families and loved ones, this choice of solution focus can be demonstrated superbly by the many people who have turned their extreme adversity *into* something good.

MADD (Mothers Against Drunk Driving) was formed in 1980 because a drunk driver killed a child. The grieving mother's determination to change attitudes and policy to drink-driving sparked a volunteer movement that went from a handful of mothers with a mission to one of history's greatest grassroots success stories. Some 924 laws to date have been changed across the world helping to save thousands of lives. No, it didn't bring her daughter back but it gave a positive purpose to her daughter's memory and to her own life. (Personally I wish it had been called 'Mothers Standing For Sober Driving' to more positively support their cause yet I do understand how sometimes we need to be more attention grabbing to reach our audience. We're back to language conditioning!)

Seriously injured soldiers attempted to climb Mount Everest to raise funds for others. They took back their power to turn their horror into triumph.

Martine Wright lost both her legs in the London bombings in 2005. She chose to take up Volley Ball and played in the British Paralympic 2012 Olympic Team. On the BBC Sports Personality of the Year, as she received the Helen Rollason award for overcoming adversity, she said she was thankful for her experience because she would never have taken this path otherwise.

Whilst not in this league, I myself have had difficult and painful life experiences in other ways. I have deep compassion for you if your partner has just left you or beats you, you've lost your job, you've been suddenly bereaved, fallen out with someone important to you, have a life threatening disease or any other significant life challenge, or indeed have a 'learned pattern' of looking at the negative aspect or learned negative things about yourself, maybe to the point of suicidal thoughts. Yet, you can still choose to look at *'what's good about this?'* or *'how can I turn it into something good?'* We don't necessarily have to do something as awesome as in the examples above, yet we can choose to find a way forward rather than be overwhelmed with misery. Palace or Rats' Den; it really is our choice.

Sometimes, as Joe Vitale advocates, we just get to say *"This is the activity I get to do now"*. Whether it's something at work, standing in a long queue, being faced with an unpleasant task, being stuck in a traffic jam, or any other undesirable scenario, accepting 'this is the activity I get to do now' stops the angst and allows the mental space to turn it into the most valuable time possible.

Demi Schneider

Every single topic has a Rats' Den side and a Palace side. If you're looking from the standpoint of what you *haven't* got you're in your Rats' Den. If you're looking from the standpoint of what you *have* got you're in your Palace. As soon as you notice the absence of something realise this is the choice you make; either to dwell on the absence (and create more absence) or focus on what you *have* got and what you want to manifest and set that part of your brain working toward creating them!

"I haven't got a relationship". "I haven't got enough money to pay this bill". "Despite life being good I still feel miserable". Notice the Rats' Den 'absence' thoughts with Rats' Den feelings and Rats' Den 'stuckness'.

Creating good life experiences is your birthright and other people can do the same. You are not robbing them or being greedy. You're not helping them by not having your good. Be the example of good living to inspire others. If they choose to shun this, that's their accountability.

Whether it's a new job, a new relationship, better health, more joy, inner peace, more confidence, better family relationships, just having more time or whatever else you may want, remember to be specific. 'Happiness' is too vague. If it's more joy, or confidence, or a new job, *be specific* about what that joy, confidence, or new job entails.

If you want a new job, what's important to you? What sort of location do you want to work in? (E.g. near a park to go for a walk in your lunch hour or near shops). What radius/journey time do you want? Do you want to work in a small company with few colleagues or a large company with lots of people? What talents and skills do you want to use? Do you want to be recognised and appreciated and valued and to earn a good income? Make a list of what is important to you and then look for a job that meets these characteristics, rather than necessarily a particular job. Some clients have done this and ended up happy in work they would never have dreamed of!

Similarly, if you want a new house, in what location? How many bedrooms? Do you want it small and cosy or large and airy? Do you want an en suite bathroom? Have every detail listed and focus on aligning the other Components of Palace living to be authentic and allow this to come to you.

For more confidence or joy, list all the detail of what that looks like for you. What would you be doing, what difference would it make, what would you allow yourself to have or be or do? Focus on these things and align all 5 Components.

It also serves us to become very aware of what we are allowing into our minds from external sources. Remember your mind cannot tell the difference between real and imaginary. What are you choosing to put into your precious mind? For example, if you feed your brain with negativity from TV, be it the 'soaps', or people suffering, or films with negative subject matter, that is effectively all 'real', taking you into your Rats' Den and going into your stress bucket!

I recommend clients stop watching all negative TV including the news and stop reading newspapers. You can see the headlines to know what's going on in the world but you don't need to see all the gory details. Instead spend your time nurturing and nourishing your mind, body and soul with positive things. You will feel all the better as a result. And you will be spreading positivity to those you love and into the world!

Component Two
Align Your Feelings

When we have negative thoughts we're generally very good at buying into the negative emotion that goes with them. Not only do we have the low frequency vibration around the negative thought, we also have the added intensity of the negative feeling. That is a very strong negative vibration to be tuning into, nurturing our Rats!

In order to have the same intensity with our *high* frequency Palace positive vibration, to create what we *do* want we need to buy into the high frequency *feeling* that goes with the high frequency thought about that desire. If we feel lethargic towards the thought or that it's out of reach, it nullifies that positive thought and takes us back to the Rats' Den.

We have to close the gap between wishing for something and having it manifest. If you don't believe what you want can happen, or you want something too much so have fear attachments to its 'failure', this will again give Rats' Den vibrations and you will continue to hold yourself apart from what you want. You will keep the distance you have now, whether it's for a relationship, a job, confidence or happiness or anything else if you are not on the same frequency to connect with your desires.

Living This Component

The trick here is to imagine how you would feel if what you want to be, or have, or do, was true here and now! Your brain can't tell the difference between real and imaginary so as you are picturing your desired scenario and feeling it as if that scenario were true *now*, you are tuning into the fullness of that positive high frequency vibration.

For what you want in the moment, such as to feel calm instead of stressed, this can be quite straightforward. However if you're wanting to manifest a wonderful new relationship or find your perfect home, it can sometimes take time to become comfortable with taking ownership of feeling like it's real and you *can* have it. Until you do, the gap will remain. As any negative contradictory feelings come up to hold you apart, use one of the techniques in chapters three or four to eradicate them. Then keep focused on imagining what you want as though it were real now and feel the joy of experiencing it in the here and now! This way you close the gap and draw your desire to you in the now.

I have found creating a Vision Board is a valuable and fun way to hone into our desires, take ownership of them and feel the reality of them. You can google 'images of' what you want (which can be feelings too, such as confidence, peace or happiness), print them and stick them on a big board. Write alongside each picture the appropriate details. For example, "I feel so good now having this wonderful job which uses all my skills and talents, where I am appreciated and I am well paid". Or "I really appreciate this exciting new relationship with my true soulmate who I'm proud to be with, who is supportive and treats me well and appreciates what I bring to the relationship too" etc. Or "It feels good to be growing in confidence everyday now that I am focusing on all that is good about me". Sometimes it can be helpful to ask yourself "For what purpose do I want this?" to move into the core of your desire more authentically. Stand in front of your board each day buying into all those words and images saying "I allow myself to manifest all this and more. I am worthy and deserving of all my good". As you focus on what you do want, ask yourself *"what do I need to work on and shift in myself to move into alignment to allow this to happen?"*

Let any negative thoughts you have show you where your blocks are and use the techniques from chapters three and four to release them.

It gives me great joy to stand in front of my Vision Board for 10 or 15 minutes each day, seeing, reading, feeling and absorbing it! I have manifested much good from doing this.

Sometimes I am asked "If everyone was getting 'all they want' surely we'd just be in competition with each other?" Notice how this is a heavily weighted belief of 'there's not enough to go round'. There is *plenty* to go around. The starvation in the world isn't because of the lack of food! It's because of the negativity in corruption, war, bureaucracy, etc not getting it to where it's needed (i.e. the lack of love)! We don't all want the same things, or jobs; we're not attracted to the same people or want the same holiday destinations or car.

Focus on abundance and feel the truth of this. You can find abundance in the world just as much as lack!

Too often our first thoughts as we're waking up can be very negative, which inevitably makes us feel bad, to a greater or lesser extent, before we've even got out of bed. What a way to start our day!

Imagine waking up with some thoughts you can genuinely feel good about and starting your day in a positive frame of mind. You'd be in your Palace mind, already producing serotonin and feeling the 'strong arm' effect in your physicality! From that empowered space it is much easier to get out of bed and be positive about your day and your life.

Grab control of your mind when you are first stirring from sleep by having appreciation thoughts and *feeling* the appreciation! I always suggest clients choose things that haven't got 'but's'. For example, if you're thinking "I'm blessed I've got a job to go to" and then immediately think "but I hate every minute of it", you've undone the good. Instead, choose things that are without contradiction, such as being thankful for the comfortable warm bed you've slept in; that you're going to open your eyes and be able to *see* (wouldn't a blind person like this gift?); that you can hear; that you are going to swing your legs over the bed, stand up and walk! Appreciate that you have running water and that you can read and write, unlike 2 billion others; that you live in a country of free speech; a country of plenty; or just feel appreciation for the beauty of the daffodils welcoming in the spring. There are plenty of people out there who would gladly swap places with you. Appreciate your very existence. Feel the appreciation in every cell of your body.

Start your day with appreciation thoughts as an automatic habit every day for the rest of your life, just like cleaning your teeth or eating. Choose to go through your day appreciating the clothes you have, the food, your ability to pay for your groceries, the transport you're using, etc. Focus on abundance and feel the truth and joy of the abundance you do have. We can perceive appreciation thoughts being on the highest frequency vibration, along with Love. Appreciation is the antidote to feeling the 'absence' of things because it focuses on what you *have* got. It feels much better and will put you in your Palace.

According to the Global Village research, if you have a roof over your head, clothes on your back, food in your fridge and a place to sleep at night (which so many of us take for granted), you are better off than around 75% of the world's population! We are also better off than the 768 million people who are without safe water, or the 2.5 billion who don't have proper sanitation. Did you know that 526 million women in the world don't even have access to a toilet?

It pays to be thankful for our blessings and appreciate them every time you turn on that tap or flush the toilet or have something to eat, as well as first thing in the morning.

(You can use the term 'gratitude' or 'appreciation' as best resonates with you. I generally prefer the word 'appreciation'. If I say I really *appreciate* having something it feels whole. If I say I am so *grateful* for something it can sometimes feel like I somehow shouldn't be having it and am 'lucky'. It doesn't feel as authentic or strong as I *appreciate*. Choose what suits you.)

We can choose to buy into appreciation feelings at any time, for example if you are not in a relationship and would like to be, appreciate any love you do have, even if it's only from your cat. The appreciation puts you in the Palace. If you are short of money toward a bill, appreciate the money you do have toward it. You'll then be in your Palace where you can come up with solutions to get the rest. If life is good yet you're still miserable, focus on what's good and *how you can embrace it,* not the feelings you are lacking. Find one thing that *does* bring a smile to your face. Then add the next thing, and the next. If you go through your day focusing on what does give you pleasure you'll be in your Palace and can't feel miserable.

Sometimes I have clients who feel guilty because they have more than others or that others are suffering and they are not. It doesn't achieve anything or help those who are less well off. This is a time to Stop It. Stop putting your energy into nurturing the Rats in your Den. Instead, be thankful, embrace and rejoice in your good, knowing the more you have the more you can help others when you choose! Choose to add positive energy to somewhere in the world right now by sending them love! Doesn't that feel better than the pointless guilt? Tuning in to negative vibrations just spreads negativity and ultimately everyone suffers. Start focusing on what you *do* want for others (be it peace, education, fresh water, or better standard of living etc) and maybe set up a direct debit to support a fund somewhere, feeling good that you are contributing to the positive improvement, or go online and sign petitions that are instigating positive change in the world. Let the guilt go and turn your attention to the good your privileged position can give.

Constantly *tune in to your feelings* throughout the day. You can't monitor 60 - 90,000 *thoughts* each day but you *can* tune in to your feelings. If you're not feeling good your thoughts can't be serving you. How do you *want* to feel? What thoughts would create that feeling? Think those thoughts! You're in charge of your mind. And remember, any 'buts' that come up, such as "I can't think those thoughts when I'm panicking" are just resistance to your own good. The truth is if your life depended on it, or someone offered you £100,000 to have a different thought, you would!

You will soon appreciate the difference between feeling good 'because something nice has happened' and feeling good 'because you are choosing thoughts that align you with feeling good'! When you are reliant on external circumstances to make you feel happy, you are at the mercy of what life gives you. When you choose to align with feeling good just for its own sake, you feel happy anyway, which paradoxically, gives you the best opportunity to manifest your good!

Component Three
Align Your Speech

We then need to bring our words and language patterning into the same alignment as our thoughts and feelings. So far we've got our mind focused on what we do want and feeling good about it. However, if for example we have been focusing on allowing more money to come to us and then go round saying "that's expensive" or "I can't afford that" this immediately takes us out of the Palace again and back with the Rats focusing on lack.

We need to Switch this to "That would look good in my home/office/etc" and "As I let more in, I can have that". Now we're back in the Palace so that part in your brain will start working on the solutions to bring you what you want. As explained, with positive and direct focus your anterior cingulate gyrus steps in to help you achieve what it perceives you want to achieve.

It is essential to tune in to a whole new language patterning that aligns with what you do want if you are to live easily and authentically in your Palace. Enjoy changing *all* your words in your conversations with everyone as well as your own attitude and self talk. It is tremendously rewarding! Moaning about things makes you feel bad; switching to the positive of everything makes you feel good! With practise this becomes second nature.

Living This Component

To best serve ourselves we really need to adopt a whole new approach to our speech patterning so that we naturally speak in positive terms. This automatically helps to keep us in our Palace!

For example:

"I don't want to be late" becomes "I want to be on time"
"I don't want to be sick" becomes "I want to be well"
"I don't want to be broke" becomes "I want to be financially secure"

With practise, catching yourself and Switching to the opposite positive, you'll find you automatically start to think and speak like this.

If someone asks "How are you?" what is your current normal response? It amuses me how so many people respond with "Not bad". If you're 'not bad' surely you're at least 'quite good'? Try saying "Bad" and at the same time, feel good. It doesn't work because they're on different vibrational frequencies!

Even if you're not feeling good "I could be better" focuses on how you want to be rather than the jocular "I've been worse".

I had a client who was very anxious about a proposed trip. Besides other techniques I shared with her, I asked her to write out every detail of how she wanted her trip to be. I teased her mercilessly about her first attempt! (We had that kind of rapport). She'd written "We're not late leaving and there are no traffic problems on the road". Eventually, after much prodding, she changed it to "We leave on time and have a free and easy journey to the airport". Her final attempt at her script was totally focused on what she did want and I suggested she read it every day. She had a really clear, detailed picture built up in her mind. I had a wonderful email on her return telling me how well her trip had gone and best of all the email was full of positive language! Well done her!

Rather than moan at someone for interrupting, pleasantly say "I appreciate it when you listen to me" and carry on. Rather than yell at a child for doing something 'wrong' give them the picture of what you *do* want from them. It's just a shift in focus!

Wherever possible include words that convey positive energetic feelings. This increases the positive power of your words. "I feel so happy now I've done that task". "I feel so ecstatic being in love with my perfect mate". "It feels so good to have this new sofa/car/job/boss/friend". "I am so blessed." Appreciation and Love send out vibrations on the highest frequency. The change in the chemicals you produce and the way you feel, plus all the vibrational effect of this, will make a huge difference to your life.

It is important to use language that brings what we want into the 'now'. If we say "I *will* get a new job" we keep it out in the future. It's hard to feel good about something we have no attachment to 'now'; it's then really just a hope. We need to say "*I now have* a new job" so we can feel the feelings of good right here and now. We can only receive in the present (the past has gone and the future hasn't yet happened) so using the present tense keeps the alignment with Component Two and with 'now'.

When I asked the client above to write her journey details I asked her to do it all in present tense. As she was reading and visualising each line she could then feel the reality of it happening 'now' to take ownership of it. Saying "I *will* get ready and leave promptly" creates pressure and is a promise to yourself that you might break. Saying "I *am* getting ready and leaving promptly" tunes in to having the experience.

Our simplest solution is to eradicate all negative words from our vocabulary! If we didn't have any negative words to think and speak, we'd find it hard to be in that Rats' Den. As it is, we can often lament about a situation with far more gravity than we can talk about a good one.

New ways of thinking and speaking could be:

I am glad to be alive! I am choosing thoughts that benefit me. I am willing to trust the process of life. I am moving forward constantly. I am committed to living the very best I can. I am willing to unlearn the old and relearn the new. I am releasing old negative thoughts and patterns easily.

I am willing to accept myself just as I am. I am willing to approve of myself just as I am. I am improving the relationship with myself every day. I forgive myself. I forgive others who have harmed me in the past. I forgive and let go of my past. I set myself free.

My body is strong and healthy. Every cell in my body is alive with health and energy. My body wants to be well and it feels good to know I am now helping it. I move and exercise in ways that feel good. I choose to look after my body - I need it to live in!

It is wonderful to be working in a job I truly enjoy. I feel valued and respected. It feels great to use all my talents and abilities and feel fulfilled. I work in an environment that feels good. I have great rapport with my colleagues.

My income is constantly increasing as I work the same or fewer hours. I have more than enough money for my needs and desires. I welcome all the abundance in the Universe. I enjoy the freedom money allows me.

I look for all the good in my day and in my life. I patiently listen to my own inner guidance. It feels good to connect with my inner wisdom and trust it. It feels good to rediscover the 'real me'. I now allow myself to be the best I can be.

I find it easier and easier to make positive choices for myself. Being organised feels wonderful. I easily express myself to others. I stand up for myself. I am growing in worthiness, deservability and self-esteem every single day.

As you were reading these, did they make you feel good or did you immediately have negativity popping up? Realise that any negativity, such as doubt, or distrust you can have this, or that this wont make any difference, or that 'this isn't real', is just your Rats getting in a panic! You have been nurturing them for so long, when they suddenly realise you're abandoning them and moving off into your Palace they do all they can to hold onto you! It's up to you to be firm and say "Thank you, but I am indeed leaving you. You'll have to go live in another mind that's still a Rat Nurturer" (Or you could use one of the other Letting Go exercises, such as hurling them in the river or sending them off on a cloud, or just 'splatting the Rat').

Read them over again. As you do, imagine them as true and allow yourself to buy in to the good feelings you'd experience. If you tell yourself often enough that you're 'glad to be alive' and then look for the evidence of that in your life and buy in to it, you will soon be embracing the joy of being alive. Or if you choose 'my body is strong and healthy' and keep focused on the parts that *are* strong and healthy, (even if it's the lesser part of you), your body will respond in greater strength and health. Your brain will respond to what you say. This is the language patterning to use on a vision board too.

Sometimes a client will say "How can I believe 'I now have a wonderful relationship' if I'm on my own and miserable?" They can choose to focus on the good feelings of being in a relationship as though it were now, rather than buy in to their misery of being on their own. All such statements (known as affirmations) are 'untrue' to begin with. If someone were already *in* a wonderful relationship they wouldn't need to be saying this! Remember, feeling the absence just perpetuates that Rats' Den negative space, keeping the gap. By saying your desire in the present tense, and feeling the reality of having it, you move into the positive Palace and tune into the 'havingness' of your desire, closing the gap.

Other times, saying affirmations about what you want in the present tense can give motivation to take action. For example, if your affirmation is "It feels great to have a job that uses all my talents and abilities" and that is nowhere near true now, ask yourself the Miracle Question "If I had such a job what talents and abilities would I be using?" Be clear on this - make a list of every tiny thing. Then ask "If I was to find a job where I could use all these, where could I be looking?" (It might be the internet or local paper etc) "If I was looking there, *when* would I be looking?"

You've now painted those pictures in your mind to know you are looking for a job that uses those specific talents and abilities, you know where you're going to start looking and when you'll be doing it. Go do it! However, if you're looking with fear or doubt realise that is a huge wave of negative vibration that contradicts your Palace mind intention so you're back with the Rats! Embrace the 5 Components and then start looking, trusting the perfect job is there for you, you just need to align with it!

If you do not follow through on your Miracle Question answers realise that is deliberate self-sabotage and you're back with the Rats. Is this an act of Loving Yourself? If you were to make a positive choice to move toward life joy, what would it be?

You cannot stay stuck when you're focused on the way forward. The dividends and benefits of living in the Palace are well worth the effort to make these new ways become second nature. You are in charge of your mind and you can do it!

Beat Your Depression For Good

Component Four
Feel Worthy and Deserving Enough to Let Your Good In

The previous Components will only bring you the full dividends if you feel worthy and deserving enough to let your good in! 'Knowing' in your mind that you deserve is not enough. It's your deeply held beliefs that count. As I said before, how can you allow yourself to be or do or have what you want, including happiness, if you don't feel worthy or deserving of having it? You either wont be able to allow yourself to have your true desires or, even if you are blessed with a life that outwardly would seem very happy, you wont be able to enjoy it. And if you can't allow yourself to embrace your good there's no point in having it. All Rats' Den living.

Living This Component

Working on your Worthiness and Deservability is another gift to your self. Start giving that gift to yourself today if you haven't already started to do so by telling yourself "I allow myself to feel worthy and deserving of all my good". You'll be taking substantial steps toward living in your Palace. See pages 19–24 to remind yourself of this in full. Or, just think "It doesn't matter if I deserve it or not; I allow myself to have it anyway" remembering the Universe doesn't measure deservability; it just responds to the vibrations you are sending out.

Choose to focus on all you *have* got, in health, time, modern conveniences, external benefits and indeed every breath you take. Be thankful for these things and let this expand your capacity to let in even more good.

On a scale of 1 to 10, to demonstrate what a 10 looks like for Deservability I give my clients a copy of the Deservability Treatment from Louise Hay's brilliant book "You Can Heal Your Life". I am proud to say I am a trained Louise Hay facilitator and am even more proud and enormously grateful to have been given permission from Hay House to reproduce it here.

I recommend my clients read this daily, or in rotation with other pages coming up in later chapters, to again paint those pictures in the mind to go there in the body. It doesn't matter where you feel you are currently on the scale; by applying what you are learning in this book you will get to a 10. Every step up on the scale as you make your positive changes will feel better and better.

When you can read every word of this Deservability Treatment and feel its truth in the pit of your belly, you'll know you're a 10. And when you get to a 10, that 10 just expands and gets bigger and bigger as you learn more and more to embrace and flow with all the good that you now *allow in!*

This is also duplicated in the Cut-Out section of this book for easy access for regular reading.

Deservability Treatment

I am deserving. I deserve all good. Not some, not a little bit, but ALL good.
I now move past all negative, restricting thoughts.
I release and let go of the limitations of my parents.
I can love them yet go beyond them. I am not their negative opinions, nor their limiting beliefs.
I am not bound by any fears or prejudices of the current society I live in.
I no longer identify with limitations of any kind.
In my mind, I have total freedom.
I now move into a new space of consciousness where I am willing to see myself differently.
I am willing to create new thoughts about myself and my life.
My new thinking becomes new experiences.
I am willing to forgive all those who have harmed me in the past.
I am willing to set myself free.
I am willing to love and approve of myself, exactly as I am now.
I accept myself as I am now. I am a magnificent expression of life.
I am worthy. I am willing to receive the very best.
I now know and affirm that I am at one with the Prospering Power of the Universe. As such, I now prosper in a number of ways.
The totality of possibilities lies before me. I deserve life, a good life.
I deserve love, an abundance of love. I deserve good health.
I deserve to live comfortably and to prosper. I deserve joy and happiness. I deserve freedom to be all that I can be. I deserve more than that.
I deserve all good.
The Universe is more than willing to manifest my new beliefs.

*And I accept this abundant life with
joy, pleasure, and gratitude.
For I am deserving. I accept it. I know it to be true.
And so it is.*

*By Kind Permission of Hay House Inc. Carlsbad, CA
copyright 1984, 1987, 2004 by Louise L Hay*

Imagine how life could have been if you'd had these beliefs in your 'blueprint' and lived this way since? Let this be your incentive to allow yourself to be a 10 now!

Choose to get off the *'I have to do this or be that to be good enough to deserve'* merry-go-round and accept that if you allow yourself to have something it doesn't matter whether you deserved it or not. Embrace all you have and know the more good you attract, the more positive the vibration is that you are contributing to the planet! Everyone gains!

I have found Inner Child work invaluable to help our Worthiness and Deservability and reprogramme our 'emotional blueprint'. This is coming up in chapter eight.

Component Five
Learn To Love Yourself

This is the greatest gift of all to your self and beyond! I said there are no short cuts and there aren't in terms of 'really living' these Components as opposed to 'knowing them and living something different', which is another popular trap to fall into. However, learning to Love Yourself is the short cut to living in your Palace and is the key to authentically sitting on your throne as King or Queen of your own life, where you can stay in your Palace effortlessly.

This is my favourite part in my courses and is the most telling about just how disconnected someone is from their real self and explains the emptiness they've consequently felt. It's so good to see the light dawn for them and to know I've given them the vital missing link from their lives to find inner peace, joy and happiness!

We will come back to this in more detail in chapter twelve when we have worked on reprogramming our 'blueprints', both mental and emotional so the path home to ourselves is clear.

Living This Component

For now, as an act of Loving Ourselves let's explore two areas that are key to living well and feeling good.

Relationship With Ourselves

Feeling good deep within starts with how we feel about ourselves. The most important relationship we have is with ourselves. On a scale of 1 - 10, what does your relationship with yourself feel like at the moment?

Again, no matter where you feel you are now, this can change and not only can you become a 10, you can stay there. When you are a 10 you feel good and inevitably your relationships with others fare better too.

Be willing to recognise what is good about your self! You can never feel good fault finding. (Choose to say "Stop It" if you do!) Choose to focus on your qualities that you do like and grow your self-esteem from there.

EXERCISE:

Get some paper and write a list of all the qualities you like about yourself - physical attributes count too. Some clients find this really hard at first - demonstrating the point! How can they have a good relationship with themselves if they find it difficult to recognise their own good qualities? The truth is we can all find qualities we like about ourselves - it's acknowledging them and focusing on them that allows us to build on them. Then we are helping ourselves be the 'best' we can be!

Here are some words to inspire and stimulate your own awareness:

Kind, honest, loyal, faithful, compassionate, resourceful, caring, creative, intelligent, trustworthy, funny, good listener, good friend, passionate, attractive, patient, tolerant, wise, intuitive, articulate, practical, clever, good clothes sense, beautiful hair, good muscle tone, nice eyes, loving, lovable, determined, balanced, inspiring, confident, sexy, flamboyant, jolly, gentle, good communicator, generous, conscientious, willing, friendly, lovely smile, competent, talented, dependable, consistent, sensible, stable, committed, insightful, adaptable, devoted, knowledgeable, understanding, sociable, strong leadership qualities, accomplished, artistic, an original thinker, a pioneer, an innovator, skilled, organised, supportive of the underdog, a great server, tender hearted, charismatic, perceptive, responsible, capable of earning a lot of money, sensitive to others suffering, high achiever..... the list goes on and on.

If any of these resonate with you write them down and add other good qualities you can think of that are part of the uniqueness of you. Add to your list as you think of others in the days ahead. Make your list up to 50. When clients have achieved this I know they are growing and can't feel negative for very long if they read over that list and remind themselves of just how wonderful they are! And yes, you do have 50 wonderful qualities.

Do this now. Even if you only get 10 to start with, that's fine. Add to your list as often as possible and praise yourself as you do! It is a wonderful way to build your sense of self-worth and self-esteem. You are creating a better relationship with yourself. Enjoy it feeling good! It is an act of Loving Yourself.

A good question to constantly ask yourself to inspire good feeling as well as positive direction is "What would be an act of loving myself?" or "Is this an act of loving myself?"

I have witnessed and experienced the power of these questions many, many times: the overweight lady who lost 3 stones by asking these questions about her food choices, the man who was good at doing things for other people but not for himself, who learned to say 'no' when he needed to as an act of loving himself, the lady who used these questions to stay strong about leaving her worn out relationship, the businessman who used them to make difficult decisions at work. *"Is this an act of loving myself?"* *"What would be an act of loving myself?"* Absorb these into your brain, body and soul and use them all day, every day. They empower you and feel good.

Relationship With Life

What does your current life look like? Do you have a good relationship with life itself? Are you living a rich and fulfilling life with plenty of variety and time to enjoy the different aspects?

Or is your life a bit empty? Or dull with not much excitement or opportunity for joy? Or is it so crowded you are constantly chasing your tail to try to stay ahead and are close to, or actually experiencing, the resulting overwhelm? Or is it ok on paper but driven by duty, with little joy for you? Or is your life governed by what you perceive to be your limitations, perhaps due to health, lack of money etc? Or is it your *life* that's ok, you're just not able to feel the *appreciation* of it? Or does your life totally revolve around your relationship, your job, your children or some other external focus?

None of these are what living well is about. We need to be responsible for creating our own happiness. To have a fulfilling life we need to create a life that looks like it's fulfilling to lead and live it to the full! Let's be in our Palace mind and create the life that reflects what we want to be living and can have joy in living.

Susan Jeffers shows a 'life grid' in her book "Feel the Fear and Do It Anyway". I feel this is a simple and excellent way to achieve this. I ask clients to draw a grid of 9 boxes, rather like a noughts and crosses board. We first put in all the aspects of their current life, which may be their work, family, hobby etc, one per box. It graphically shows their relationship with life. They can then add other things in other boxes, (or add more boxes as appropriate) that they would like to be experiencing, to build that picture clearly for their Palace mind to go to work on achieving them.

EXERCISE:

Draw your own grid and fill in each box with what currently exists in your life. Perhaps you'll have a box for work, for parents/family, for your relationship, for your children, for hobbies, exercise, leisure, 'you' time, personal growth and whatever else is part of your life.

Does your grid look like an exciting life to lead? If not, it's a good indicator of why you feel depressed! Even if you have all 9 boxes filled, what feelings does *each box* give you? If most of the boxes you're looking at feel negative you will not experience joy living them.

If you have a grid with only 3 boxes filled in, for example 'work/family/kids' does that look like a fun life? What else would you like to include? Fill in the others with things you *would like* to have in your life - anything from the list above that you're not currently living, or whatever is meaningful to you, be it Weight Watchers or a meditation group. Paint those pictures in your mind and allow yourself to create them.

If you have so many boxes filled in you can't possibly fit them all into your life comfortably, this is not living well either. (One client had 16!) What could you drop or re-organise or delegate? It may seem difficult to do this, yet realise you are not serving yourself or, in truth, anyone else by running around depleting yourself, and may well be brewing resentment and other negative feelings which are damaging to your own health and wellbeing.

If your choices are restricted because, for example, you are a carer for someone, make sure you have other time 'just for you' to have fun or relax or emotionally nourish yourself. You will feel better and have more to give when you want. If 'poor health' prevents you doing as much as you would like in certain ways, find other activities you could enjoy.

A quality life is a grid filled with meaningful things that you either already have or are committed to working towards. It's your life: how do you want to live it?

When you have a grid that makes you feel good looking at it, align the 5 Components to create it for yourself. Work to make each individual box as near

Beat Your Depression For Good

a 10 as possible. If, for example, you have a 'family' box on your grid, there is little joy for you if you score that box '3' out of 10. Given you can't change your family, what different thoughts would you need to cultivate in order to improve the scenario? If the score was to improve to a '5' or '6', what would *you* need to change to achieve that?

The truth is you can be, or do, or have almost anything if you allow yourself to. Be committed to manifesting a rich and vibrant life. It may take time to manifest some boxes. 'Join Weight Watchers' may be a quick box to fulfill yet 'new relationship' may take a while longer. *Trust* the timing of such things - as explained in the next chapter.

What would a quality life look like for you? Your Life Grid may end up like this:

WORK	RELATIONSHIP	KIDS or ANOTHER INTEREST
EXERCISE	FAMILY	'ME' TIME
PERSONAL GROWTH	FRIENDS	HOBBY / LEISURE

Reserve a box for 'personal growth' to build in time to activate the content of this book and reach out for similar material to help you grow. You can't just 'do this stuff' for a little while and expect to magically stay in your Palace. *It must become a way of life.* You have to constantly clean your teeth, have showers, fill your car up with petrol, go to the supermarket, and a million other things that are choices you make for a positive purpose. The purpose here is to live well and be happy! Surely that's worth some ongoing attention.

Also, do reserve a box for *exercise* as it is now known this is fundamental to one's mental wellbeing! Did you know it's *physical exercise* that keeps our brain cells alive? Going for a half hour daily brisk walk (or an hour if you can), doing gardening, or sweeping leaves off the drive all count. I'm not one for the gym or classes so I do the old fashioned Callanetics or my DVD of 10 minute workouts. If I really don't feel like doing much I can Miracle Question myself into doing a 10 minute programme and always feel much better afterwards (and often end up doing two!) If you're feeling down, exercise will lift you because you'll be producing serotonin. Sunshine is good for serotonin production too, so a walk on a sunny day is very beneficial.

To make the intentions of your life grid become reality I recommend you adopt a strategy I began a few years ago and live to this day – and will continue to. Spend 10 minutes at a convenient time (mine is usually Sunday evening) to sketch out a timetable for the week ahead. Make sure you allocate time for each box. *When* will you be working, spending time with loved ones, starting that new project, doing exercise, having time for yourself, working on your personal growth etc?

If you come to a box on your grid that is not currently in your reality, use that time toward creating it. Find the local gym/group, do your CV, make a vision board for that holiday, visit a travel agent or go online etc.

I find this ensures I maintain a balanced life and am automatically organised for everyone's maximum benefit. Of course sometimes things change. I just make sure whatever had to slip becomes priority the next week. This is also helpful toward rehearsing the following day in my mind the night before (page 129 in chapter ten) because I already have it set out. It is great for getting some discipline going if you're a procrastinator too.

Most importantly, whatever you are doing at any point, give 100% attention to the task in hand. For example, if you are at the gym but thinking about work or your relationship, *you are not in the gym as far as your mind is concerned.* As your mind can't tell the difference between real and imaginary effectively you'll still be at work or in your relationship and wont feel the mental benefit of having been away from them in the gym. When you are at work, be at work 100% or when you are with your kids, be 100% with them etc. It is about Staying in the Moment again.

Life will feel very much richer and you will have awareness of living these experiences. Your time will be more meaningful and, if you are inclined to feel 'constantly over-rushed' time will seem to slow down. When there are times to plan ahead, still keep your awareness of the moment you are in while you do so.

Feel the empowerment of being in charge of your life, creating the 'life grid boxes' that most resonate with you and making each box the best possible. Feel the empowerment of being 100% in the moment and living the full awareness of each moment of your precious life. Your relationship with life will improve and you will feel better about yourself.

It is an act of Loving Yourself to take back your power and create a life of meaning, purpose and fulfillment. If you have any trouble coming up with these details, think of this: on your deathbed what do you want your memories to be? Specifically. That is what you need to create.

Chapter Seven
Palace Protocol And Etiquette

Sometimes we can think we're 'doing it right' and then feel the frustration and disappointment of things still not going how we want.

Notice how this is focusing on the 'absence' again. We need to Switch to the sense of 'having' to be in our Palace. It is a fine line to tread yet is only the same as many other things we do. If we press a thousand right keys on our computer but one wrong one we wont get the result we want. If we do a text message but then forget to press 'send' it wont be received. It needs to be exactly the right atmospheric conditions for it to snow. There are zillions of examples of how nature needs exact conditions, or we have to function in an exact way for things to happen in a certain way, without any room for deviation. It is the same here.

I can visualise getting a parking space and it happens. I can visualise having all green traffic lights on my journey and it happens. I can visualise an exact time I arrive at a destination and it happens. However, if I've got out of my Palace, say because I was cross with my daughter for messing about and making herself late for school, I do the same visualising but *don't* get the parking space, the green lights or the time of arrival I want. My *thought vibration* is no longer coming from 100% Palace space.

It is quite profound how things seemingly out of our control, 'pop up' and go against us when we're not genuinely in our Palace. Our vibration is shifted. Just as tuning in to a radio station has to be precise to get the programme you want, you've got to be precise in order to get back from life what you want.

To this end, there is some finer tuning we can do:

Cultivating Trust.

We need to cultivate trust in our own abilities, trust in the process of life and trust the timing of what comes to us.

When my daughter's dad left me it took ages for our house to sell. It was a very difficult time and I was at such a low ebb but just kept repeating over and over "Everything is working for my highest good", "Everything is working for my highest good" although I couldn't see for the life of me how! I sunk myself into trusting and *surrendering to that trust* that things beyond my unhappy situation would unfold for the better.

Although I didn't want to leave my beautiful five bedroom house I couldn't financially stay there. I made a very specific list of all the things which were important to me in a new house. I wanted to stay in the same area. I wanted three bedrooms, even though my budget really only allowed for two. I wanted a separate playroom area for my little girl, either perhaps a garage to convert or space to add a conservatory. I wanted an en suite and a place for my huge Christmas tree. I wanted an accessible loft. I wanted a living flame fireplace. I wanted to not be overlooked. (See what I mean about words? How can I Switch '*not* be overlooked' into the opposite positive of what I *do* want without writing an essay?) Then I added to my list "at a price I can easily afford".

I heard myself saying "I am so happy in my new little house" and then realised I didn't want a *little* house - I wanted a big one even if my budget was little! I changed it to "I am so happy in my new *big* house" but somehow that never quite came out. I invariably ending up saying "I am so happy in my little - (whoops) big - house that meets all my needs and desires".

As I went house hunting nothing I looked at came remotely close. I really had to dig deep to stay focused on my list of what I wanted and keep up that trust! "I am so happy in my little - *big* - house" over and over as I read through my list. Though it was hard to imagine good feelings about being in that situation, especially as I wasn't seeing anything to justify my optimism, I just kept focused on what I wanted very clearly, trusting it was there for me.

One day, my daughter's dad told me he'd spotted a 'new build' in the garden of an existing house on an estate near where we lived. I went along to see it immediately. The builders were very friendly and showed me round - albeit still at breeze block stage.

The reason my other house had taken so long to sell is that this one wasn't built yet! I was able to meet with the private developers and have some things changed. And it had every single thing on my list and more benefits beside! It is true there were a few hiccups at the end so the move wasn't as smooth as I'd have liked but I can understand why. With one thing and another I'd inadvertently been thinking "this has to happen in this set time frame or else it will be catastrophic", to the point where my focus was on the 'fear of things not happening as I wanted' rather than on my 'trust that it would all work out for my highest good'. I was back in my Rats' Den for that time so just attracted more Rats (problems).

It did all come together and although from the outside my house looks small, once inside it's really quite large! I even got my 'little - big house'! And with the extra large conservatory I had put on (at a bargain price!) it certainly feels spacious enough. I have loved making it beautiful without having to compromise on a partner's choices, I have loved putting up stunning Christmas trees that rival Harrods, I have loved that it is perfect to work from and I've never been happier.

We can often see with the benefit of hindsight that something we were upset or frustrated about actually worked out well. The key is to be in the state of trust *at the time it didn't work out*. This saves us much angst and keeps us in our Palace mind at the difficult time. The Universe is always saying 'yes' to us; just not always in the way we might anticipate!

When we trust the process and timing we live much more comfortably. If we want a relationship and keep noticing the absence of it we're back in our Rats' Den. When we trust the perfect relationship is out there for us and focus on getting ourself ready to *receive* it, we can feel content. There are all sorts of reasons why that special person isn't yet appearing. We can trust they will come at the perfect time and space and enjoy all the things we *can* do whilst on our own that wont be so easy with a partner around.

I have had to make a lot of changes within myself to be able to now *receive* what my mind has known I've wanted in a relationship (and other areas of life) for many years. When I was a '1' out of 10 in self-worth, self-esteem and deservability and lived from a point of total disconnection from my real self, I could never have 'let in' the wonderful man my heart desired. If I want a 10 man, I have to be a 10 myself, not only to be able to 'receive' him in my life but to be attractive to *him!*

As I've learned to trust myself I have been able to cultivate the trust in life and the process thereof. Of course there are challenges in life. It's all part of growth. If there were no challenges there would be no growth, on any level. The difference is in the way we handle them. Trust helps keep us securely anchored during 'life's storms' and it is Loving Ourselves that creates the space for trust. A willow tree has the flexibility to sway and bend in a storm and then become upright again afterwards and in time, any damage will repair. It is the solid rigid oak that breaks or gets uprooted and falls over. Cultivating self-love and trust helps us be the willow!

Letting Our Thoughts Go Out Uninterrupted.

When we are focusing on something that we do want and aligning the Palace Components it is necessary to keep an open mind as to *how* our desires will manifest.

If we start deciding "A new job will come through the Job Centre" or "I'll join a dating agency and meet my partner" we limit ourselves. If we were tuning into a radio on a narrow band instead of the full range of frequencies available, we could only receive the restricted number of programmes. Essentially it is the same with our thoughts. Once we've thought about what we do want, we can focus on aligning the other 4 Components, cultivate trust and then pleasurably await what comes to us, keeping a completely open mind so we tune into the widest frequency band possible to access our good. It is wonderful how unexpected good comes our way when we're not in the way of it! The less attachment we have toward something manifesting, the more open we are to allowing it.

It is also no good to say "I'm doing all this and when I see the result I want I'll believe it". I had a client who came to me for hypnotherapy for improving her confidence. She soon understood how she needed to shift her focus to *being* confident and not on the 'absence of' her confidence. The following week it was apparent that she was implementing this and was putting the new ways I'd shared with her into practise. However, she was waiting to *see the evidence* of her "I am now confident" space so she could prove to herself she'd changed, in order to believe it.

Notice this is not the same at all as saying "I am confident" and being in Palace mind. Saying "I am now confident" and looking for external validation so she could believe it, was then just a wish. She was really sending out a vibration of *doubt* about it happening - Rats' Den again.

Similarly, if you decide something like "This new job will be a turning point for me" you are setting yourself up for disappointment if it doesn't work out that way. It may end up being a turning point or it may not. It's not your prerogative to decide. This kind of 'fixed agenda' living is tight and often joyless. Surround the new job with positive thoughts and feelings and wait to see how it unfolds. May be you need to work on yourself more before you reach a turning point or maybe there is something else ahead which is even better.

Feeling any sense of limitation, impatience, observing what hasn't happened yet, or feeling frustration or disappointment, all put you back with the Rats. Trust the process of life and work on yourself to be open to receiving, allowing your thought vibrations to go out unblocked or uninterrupted, and let your good come to you in the way the Universe decides!

Understanding The Balance Between Action And Allowing

Sometimes we can decide what we want and then go all out to obtain it at all costs. We often end up disappointed or worn out. Even if we achieve what we want, it can often be unsatisfying. In essence we are saying "The only way

I can have this is by putting in 100% Action Effort" and we're falling into the trap of all sorts of negative attachments described before.

I used to put *so* much Action Effort into life! Yet I seemed to get very little back, primarily because I had such a mis-programmed 'blueprint'. Even when I had worked on this I still needed to understand the difference between Action Effort and Allowing Effort. *Allowing Effort is when we focus on aligning the 5 Components and become the magnet for our good instead of chasing it with Action Effort.*

Of course effort is necessary to achieve things. Effort is necessary to choose to be in your Palace mind until it is second nature. However if, for example, you are desperate for a job and put lots of Action Effort into applying for as many as possible, the negative desperation will likely sabotage you to a greater or lesser extent. If instead, you first work to align the 5 Components of the Palace mind, particularly Loving Yourself to connect with your inner guidance, you'll become the magnet for a job that really suits you. Similarly, advertising all over for clients, or doing everything you can think of to meet a partner will tend to push away what you want, chasing it with Action Effort. When your vibrational space is aligned with the 5 palace Components, you'll draw in clients or an ideal partner with Allowing Effort.

Allowing Effort starts from within. When you are aligned and connected with your true self, able to access your wisdom, you then intuitively know the Action Effort that is required. The balance comes in cultivating your ability to listen to your own intuitive inner guidance and only take action when it *feels* right, deep within, i.e. *inspired action.* If you take action and it seems an uphill struggle, back off and re-assess. When things feel right, things flow and manifestation tends to come easily.

Enjoying the Journey

One of the biggest 'mistakes' I made on my own life path was to be completely attached to the end goal. I would put out my desires, imagine them as 'true', practise the correct speech patterns - and then feel the disappointment and frustration of very few of them actually manifesting.

Besides realising I never felt worthy and deserving enough to *have* what I truly wanted, let alone love myself, I also had to learn it isn't all about 'getting what we want'; there's a journey to be had. Of course the purpose of thinking about what we want, feeling it, speaking appropriately, working on our deservability and loving ourselves is to get us from where we *are* to where we want *to be* - or what we want to do or have. However it is *mindfulness of the journey* that has to be our focus too.

Suppose we want to get from Cornwall to Scotland. For most of our experience we will not be in Scotland. Most of the experience will be about the journey. If we're constantly feeling frustrated or disappointed we're not in Scotland we'll have a pretty miserable journey and also a very narrow one. If we're so focused on getting to our destination as quickly as possible there is so much we could miss out on - enjoying the scenery, stopping off at a village pub for lunch, meeting someone who turns out to be life influencing in some way, choosing to stay at a delightful B&B to make the journey easier, exploring some of the sights and places of interest along the way, etc.

Even if we never got to Scotland for some reason, we'd still have had a happy life experience in the process. And maybe Scotland wouldn't have been what we'd anticipated anyway. Or maybe we'll choose to change our destination as our experiences along the way give us different enlightenments. And if we do get to Scotland we'll be all the better for the richness of the journey.

My point is to absolutely have your desires and goals; it brings meaning and purpose to your life. However if 'getting them' feels crucial to your enjoyment of life, besides tuning into a negative vibration to block them coming, if they don't happen life will be a big disappointment. Align the 5 Components for Palace living and then focus on your journey, first and foremost appreciating each day just because you're alive.

Realise there are many things that are more important than the important things on your list. Cultivate happiness without needing more. You then become the magnet for more!

The key to living well is to be so happy and connected with 'who you are' deep inside you feel completely content regardless of what manifests.

I used to think I needed certain things to 'be happy' - such as a big house, a relationship, lots of money etc and constantly felt the disappointment of them not being in my life. Then, when I did have them it never brought me the happiness I wanted! I was looking for these external things to fulfill me. Now I know I can be happy anyway - and I *am* - and as of the time of writing I don't have any of those things in my life. I am happy because I've learned to be happy with myself, connected deep within and I've learned to enjoy the journey. Sure, those things are again on my vision board - yet now they come from a deeper space within me, have more meaning and purpose and feel authentic. If they happen they happen - and if they don't, I'll enjoy life anyway! It took me years to get to this point. I do hope this book will allow you to get here very much quicker!

Chapter Eight
Boarding Up The Rats' Den
Part One

It's time to start reprogramming your mental 'blueprint'. You'll need to rid yourself of the deep-seated negativity constantly pulling you back to your Rats' Den if you are to pack your bags and move to your Palace. With the insights gained from the last chapters we can now work on the blocks you identified in chapter two.

Dissolving Resistance

Let's go back to pages 14–16 to all the Resistances you underlined that you have in your way and which are blocking you from living well. These can now be dissolved and replaced with nourishing things that serve you much better. I have found a very effective way to achieve this is to use the following exercise, based on an NLP (Neuro Linguistic Programming) technique. Whatever time it takes will be well worth your investment as it will give you the template for a whole new way of thinking and living!

EXERCISE:

Copy out each sentence you underlined and write *'I used to'* in front of it. For example, I used to believe I wasn't good enough. I used to think no one understood me. I used to believe life was hard and lonely. I used to fear I might be worse off. I used to procrastinate and put things off. I used to avoid doing things even though I knew they would benefit me. I used to blame others. Etc. Add words to make it flow into a paragraph.

Then write a paragraph with *'I now realise'* at the start of each sentence and write as many things as possible, incorporating what you've learned. This can be general, for example: I now realise these negative blocks need no longer be true for me. I now realise these old ways do not serve me. I now realise I am the only one who thinks in my mind and I can change these old patterns. I now realise I can connect with my own power and reprogramme my mind in ways that do serve me, etc. You can also be specific, for example: I now realise I am good enough just because I exist. I now realise I just learned that life was difficult and lived that out, it is not 'true' as not everyone thinks this and as a result they live more happily. Etc.

Then take each sentence you wrote for 'I used to' in your first paragraph and turn it around to the *direct opposite*, putting *'I now choose to'* in front. For example (the opposite of the examples above) I now choose to believe I am good enough exactly as I am. I now choose to stop giving my power to other people and take it back for myself, focusing on building my own self-worth and esteem. I now choose to trust and flow with life and grow in confidence to embrace relationships with others. I now choose to feel the fear and do it anyway, knowing in my Palace mind I can handle things. I now choose to deal with tasks as they crop up knowing this will make me feel good. I now choose to accept accountability for myself regardless of others. Etc.

(If you had 20 statements in your 'I used to' paragraph you'll ideally need 20 direct opposite statements in your 'I now choose to' paragraph. You can then add any general choices that feel right for you).

Two examples of completed scripts are shown below to help. Take as much from them as you wish especially the 'I now realise' paragraphs, as well as using your own words to create your powerful reprogramming script. Know that just in doing this exercise you are starting the process of change because your mind has to come up with the opposites you want in order for you to write them down!

This first example is to help you turn around the Resistances you underlined on pages 14–16.

Dissolving Resistance
Example Script

I used to believe I wasn't good enough. I used to believe I wouldn't find something to help me. I used to let myself believe there was

Beat Your Depression For Good

nothing wrong with me and that I'd 'get by' like I've somehow done before. I used to believe "that's just life" and that I couldn't live without my cigarettes/drink/drugs. I used to put things off, telling myself "I'll do it later" or that "I don't have the time right now", despite actually having plenty of time, often being bored. I used to keep up appearances, not wanting to let anyone know I have a problem. I used to use self-diminishing language such as "I'm sorry" or "I'm probably wrong but....." to cover my lack of confidence. I used to judge others according to my values and perceptions and allow self-righteousness to cloud my vision. And, worst of all, I used to believe that my only way forward was for someone else to wave a magic wand to enable me to be happy, having always been surrounded by people who have always done everything for me and never learning to do things for myself.

I now realise it is up to me to take accountability for my life and this is something I CAN do. I now realise it is MY life and no one else can live it for me. I am the only one who thinks in my mind. I am responsible for the thoughts I allow to live there and for my reactions to each thought. I now realise I have complete choice in the way I go and what I do. I now realise I can take back my own power and make positive choices. I now realise I can handle everything that comes my way as I can always choose to come from the point of power rather than the point of helplessness. I now realise I can choose my thoughts with care, understanding that each and EVERY thought I have tunes me into my Palace or my Rats' Den with all the consequences thereof. I now realise I am good enough exactly as I am. I now realise I can let go of old habits that don't serve me. I now realise I can face up to things. I now realise it serves me to lay down all judgment. I now realise I can change my language patterning. I now realise I am the one who holds the magic wand in my life as I learn the new ways of thinking, feeling and speaking to create all that I DO want to be and do and have. I now realise I am worthy and deserving of all good, including an abundance of love, joy and fulfillment.

I now choose to lay down all my resistance to my own good. I now choose to embrace my worth, knowing I am good enough exactly as I am. I now have the answers to help me move forward and I choose to face up to things. I now choose to embrace life and nurture myself, respecting my body and only giving it nourishing foods and beverages. I now choose to allow myself to be efficient and get things done as they crop up. This way I feel good about myself. I now choose to be free of past limitations as I choose to handle challenges positively. I now choose positive language that aligns with my positive thoughts and feelings to create all I want, including confidence, self-respect and self-worth. I now choose to lay down all judgment, welcoming in acceptance, including self-acceptance. I choose to be accountable for my life, pick up my magic wand, take back my own power and live life to the best of my ability, knowing life will improve daily as I move toward and into the 'Palace', ultimately to sit on my awaiting throne and be King/Queen of my own life. It feels so good to know this is so easily within my power!

I now choose to forgive the past and all who have harmed me. I now choose to forgive myself for all I have and haven't done. I now choose to set myself free. I am worthy and deserving of all my good and I let it in because I believe this. I am willing to approve of myself and accept myself as I am and LOVE MYSELF because this aligns me with my true source and soul from where I can truly LIVE IN JOY.

When you've finished your script, feel a sense of achievement and say 'well done' to yourself! Read it as often as possible for as long as it takes to suddenly find you've stopped thinking the "I used to" statements and find yourself living the "I now choose to" ways automatically. Remember it wont *all* be from black to white; some things you'll be able to embrace swiftly, others may take more time. Be gentle with yourself. Choose to Love Yourself enough to embrace living your new choices. Keep reinforcing them until they have filled your entire being and the old resistances no longer exist.

You can also write an additional script for any other things that you want to change. For example "I used to attract violent relationships" "I used to shout at my children" "I used to believe I wasn't worthy of....." etc and write the appropriate "I now realise" and "I now choose to" sentences to turn them around.

This second example is an additional script a client wrote. I am immensely grateful to her for allowing me to share it with you here.

Dissolving Resistance
Example of an Additional Script

I used to believe I was lost and alone and nothing would ever change for me. I used to believe it was all my fault and I just had to accept how things were for me. I used to believe life was hard and harsh and there wasn't any good for me. I used to believe it was impossible to stop smoking. I used to believe I was mentally ill and needed drugs and counseling. I used to believe I just wasn't capable of living life. I used to believe it was hard to change. I used to isolate myself and not see anyone. I used to be weak and completely lacking in confidence and power. I used to give my power away, looking for love and acceptance. I used to feel like I didn't belong anywhere. I used to feel I was a bad person. I used to live in fear.

Now I realise I have the power to change everything. I now realise I can understand the past, forgive it and let it go once and for all. I now realise I really am worthy and deserving and I have the power to choose the life I truly deserve. I now realise how the mind works and therefore I recognise what is happening when a negative thought arises and have all the power to change it. I now realise resistance is futile and by allowing and accepting I have all the power and control I need to redirect my thoughts and feelings. I now realise that I really do have a choice in every area of my life in every moment and that I can choose love, health, joy and abundance. I now realise I can stop smoking. I can love and heal my body. I can be free. I now realise I can be happy in every moment. I now realise I am powerful.

I now choose to love myself. I choose to love life every moment of every day. I now choose to completely let go of all that has been and live only in the present, open to all that is wonderful, loving and good. I now choose to really love and nurture my body and mind and soul. I now have all I need to face any challenge with peace, grace and love. I now choose to completely forgive myself and set myself free. I choose to open my heart to life and live it fully. I now choose to give myself time every day to work on my personal growth because I am worth it. I now choose to believe in the goodness of my being and share it with the world. I choose to believe in the unlimited power of love. I now choose a happy, healthy, fulfilling life. I choose to become all I really am and enjoy the discovery. I choose to live in the moment and be grateful for all I have and all I am receiving and all that I have coming to me.

New Beliefs

I do hope you are already constantly repeating "I am worthy and deserving of all my good", or your chosen equivalent, to help reprogramme your Worthiness and Deservability beliefs.

Let's now go back to the Beliefs you wrote in chapter two so you can reprogramme any of those that aren't serving you. Referring to pages 18/19 read over what you wrote.

It may become very clear the extent of the negativity from which you have unknowingly been functioning! If you have any doubt about which beliefs are negative and which are positive just notice how they make you *feel*.

Some of what you've written may well be positive and serve you well, which is wonderful. No doubt those areas of your life are working favourably for you.

If you have written "Work - necessary to earn money" realise this is *not* positive. Anything that gives a neutral feeling is not really serving you as a 'blueprint' belief. "Money - it doesn't grow on trees" isn't positive and does not serve you either.

Now is your opportunity to create the best 'blueprint' you could ever have chosen to have had programmed into your mind when you were very young. If you had received these positive messages in the first place and consequently given this data your attention, you would automatically have these beliefs today. If you had unhelpful programming you can use your own power to change this now. Remember this is not about blame; that gives your power away. Cultivate acceptance and take accountability for your life now. Of course the new choices wont feel true yet – you first need to get the template in place to then be able to internalise them as your new truths.

If you can identify with any of the following negatives, you might like to consider the alternative positive suggestions laid out here for your own set of new beliefs.

Depression: Clients always put negatives here! "Feels bad", "Stuck", "Endless misery", "Overwhelming", "A black hole" are just a few of the selection I hear.

However, *isn't it true that if you weren't having the negative depressing thoughts you couldn't feel depressed?* Isn't your body just feeding you back physical reactions due to the fact that your thoughts are in the Rats' Den?

If your belief about depression was "**I** am in charge of my thoughts and by living in my Palace and Loving Myself I need never know depression" what difference could that make for you? How much more empowered might you feel?

Imagine having had this truth in your 'blueprint' since childhood. You would never have given your power to your Rats. We can feel shock and horror and have negative emotions for a while without slipping into depression. Embrace this as a new belief now and know that you need never know depression again!

Yourself: If you believe you are incompetent, weak, worthless, unimportant, inferior, resentful, fearful, unlucky, etc, how can you possibly live well? What do you wish you had grown up believing about yourself?

"I am confident, motivated and have purpose" "I am worthy and deserving of all my good" "I am strong and powerful" "I love myself". Imagine the difference in your life if these were your beliefs.

Men/Women: If you have written negatives about the same sex or the opposite sex you are setting yourself up for those negatives to show up again and again. I remember years ago a therapist asked me ten things I believed about men. They were all negative! How could I expect to find a wonderful man if I essentially believed men were all those negative things? Of course there are some men out there who fitted my list (which, not surprisingly, were the ones I found!) yet there are plenty of men who are the very opposite! To attract one of *them* into my life I'd have to change my beliefs to positive things about men in order to set up that pattern match. If I'd known this years ago my life would have been very different! Instead, I was waiting for a good man to come along to disprove my negative beliefs! Perhaps not exactly an ideal basis to form a wholesome relationship!

Healthy beliefs might be "I am comfortable with men/women" "I enjoy working with men/women" "I enjoy friendships with men/women" "I attract intimate relationships with those who reflect my positive beliefs about men/women" "I attract intimate relationships with those who reflect the positive beliefs I have about myself".

Friends: Maybe you've had poor experiences with friends letting you down, or too few friends. If so, ask yourself, very gently, why you made friends with people like this in the first place or why you don't have many friends. What is inside *you* that creates this? Do you have beliefs that you're not worthy of being liked/loved and therefore keep this distance by vibrationally inviting others to prove this to you? Or are you easily jealous or judgmental? The first shift is to work on the beliefs you wished had been in your 'blueprint' and then work on yourself to align with that same space to attract and allow friends like that to come into your life. Be aware of any negative thoughts that doubt this shift will change anything! It's just your Rats complaining again. If you keep feeding them the negatives will keep flourishing.

Your new chosen beliefs may be "I always have wonderful friends who are reliable and fun to be with" "I make friends with people who are mutually supportive and positive" "I value my friends" "I easily make new friends" "I am a good friend". If you'd had these beliefs in your 'blueprint' you would be experiencing these today.

Love: I have found so many people don't even feel they know what love is, or certainly have many negative notions about it. "Love hurts" "You have to earn love" "Love is difficult". The truth is *Love is the greatest and most powerful emotional force we have.* All that's happened is that you didn't get the right images of love 'programmed in'. Choose new beliefs that inspire you and encourage you to find the love within yourself and around you. Loving your self is the ultimate antidote to depression because when you Love Yourself you feel good!

What do you wish you believed? "Love is wonderful" "I am loving and lovable" "I find love wherever I go" "I give love easily and enjoy receiving love" "I love myself" "I attract true love in an intimate relationship that reflects the love I have for myself" "Love makes me feel good".

Work. If you are in a job you dislike, realise that staying there is not an act of Loving Yourself and is not living well. Even if temporarily you have to work at something or somewhere you'd prefer not to, *find the good in it* and focus on what you *do* want. Believing 'it's hard out there' will only make it harder for you.

Your desired work beliefs may be "I always enjoy my work" "My work is rewarding and fulfilling" "I always earn an excellent income" "I have plenty of clients for my services" "I work in places where I am valued and respected".

People who already live these things certainly didn't come from a space of believing they hated work or never got paid well or got taken advantage of. Installing these new beliefs will help enable you to shift into that new desired space. Love Yourself enough to allow yourself to be the best you can be and to have a wonderful job!

Money. This is really interesting. People are *so* tied up in their beliefs about money. Are yours positive or negative? Be aware here:

"I have to work in order to earn" is negative because it is *limiting*.

"Money is the root of all evil" is not true; the correct quote is *"The love of money is the root of all evil"*. There's nothing wrong with money.

"Money isn't important" is a really common trap to fall into thinking it is positive. It's not. Believing money isn't important to you or that money doesn't make you happy aren't helpful beliefs. Try being without money and you'll soon find out how important it is to you.

It is true money *in itself* doesn't make you happy yet it is your choice of what you *do* with your money that will bring you happiness. Having the money to experience wonderful holidays, or to buy your children nice things, or to have the joy of a car to drive around in that isn't falling to pieces are all advantages that make life more pleasurable.

Equally, "I don't need or want lots of money" doesn't serve you. If you are willing to be *open and receptive to all your good* it is contradictory to then say you want to limit the amount of money you have. If you become aligned enough to have surplus wealth, welcome it and give some away to where it will do good. Feel the joy of knowing you just paid for a child's operation, or funded some local project, or helped some animals somewhere in the world and made a difference.

If you feel guilty about having more than others, once again realise this does not serve anyone. It doesn't help others and it keeps you in your Rats' Den! The guilt is pointless. If you are aligned enough to tune into abundance on *any* level embrace it with gratitude and appreciation and praise yourself for this achievement! Feeling guilty about having 2 legs or eyes that 'see' would amount to the same thing. It doesn't help the amputee or the blind person and just sends out negative vibrations into our incredible Universe. For what purpose? Instead, choose to embrace the abundance and enjoy the extra freedom you have and share it with others when you desire.

As a nation we are notoriously generous to charities, be it at home or for some disaster that happens abroad, yet I often find people say *"If I had the money I'd give to charity"*. What are they really saying? They are saying they would rather buy their newspaper, their lottery ticket, their own food and so on than give £2 per month to a charity. Giving £2 per month wouldn't actually change these things, or even be missed, yet it would do immense good elsewhere. The damage to themselves is that they are giving out a poverty thinking message of *"I don't have enough money"* which takes me back to the first point I made about negative beliefs about money. Be honest! If you don't want to give to charity, *don't*, and be comfortable with that choice and *keep your beliefs positive and authentic.*

We've all heard 'money comes to money'. Why is this? It is because people who've got plenty of money have a good mental relationship with money. People who don't have much money invariably believe "Money is hard to come by" or "I have to work hard for money". We will experience what we have tuned into from our deepest 'blueprint' layers.

Consider embracing beliefs such as "I am comfortable with money" "Money is my friend" "I love the freedom that having money brings" "I am a magnet for money" "I enjoy the good I can do giving money away" "The more money I have, the more I can contribute to the good in the world" "I enjoy the experiences money allows me to have" "I am worthy and deserving of all the money to meet my needs and desires".

If you already have these as beliefs you are blessed and no doubt live in financial comfort. What we think about *and believe* becomes true for us.

Health. Often clients write "You're lucky to have good health" or similar, to suggest it is in the lap of the gods. Your thoughts affect your health too! Your body feeds back everything you are thinking. For example, if there are two people going for an interview, one of whom is very anxious and one of whom is confident, which one is most likely to have 'butterflies in the tummy' and even end up in the lavatory with 'the runs'? Of course it's the anxious one. If they weren't having the anxious thoughts, their body wouldn't reflect this with the physical response.

Louise Hay did a great deal of research on the thoughts behind almost every ailment known. You can read about these and the appropriate changes to make in your thoughts to regain health in her books "Heal your Body" or "You Can Heal Your Life". She says the 'mental causations' have been found to be about 95% accurate. In my experience, they're about 99% accurate!

Here comes a curious thing. I have known so many people ailing, who profess to want to be healthy, yet aren't willing to entertain this notion at all, including my own darling sister who died of an epileptic fit when she was 34. I have found this to be for many underlying reasons including: "It's too awful to consider that I would have inflicted this on myself"; "That would make me feel too vulnerable, whilst I see myself as a victim I can cope"; "It's the only way I learned how to get attention"; "Being ill means I escape other responsibilities in my life that I fear I can't handle"; "My parents were always ill and so I will be" and many more.

It is also true we live in a culture where we have given our power to modern medicine so have forgotten we have our own innate ability to heal. When we have symptoms that we didn't have before, we go to a doctor who then gives us a name for those symptoms in the form of a diagnosis and then we are prescribed medicine or an operation to stop those symptoms. Alternatively, we could choose to explore the concept of *"How is it I have symptoms now that I didn't have before? What Rats' Den thoughts have I had to make my body give this particular physical response?"* When we release the negativity, we can see dramatic health improvements.

Of course I am not suggesting that we don't get treated. I am suggesting we don't have to give *all* our power to modern medicine. As I write this I am working with a lady who has a potentially cancerous lump around her submandibular gland on the right side of her neck. It is wonderful that this can be diagnosed and treated these days. It is also a blessing we live in a country where treatment is relatively easily accessible and free. Yet we are also working to dissolve the *mental causations* for this dis-ease and to prepare her to be in the best mental state for her operation; securely in her Palace mind, strong, authentically forward focused (not just superficially 'thinking positively') and at peace. We are visualising her being healthy and aligning those 5 Components to cultivate good health from now on.

Another lady I had as a phone client had been suffering for nine years with a rare condition called conversion syndrome for which she'd had many treatments, both physical and psychological. She had terrible attacks of 'shakes' that took over her entire body and clearly affected her life very detrimentally. After a few months of weekly sessions she felt so much better mentally and her shakes reduced dramatically. By the end of our sessions she was a different woman and 'shake free' and was even able to attend her son's wedding. I shall treasure her lovely thank you card and letter forever. You can read her testimonial on my website www.depressionbustingcourses.com

It is amazing how much we can help ourselves to good health when we take back our own power and live in the Palace. I explained in the section on 'Anger' how I used the Balancing the Power visualisation to heal myself and no longer need that operation.

What do you want your health beliefs to be? You might like to consider "I am filled with vibrant health and energy" "I use the power of my mind to be in my Palace and create great health" "I go beyond my parents' ailments as my own person and enjoy good health" "I am blessed with health and vitality".

Success. So often success is perceived as something external that we achieve or is perhaps beyond our scope to reach. Whenever we feel the *absence* of something we're in our Rats' Den, keeping us apart from our good. Realise you are already a success because you're here! The odds against a sperm and an egg coming together to create you is zillions to one against. Well done! You made it! Then consider this:

Imagine an Olympic Swimmer who has won the gold medal. Is he a success? Of course. Was he a success when he won the bronze medal in the Commonwealth Games? Yes! Was he a success when he was Junior Champion? Yes. Was he a success when he was best in school? When he could swim a length? When he'd learned to swim? When he first got in the pool? Absolutely. Each stage was a worthy goal in itself.

Now imagine if he'd learned to swim and then said "But I haven't won the gold medal yet" and when he was best in school he said "But I haven't got the gold medal yet" and so on. Where would the joy have been in his achievements? Would he have moved joyously from stage to stage or would it all have been pretty meaningless because he 'hadn't got the gold medal yet'? If he never got the gold medal his ambition would be down the drain and he would feel the misery of what he'd striven for all his life not happening. Instead, by recognising every step of his achievements and feeling the good feelings about himself along the way, not only would his journey be much more positively motivated, how much more would he have been in his Palace mind to help him achieve his goals? If he hadn't won the gold medal it would have been *one disappointment in a lifetime of achievement.*

Consider your beliefs about success from what you *have* done and achieved. You successfully got your job or bought your car or went shopping or perhaps made someone else happy today. You achieve success every day! Embrace it and acknowledge yourself for it! You can also see success as *any* step towards a worthy goal and praise yourself all the way.

You might change your beliefs to "I am a success because I am here" "I am successful every day in many ways" "Success is every little step I take toward any worthy goal" "Success breeds more success" "I willingly recognise and embrace all my successes" "I am a magnet for success".

Light bulb inventor Thomas Edison said "The most certain way to succeed is to try just one more time".

If these beliefs had been programmed in when you were little you would feel successful today. Embrace the change now.

Failure. If you feel bad because you feel you've failed at something that's guaranteed to put you in your Rats' Den! For what purpose?

Doesn't failure just mean *something didn't work out the way we wanted it to at the time?* Why do we need to beat ourselves up about it? Even if we feel we 'should have known better' beating ourselves up doesn't help! Your Palace mind can make a sensible assessment and is rational and has your solutions to move forward.

As Edison also said "I have not failed. I have just found 10,000 ways that won't work". I have adapted this for myself in the form of *"I spent today finding out how not to do things",* feeling acceptance rather than frustration.

You might choose the beliefs you wish had been fed into your 'blueprint' to be "Failure just means it didn't work out how I wanted it to at that time"

"Failure is an opportunity to do things differently next time" "There is no such thing as failure, just lessons to be learned".

Sometimes people get confused over the difference between a 'belief' and an 'affirmation'. Whilst the wording can be similar or even the same, an affirmation focuses us on what we want to change or manifest now; a belief is something we've stored deeply that we need to change deeply.

For example, an affirmation could be "I now have many new friends" or "Money now comes to me easily and I welcome it". If your deep-seated belief is "I find it difficult to make friends" or "Only bad people have money" this will inevitably pull you back and hamper your affirmation manifesting. Changing your *belief* to "I always have plenty of great friends" or "I always have plenty of money" enables you to be free of the contradiction.

As you do the following exercise, think in terms of what you would have wanted your four year old self to have taken on board, rather than wording things in terms of what you want to change now.

EXERCISE:

Write out, with pride, the new beliefs you want to programme into your mind. You could do this straight onto the relevant page in the Cut-Out section of this book. Read them over and over and over until they are as entrenched in your brain as your date of birth. With enough attention you will find these new beliefs take over and the old ones disappear. Focus on a new belief one at a time and look for the ways it then shows up. What we focus on grows. It may take a little time to see the manifestation while you are in the process of re-educating your mind yet the more focused and trusting you are the quicker the results will be.

You might end up with a page that looks something like this:

New Beliefs
Example:

Depression - is just my body telling me my thoughts are in the Rats' Den. I am in charge of my mind and I choose thoughts that serve me. I live in my Palace where depression doesn't exist.

Myself - I am blessed to be alive. I am confident, secure and full of self-worth and self-esteem. I love myself. I am worthy and deserving of all my good. I am in love with life.

Men - have lots of qualities and skills to serve the world positively. Men are good fun. I am comfortable with men. I like working with men. I have harmonious relationships with men. I have good relationships with the men in my family. I attract intimate relationships with those who reflect the positive beliefs I have about myself. I always have the courage to end intimate relationships that no longer serve me.

Women - have lots of qualities and skills to serve the world positively. Women are good fun. I am comfortable with women. I like working with women. I have harmonious relationships with women. I have good relationships with the women in my family. I attract intimate relationships with those who reflect the positive beliefs I have about myself. I always have the courage to end intimate relationships that no longer serve me.

Friends - I always have lots of wonderful, caring, supportive friends. I value and respect my friends and they value and respect me. I make new friends easily. I am friends with people who are mutually supportive and positive. I am a good friend.

Love - I am loving and lovable. Loving myself makes me feel wonderful. I love myself more and more. I find love wherever I go. I give love easily and freely and I willingly and easily receive it back.

Work - I always have great jobs. I love going to work. I am passionate about my work. I feel valued and respected at work. I enjoy what I do at work. I always work at the right job at the right time and space. I am always well paid.

Money - I am comfortable with money. Money is my friend. I love the freedom that having money brings. I am a magnet for money. I enjoy the good I can do giving money away. The more money I have the more good I can contribute to the world.

Health - I am filled with vibrant health and energy. I use the power of my mind to be in my Palace and create great health. I go beyond my parents' ailments as my own person and enjoy good health. I am blessed with health and vitality.

Success - is any step towards a worthy goal. I am a success because I exist. I am constantly successful in many ways every day. I embrace all my successes.

Failure - just means something didn't work out the way I wanted at that time. It is an opportunity to do it differently next time. A lesson to be learned and to grow from.

Now compare what you've written with your original beliefs list. This may show you graphically the reason you've been in your Rats' Den! How exciting to be taking back your own power in this way instead of living from the data someone else programmed into you - by default! Choose to start your own reprogramming now this minute. The fact that you have written your new list is already evidence of you making positive change; your mind has now got the data for where you do want to be and when you go there in the mind you go there in the body. When you have made this shift authentically you'll have made permanent life change!

If you still need convincing that it's worth the effort to do this and to read your new beliefs *constantly* so they become part of you, (just the way your old beliefs did when you gave *them* the attention) consider this:

I was working with a client who was in a pretty deep dark space, well and truly entrenched in his Rats' Den. When we went through his beliefs as they were then, every single one of them was negative except money. He had come from a privileged background where he'd frequently been given money. He confessed he'd put an enormous amount of money into drink and drugs over the years. His beliefs about depression, himself, men, women, love, work, success and failure were all doom and gloom. When it came to money he'd put "money grows on trees and is easy to get". When he left after the 2 day course with me, feeling that life perhaps *was* worth living and with some positive focus, he'd decided he needed a camera to photograph some things to sell, plus a computer of his own. Later he called me to say that he got home to a host of calls about work, which had been practically non-existent prior to him coming. He'd been dog walking for a sick neighbour who, out of the blue, gave him money. Within *one week* he'd got enough money to buy an ipad and a quality camera. I guarantee if his beliefs about money had been "I have to struggle for money" or "money is hard to come by`" he would not have had this experience. Oh what incentive to change his other beliefs!! And, I trust, yours.

Core Beliefs

It is also worth pondering on other core beliefs that hold you back and lead to disappointment and frustration. These are often the root of, or linked into, lack of deservability feelings too. For example, if you have a deep-seated belief that you're alone or unwanted it may leave you feeling somewhat detached or disconnected from others and from life. Perhaps you therefore find it difficult to build fulfilling relationships. If so, how can you then feel worthy and deserving with this contradiction in the way? The core belief that you're alone or unwanted will always prevent you closing the gap from 'where you are' to 'where you want to be' because it will always pull you back to that negative belief space in your

Rats' Den. This is why it is imperative to change your beliefs at this deep level. Otherwise they will keep pulling you back to your Rats' Den regardless of how much other work you do on yourself.

Do you feel generally unwelcome or that there's no place for you in the world? Do you have a core belief that you don't belong? Or are you overly self-blaming or overly responsible (it's all my fault), believing you're innately wrong? Or do you feel you somehow deserve to be punished because you're innately bad? Perhaps you feel inadequate and that you are 'not enough', consequently being too self-sacrificing or living in deprival.

I've had clients whose Deservability issues stem from a core belief that they have no right to take up space, or some feel a burden just because they are alive. Others have felt cursed by being too different to comfortably fit in with social circles or with life. These beliefs need to be shifted before they can truly feel worthy enough to let their good in or live well.

Do you feel you're too much or too big and loud or too self-contained and inadvertently shut yourself off from convivial relationships or the ability to truly express the fullness of your gifts into the world? Do you give the impression of being totally self-sufficient as a subconsciously adopted strategy to overcome a deep feeling of powerlessness? Does this manifest in you being distant with people whilst in fact you deeply crave connection with others?

Perhaps you were raised in circumstances or with messages that have made you feel unsafe, so find it difficult to connect with others in a wholesome way. Perhaps you feel unimportant or inferior, making it difficult to be seen or heard by others. This can also bring a paralysing level of perfectionism, insecurity and lack of confidence. Perhaps you just feel plain unworthy or worthless.

If we grow up with 'lack' messages we can easily take on beliefs that we 'can't have' and no matter how much effort we put in, or how capable we are, we end up 'not having' what we want or have worked so hard for.

Arguably, the most damaging of all is if we've grown up without a firm foundation of being and feeling loved. We are often unable to truly thrive and flourish in life, or feel empty regardless of 'successes'. When we come from a space of not feeling lovable we can only create situations that support that belief and we end up worn out just trying to get our basic needs met.

Realise all of these have come from what you've learned from the influences around you and have created the basis of your experiences. They are not *true*.

Sit quietly, close your eyes, relax as deeply as you can and reflect on *any* core beliefs that don't serve you. Whatever comes to mind or if any of the above resonate with you, write them down. Determine to change those core beliefs now at this 'blueprint' level and reprogramme your mind with new positive choices that *do* serve you to believe.

EXERCISE

Write a 'Dissolving Script' as you did for your Resistances: I used to..... I now realise..... I now choose to..... Create the template for this change and read it regularly for as long as it takes to rid yourself of this untrue damaging data and embed your positive truths. Be gentle with yourself and know that you have all the energy and resources to do this.

Although not yet entirely sure how it happens, neuroscientists know that data is fed from our conscious to our subconscious. However, to speed up the process we can use visualisation to directly help on a subconscious level.

The Two Islands visualisation shown below enables you to destroy your damaging beliefs and replace them with new wholesome ones on this deeper level. This again can be found on the free audio download (or purchasable CD) with this book. In addition, I thoroughly recommend you talk to your Inner Child (the 'younger you' who took the false nonsense on board) and heal your emotional 'blueprint' too. That's coming up in part two of this chapter.

Read through your list of negative beliefs that you've identified. Read through the positive beliefs that you want instead. Have them fresh in your mind. You can do this with your resistances and old patterns too. You may choose to do this visualisation with just 2 or 3 things at a time; whatever works best for you.

VISUALISATION: THE TWO ISLANDS

Close your eyes and allow the little muscles on your scalp to relax and feel a sense of peace and calm flowing down over your face. Let go of your cheeks and jaw, letting the peace and calm flow down the back of your head, slowly down your back, relaxing every part, now gently breathing in peace and tranquility, relaxing your chest as you exhale, letting go of your stomach, your hips, buttocks, feeling the calmness coming into your legs, relaxing those heavy thigh muscles, letting go of your knees and lower legs, slowly into your feet and toes.

When you are feeling relaxed and comfortable imagine you are in a boat floating in the sea. It is laden with all the old negative patterns and beliefs you have just identified. You are so aware of the weight and burden of them! How they've held you back and caused you pain! A little way off you notice a small desert island. You steer your boat to the shore and heave out every last bit of what you want to get rid of. Let it feel good to be taking back your power and dealing with this! See the empty boat and look at the pile on the island. Doesn't it feel good to know you are letting this go?

As you move away from the shore, feeling so much lighter, the boat moving easily now, taking you away from the negativity, you suddenly hear a massive blast! You look back and see the island has exploded into tiny little pieces, floating in the sea, sinking and dissolving into the vastness of the ocean. It's all gone! There's no trace of the island or any of the negative beliefs and patterns. Gone! Forever!

As you breathe a sigh of relief you notice how free you feel, how much bluer the sky looks, how much brighter and warmer the sun. You feel a sense of calm and peace within. As your boat moves easily through the gentle swell of the water, you notice another desert island ahead. This one is bigger and very beautiful with trees and brightly coloured flowering plants. You steer your boat to the shore and marvel at the beautiful sights and sounds. In the centre of the island is a tree, the perfect height for you to reach its wonderful fruit. You realise this is *your* tree. Each fruit contains the *opposite positive aspect* of what you dumped off before!

A little sceptically at first you pick the fruit of Confidence and start to eat it. It is delicious! Then you pick the fruit of *I am Worthy and Deserving* and eat that. It tastes even sweeter. One by one you pick and eat all the fruits of your New Beliefs, taking in this wonderful nutrition deep into your belly, savouring them, assimilating them into your system. Take all the time you need. Eat and absorb the positivity. You feel strengthened, empowered, somehow elevated as you take in the basis of a whole new way of being.

Feeling comfortably full, knowing you can visit this island any time you like to replenish or fill yourself up even more with all the beliefs and patterns that will serve you and do serve you from now on and into your future, you just drift in your boat for a while, in comfort and joy, feeling good.

And when you're ready, bringing all of these changes with you and anchoring them in the life force in your belly, you can come back to the room and time and space you're in and open your eyes.

Boarding Up The Rats' Den Part Two

Even when we make radical changes to our 'mental blueprint' and are equipped to move forward positively from now, it still leaves all the years up to this point that need to be healed emotionally for us to have true peace within ourselves. To this end we also need to make changes to our 'emotional blueprint' in order to come home to our true self and feel whole. I have found the best way to do this and to heal nearly all past childhood emotional negativity, even that which we're not necessarily aware of, is to discover and cherish our own Inner Child.

Who you see in the mirror today that you know as *'you'* is only a tiny part of you. You are also the *'you'* of last year and the year before and the decade(s) before, back to your teens and a small child. You are made up of all the *'you's'* you've been since you were born. It is *all* your experiences that have created you and brought you to who you are today. To truly Love Ourselves, all of our selves need to be on board.

Particularly if we are coming from a dysfunctional 'blueprint' for love we'll have no true vibrational connection for love. If our parents didn't know how to love themselves, however much they may have loved us or done their best to, we wont have that foundation within us. We will need to install this on our deepest layers if we are to truly come home to ourselves.

When I'm working with a client I don't say very much before I start this exercise as I don't want to create resistance in them if they feel it is 'too alien' or 'not what they've come for'. After the whole exercise it is often humbling to witness the enlightenment and shift that has taken place on this very deep level. I can literally see people start to change before my very eyes.

As you're going through this if you feel any sense of 'switching off' just take a deep breath and choose to follow it through. I find it heart-warming and very special when clients talk so naturally about their Inner Child in subsequent conversations, even my clients who are big burly lorry drivers or successful businessmen. They feel much deeper connection with themselves.

Demi Schneider

EXERCISE:

To obtain the benefit from this process you will need to carry out each stage before reading on to the next. If you just read through this section you will not be able to return to the exercises to do them authentically afterwards.

Gather a piece of plain paper and some pens, pencils or colour felt tips. (If you're not placed to get paper right now there are some blank sheets at the end of this book). If you only have one pen with you, imagine any colours you would use as you do your picture or write the name of any colours on the picture where appropriate).

With your non-dominant hand (i.e. your left hand if you're right handed or vice versa) draw a picture of yourself as a small child. If you choose you can add things around you such as your bike or your dog or friends or even draw a whole scene to depict you in your childhood. Just draw a picture of you as a small child. This is not an art exam - 'stick people' will do if needs be.

~~~~~~~~~~

When you've finished take a good look at the picture. Through your non-dominant hand your Inner Child has spoken. What you are seeing is your emotional 'blueprint' from the time you were that small child. I feel so privileged to have witnessed so many souls that have been laid bare in clients' pictures. I wish I could see yours now to give you my interpretation. Instead you can make your own assessment based on the guidance below.

What your drawing tells you:

How big are you on the page? The size you have drawn indicates your self-worth and self-esteem. The smaller you drew yourself the lower your self-worth and esteem, even at that tender age. (Sometimes people say "oh, I'm that small because it's relative to the scene I've drawn". I asked for a picture of you. If the scenery or other people/things in the picture have caused you to be 'small' it still spells the same story; you lack(ed) self-worth.)

How colourful is your picture? I give clients a huge choice of pens and colours. The more bold and colourful the picture, the more sense of deservability they have. Some do use lots of colours; their core being sees life as colourful and interesting. Others only use one dark pen - even if they've drawn a sun in their picture! They come from a belief that life is dull and 'less than', or that they don't know 'how to have', or don't deserve an interesting, colourful life. Sometimes clients only use very light pencils that are quite faint on the paper. These people have learned messages that have caused them to become diminished shadows of who they really are, with low deservability.

What details have you drawn? This is both telling and revealing.

Hair - is about strength. If you've drawn lots of hair, particularly if coloured, you have an innate strength. If you've drawn yourself bald, you don't feel strong. You may never have been allowed to discover your own power or you give away your power.

Eyes - the bigger the better. This is about your ability to see your world. What does your picture tell you? How much can you/are you willing to see?

Nose - this is your ability to take in life. So often people draw pictures of themselves with no nose; they have no idea how to take in life and then wonder why they feel detached.

Ears - are for listening. No ears means you do not know how to listen to your own inner wisdom and guidance and/or didn't want to hear what was happening at home.

Mouth - is for communication and our ability to speak up for ourselves. Is it a big smiley mouth or a miserable one? Or have you drawn no mouth and have no ability to speak out, or feel wrong about speaking out, or are afraid to?

Have you drawn feet? Pictures that show big sturdy feet belong to people who have understanding, who know how to stand on their own two feet, who can stand up for themselves, who are grounded. No feet means none of the above.

Have you drawn hands? Pictures that show hands (the bigger or more defined the better) belong to people who know how to 'have and hold'. No hands drawn means you don't know how to receive and hold your good. Perhaps you were taught you are not allowed to, or perhaps you don't feel worthy enough so when good comes to you it slips through your fingers.

Have you drawn a big head? This says you believe you are intelligent!

Where are you in relation to the page or other people/things? If you have drawn any more than just yourself what does your picture say? Sometimes clients will draw pictures where everyone else is bigger than them. Sometimes there may be a group or line of people all holding hands - or maybe all standing a big distance apart. They all tell a story. Sometimes the drawing only covers half or two thirds of the page. This indicates the amount of life they feel is empty or missing on that core level.

What else is in the picture? Sometimes there is a sense of positivity, perhaps with the scenery, especially a (yellow) sun, or a happy scenario. Other times the picture tells a gloomy or sad story. What, overall, does yours say?

Demi Schneider

To help your assessment, here are some real life examples of clients' drawings clearly showing the 'blueprint' that was in place by the time they were that small child, from which they have lived:

1) One lady spent ages doing her picture. It was very detailed and colourful and beautiful, of allotments with carrots growing and her granddad there. If you looked very carefully you could just see the profile of a tiny figure kneeling down in the middle of one allotment. This figure had no features and hardly showed. It absolutely told the story of her self-feelings and consequent life. Her picture was really about everything else *but* her, showing her 'blueprint' lack of self-worth, ability to see her world or take in life or take up space at all. Her life was all about other people and what was 'out there', constantly giving her power to them and looking to others for her happiness and peace, not realising or feeling she could create it for herself, or feel worthy and deserving enough to do so.

2) A young man drew a very large figure that totally dominated the page - but stopped at the hips where it went off the paper. He was very sensitive and intelligent and was already very knowledgeable on what I was teaching him. Seeing his picture told me exactly what was going on: he could 'talk the talk' with the large mouth on the large head, yet he didn't 'walk the walk' as he had no legs! He had immense knowledge yet didn't apply or *live* any of it authentically!

3) Another man drew four people, all from the waist up, close together in the middle of the page with big straps across them to represent them being in a car. He saw it as a picture of a family going out for the day. I saw it as very stuck people not going anywhere! He hadn't actually drawn a car other than the seat belts - no wheels to move. The people didn't have legs although they all had eyes and mouths. It became evident this man was very observant and very good at talking and communicating, yet he was trapped in negative feelings (the seat belt holding him fast) and was very rigid in his thinking (not able to move). It was easy to see his blocks to happiness from this drawing that we might not have identified otherwise, or certainly not so easily.

4) A bright, clever, intuitive lady in her late thirties who felt lonely and unfulfilled drew herself with a bike in a single pale orange pencil. The whole picture took up less than 3 square inches on the A4 piece of paper. It was so faint it could only be seen if you turned it towards the light. This is what she'd learned about herself by the time she was five. I could readily see why when it transpired she was the result of an unwanted pregnancy and had been blamed for all

the mother's problems in life. No wonder she dare not take up any space or 'show up' on the page.

5) Another man drew a picture that indicated many positive aspects about himself at that young age. Yet he drew himself bald, indicating a complete lack of strength. It quickly became clear that despite his obvious capability and many attributes he felt powerless. His mother had been over-protective and had disempowered him to the point where he had nothing in his 'blueprint' to allow him to take accountability for his own life. It shed much light on his failed relationships, him jeopardising his job and living an uncomfortable, powerless, unfulfilled life.

These pictures are very powerful and in a few minutes I can get more relevant information to help a client move forward than in any other way I have ever come across - and painlessly! They've only had to draw a picture.

Take a few moments to study your picture and what it tells you. Allow yourself to view it with honesty and compassion. To be whole you need to heal the space this little child is coming from. Even if you had a happy childhood you didn't necessarily learn to Love Yourself and embrace the fullness of your life.

EXERCISE:

Take another piece of paper (at the back of this book if needs be) and, with your non-dominant hand, draw a picture of a really happy child. Please make sure they are big in relation to the paper and have hair, their features, strong hands and feet etc. Make them really bold and colourful.

(If you find it difficult to draw a 'happy child' picture, you may well have a deep fear of moving forward. Those who struggle with this or who draw a similar picture to their first one are holding themselves back. Realise 'difficult' = 'stuck' = this negative choice is preferable on some level. You are reluctant to leave your Rats' Den. Work on giving yourself permission to move forward. Re-read the blocks to 'packing your bags' on pages 11–13 and examine other beliefs that might be in your way. Allow your self to release them and focus on being willing to Love Yourself; enough love heals anything. Then come back to drawing your picture of a happy child).

~~~~~~~~~

When you've finished compare the two pictures. Which child would you want to be in the playground at school?

It is very clear and inspiring to see the difference in clients' pictures and to observe the difference in their posture and facial expressions as they create this second drawing. They are already 'shifting' their inner space. The task now is to enable the child in the first picture to become the bright happy child in the second picture.

Still with your non-dominant hand, write this child's name at the top of the paper. It can be your own name or a favourite name, or a nickname - whatever feels right. This is your Inner Child at their best.

With your non-dominant hand, write down 6 - 8 deeply relevant emotional needs this child has. For example they might include: to be loved, supported, accepted, approved of, noticed, be listened to, cuddled, praised, encouraged, cared for, protected, understood, played with, given time, wanted, valued, respected, etc.

As an adult, we can now give these to our own inner child to reprogramme our 'blueprint' and allow ourselves to live from this wholesome emotional space.

We can do this very effectively and pleasantly using visualisation. Remembering how the brain cannot tell the difference between real and imaginary and therefore how powerful visualisation is to work on our subconscious mind, we can use this technique to heal our Inner Child and reprogramme our emotional 'blueprint'.

Louise Hay's 'Inner Child' CD (which also has the 'Forgiveness' track as mentioned before) takes you through a visualisation to meet your beautiful Inner Child and love them at all their ages. I generally use it on my courses. It can be purchased on Amazon.

The Tree visualisation below offers a lovely way of filling yourself up with all the emotional needs you lacked as a child. If you do this often enough and with enough commitment, you can heal that younger part of you just as though you'd experienced these for real in the first place. This is on the accompanying free audio download (or purchasable CD too.

VISUALISATION:
THE TREE

Close your eyes and gently relax each of your muscle groups in turn, slow your breathing and drift into a beautiful relaxed state. Then imagine you are standing in front of a large solid tree, perhaps an oak. Notice how wide and deep the roots go into Mother Earth and how the vast canopy of leaves spreads out under Father Sun. Move closer and closer till your nose is touching the trunk. Then melt into the tree, with your legs and feet entwining with the roots and your arms and hands entwining with the branches. Then slowly take in through Mother Earth all the emotional needs you had that your own mother wasn't able to give you. Take in everything you ever wanted, including those emotional needs listed on your Inner

Child drawing. Take all the time you need. Anchor them deep in your belly (lower chakras). Then slowly take in from Father Sun, through your hands and arms, all the emotional needs you ever wanted, that your own father wasn't able to give you. Take in those listed on your Inner Child drawing. Take all the time you need. Anchor them deep in your belly. When you have filled yourself up with these and securely anchored them, allow yourself to melt back out of the tree. Stand back a little and look at your tree and thank it, knowing you can come back anytime you wish, over and over to completely fill the voids you had. It is a beautiful way to heal your 'emotional blueprint' and feel good.

Then imagine a small child coming towards you who you realise is 'you'. Go down on your knees and hold out your arms to them. Even if they approach tentatively, keep smiling at them putting all the love you can into your gaze as they come towards you. Then embrace them and tell them you are their future and you are here to love them, to cherish them and give them all they lacked back then. Tell them you are here to give them all the nourishment and support they ever needed. Feel the connection with your child. Hold them. Allow yourself to feel love for them. Then take them by the hand and go off to celebrate this reunion. Go to the beach or the park or anywhere else that appeals. Celebrate this connection with yourself.

When you have spent time loving them, giving them all the other needs you listed on your picture, shrink your little child down smaller than small, to the size where you can put them into your heart where they can feel safe and loved until the next time you visit them. Enjoy the good feeling.

When it feels right, come back to the room and time and space you are in, bringing this good feeling with you.

You may have to do this in very small steps to begin with, especially if you had a particularly difficult childhood and can't relate to these feelings. For deeper emotional severance from negative beliefs or pain from childhood, I recommend the beautiful visualisation I created especially for this which can be found on my CD/download 'Free to Be'. The track is called 'Severance From Negative Self Feelings'. You can read more about it on the Recommended Listening page at the back of this book.

The truth is that you do have infinite wells of love and *all* good feelings within. Be willing to allow yourself the time and commitment to connect with them. The reward of reprogramming your 'emotional blueprint' will be immeasurable. I recommend you visit your Inner Child for at least 10 minutes every day for a month, using visualisation to get to know them, connect with them and have fun with them. Feed them all the emotional needs you listed on the second drawing you did. It is a very pleasant way to spend some time, giving enormous long-term benefit as well as being time spent in your Palace mind with those advantages too.

Demi Schneider

After the first few weeks, or when you feel connected if it takes longer, you will find you will be able to go out with your Inner Child for a whole day in your mind in just a few minutes. Time in your mind has no relevance to 'real' time. You can support yourself through challenges in the day by going and hugging your Inner Child. It can feel very alien and even 'silly' to start with but if you persevere, the relationship you develop will be life- transforming in its self

When you want to release an old belief it can be very powerful and helpful to visit your Inner Child in your own visualisation and say to them, for example, "I've realised we have a belief that we're not worth loving. I've learned this isn't true - we just learned it from people who were coming from their own disconnected space. Are you prepared to let that go now so we can move forward and embrace the truth that we *are* worth loving?" With a bit of practise you'll find your Inner Child will respond - you will *feel* their reaction come up. When they are ready you can ask how they want to destroy that old belief - maybe burning it or throwing it off a cliff or sending it off in a space rocket - and then do that with them. When it's all gone embrace your child with a big hug and tell them *"well done and thank you"*. You are now free to adopt your new 'true' belief that you *are* worth loving, from that deep level. Repeat over and over "I am worth loving!" and tell your Inner Child often that they are worth loving and that you love them, until your brain has taken it on board, just as it did with the 'false' message before. You can do this with whatever other deep-seated belief or pattern you want to release. It is very helpful to do this for negativity about your Worthiness and Deservability too.

I once realised that with reflection, I had repeatedly experienced situations that 'should' have been triumphant and joyful yet had consistently ended up in disappointment, let down, or even shock and horror, even though on the surface there was no way I could have forseen this. I had to go back a very long way with my inner child to dissolve this pattern and to encourage her to believe "I can have. I do count. I am worthy and deserving of receiving abundant rewards for my efforts. I am lovable and deserve wholesome meaningful love. I can be the fullness of who I am and actualise my gifts into the world". When I shifted the old emotional attachments in line with the mental changes I was making I could feel the authenticity in my gut! That was a huge breakthrough for me.

It can also help to connect with your Inner Child by having them 'with you' sometimes. I always have my inner 'little girl' with me when I'm gardening. I let her help me and talk about the plants and so on and have a wonderful time!

Other times it helps to *be* your Inner Child. If you have your own children this is often more relatable. Having a young daughter myself it is easy for me to feel the child-like joy of throwing myself down a death slide with her or going on a roller-coaster at our local theme park. If you don't have children you could use pen and paper and with your non-dominant hand draw a child-like picture or buy a colouring book and get busy with it. It can be very therapeutic in itself! One client, a career lady who has a very stressful job, does that now for 20 minutes every day when she comes home from work. She says it takes her totally out of herself, *being* her child and she feels beautifully 'unwound'.

Allow yourself to enjoy connecting with your Inner Child in ways that work for you and feel the 'wholeness' of you being restored. You will be able to Love Yourself authentically (more coming up in chapter twelve) and open your chakras to let the energy settle in your belly, feeling deep inner peace, calm and strength. Yes, this really does mean you too!

Chapter Nine
Staying In The Palace

This page is duplicated in the Cut-Out section at the back of this book to learn off by heart so you can turn to these thoughts immediately and act on them when necessary. In time they will become second nature and enable you to stay in your Palace easily.

1) Ask **"WHAT PART OF THE BRAIN AM I IN?"** You can't catch 60 - 90,000 thoughts but you *can* tune into your emotions. If you're not feeling good you've not been having 'good' thoughts - you're in your Rats' Den. Immediately Switch to a thought that brings you back to your Palace, such as something funny, beautiful, or a happy song. Using an 'anchor thought' can also be very helpful. This is just a specific image that's guaranteed to put a smile on your face that you can turn to in an instant, be it your child, your pet, a loved one, or anything else that appeals. One client chose the image of actor Robin Williams' bottom at the end of a film she'd seen and laughed at! Alternatively you could Switch to thoughts of appreciation, e.g. gratitude for your eyesight or what you *do* have to be thankful for. This too will instantly shift your mind space. Now you've regained command you can choose helpful thoughts from your Palace mind. Always choose a thought that makes you feel a little bit better rather than a little bit worse. *You are in charge and always have the final say.* When you change your thought to a positive one, you're in your Palace with all the benefits, you're producing serotonin, and you've saved a negative thought going in your bucket! Win, win, win!

2) Ask **"HOW DO I WANT TO FEEL RIGHT NOW?"** If you're feeling stressed and you want to feel calm, choose calming thoughts and images to focus on and buy into the feeling of them. Say "I am calm" ten times (the 'strong arm' effect on page 45) or imagine cool waterfalls or strolling along a beach in a beautiful sunset. If you want to feel safe or in command, choose images which give you that feeling in this moment. For example, you might imagine being in your bubble or being surrounded by angels to feel safe, or imagine being Nanny McPhee or Arnold Schwarznegger to feel in command or empowered.

Choose whatever works for you. 'Paint the picture' of how you want to feel, buy into that feeling and then choose your next thought from this space, perhaps using Miracle Questioning if appropriate. (See page 30).

3) Ask "WHAT'S GOOD ABOUT THIS?" Whatever has happened or is happening, find something, however small, that's *good* about it. Focus on that. Grow the positives from there. It keeps you in your Palace and you will find solutions and the way forward. If there really is nothing good about a situation, *turn it* into something good. (See page 71).

4) Say "THIS IS THE ACTIVITY I GET TO DO NOW." Acceptance saves so much stress! (See page 71).

5) Ask "IS THIS AN ACT OF LOVING MYSELF?" "WHAT WOULD BE AN ACT OF LOVING MYSELF RIGHT NOW?" Follow through on your answers. When you are moving towards Loving Yourself, you are moving towards the magnificence that is you, to be at one with yourself, which is where your true happiness lies.

6) Ask "FOR WHAT PURPOSE?" This question sheds a whole lot of light, making things clearer and allowing you to focus even more. I have used it several times in this book! I find it invaluable and use it many times every day on myself, my daughter and to help clients. For example: if I think "I really must go and do a work out" and it feels a bit of a drudge, I ask myself *"for what purpose?"* This focuses me on why I'm doing it - because I want to get fitter and more toned so I can look good in clothes that are currently somewhat tight - which then reinforces my desire to get on and do my work out.

If my daughter asks for something I don't feel is a good idea, rather than say 'no', even with an explanation, I ask *"for what purpose?"* Invariably she will realise herself it's not a good idea, which is also so much more beneficial for many reasons - her self-worth, her learning to make sensible assessments, feeling valued and not just hearing 'no' from me, etc.

With a vision board 'for what purpose' really enables us to hone in on the crux of our desires to strengthen our resolve and 'vibration'. For example, "I want a wonderful relationship". *"For what purpose?"* "To lovingly witness each other's lives, share wonderful experiences and companionship for mutual joy". Now we have a more specific picture, with more depth and feeling.

Sometimes we can think we want certain things yet when we ask "For what purpose" we realise there is something deeper involved. For example "I want to work in a large company". *"For what purpose?"* "To meet lots of people and make friends". Aha! What we really want is to make new friends - which we could do in other ways too. (You could then continue with Miracle Questions).

Beat Your Depression For Good

There are countless ways to use this and only 3 words to learn!

7) CATCH NEGATIVE THOUGHTS AND ELIMINATE THEM. Use the Letting Go exercises (pages 27–29) or Switch the thought (page 29) or simply Stop It! (Page 25).

8) USE THE MIRACLE QUESTION TECHNIQUE. (See page 30). Ask yourself "If I was a '10' how would I handle this?" "If I was being positive what would be different?" "If I was more confident what's the first thing I would notice?" "If I was being more assertive/efficient/tolerant how would this show?" Follow through on your answers. If you *were* this way what could your next question be? What else? You have your way forward. Practise to perfect the art so that it becomes part of your normal vocabulary without thinking. The dividends will be well worth the effort expended in doing this.

9) ACCEPT THINGS AS THEY ARE BECAUSE THAT'S HOW THEY ARE. Trying to change things from a space of judgmentalism and self-righteousness, however well intentioned, focuses on 'what's wrong' and keeps giving the energy to 'what's wrong'. This feeds it even more and will only keep you in the primitive part of your mind nurturing the Rats. Acceptance neutralises the negative energy and allows the authentic space for change; whether that be *accepting* there are people in the world with a different view point to yourself or *accepting* that a loved one has died so you can lay down the angst and allow yourself to grieve and let the pain go.

10) ACCEPT PEOPLE EXACTLY AS THEY ARE. It is not your prerogative to decide how anyone else should act or behave, or to decide what they should want or do etc. *Accept* everyone is on their own journey, doing the best they can from where they've come from. If you had had their influences you may be that way too. It is only *your* job to be accountable for yourself. How can *you* best handle things you don't like? How/what can *you* change to alter the situation. It is amazing when we change *our* perspective how other people change too. Accept others as they are; you don't have to agree with their beliefs or standards or behaviours or have them as part of your life - just accept they are the way they are and it's not your prerogative to judge. *Work on yourself.* Wanting others to change never works.

11) CHOOSE, WRITE DOWN AND USE MANTRAS: for example "I am worthy and deserving of all my good", "I approve of myself", "I love myself".

12) LOVE YOURSELF - EVERY MOMENT OF EVERY DAY. Embrace the 'Acts of Loving Yourself' list (page 156/157) and live it. Nurture your Inner

Child to fill him/her with what you lacked as a child. You are effectively feeding yourself all this nutritional emotional support. Spend quality time with yourself. Sit for 2 or 3 minutes breathing in through your nose, tummy pushing forward, saying "I am" and out through your mouth, tummy relaxing back, saying "at peace". Build up to 15 minutes a day if you can. Allow yourself this time in silence, 'being' instead of 'doing'. The rewards will be well worth this commitment. Allow yourself to reconnect with the core of your real self. Come home to yourself. It is the way to great health, great relationships, great experiences, great self-feelings, and a great life! And you are automatically in your Palace mind!

Chapter Ten
The Palace Regime

This page is duplicated in the Cut-Out section later in this book to carry round with you so you can check it regularly to help install the new ways until living them is second nature. You'll need to revisit this from time to time to reinforce them.

1) START EACH AND EVERY DAY WITH GRATITUDE *whilst you are first waking up. Feel* the appreciation of the things you are saying. Be thankful for the comfortable bed that you've slept in; appreciate your eyes that see, ears that hear, legs that walk; that you have fresh running water without walking miles; that you can read and write; that you live in a country of free speech, a country of plenty; or feel the appreciation of the beauty of the daffodils welcoming in the spring; etc. There are plenty of people out there who would gladly swap places with you. Appreciate your very existence. Feel the appreciation in every cell of your body.

2) GO THROUGH YOUR DAY STAYING IN THE MOMENT. There is no past and future – there is only now. The Universe only works in the now. You can only receive your blessings in the now. When thinking about the past or future, bring your attention back to *now* by looking at the clothes you're wearing, the decor of the room you're in, the view out of the window. Practise giving 100% attention to the task/experience in hand, be it showering, working, being in the gym, spending time with your family etc. Appreciate *this* precious moment of your life - before that too becomes the past. Then move to your next task/experience. You will get lots more done and feel good in the process. Living in the moment is the key to so many benefits: more efficiency, more joy and peace, more awareness, and *living!* (See page 45).

3) GO THROUGH YOUR DAY SMILING AT PEOPLE, even if you don't feel like it. Notice and appreciate the smiles you get back!

4) LOOK FOR ALL THE POSITIVES IN A DAY. Look for what's good about things, how the old patterns are changing, how your increased sense of Worthiness and Deservability is showing etc. What you focus on grows!

5) CHOOSE CONSTANT POSITIVE SUPPORTIVE TALK ALL THROUGH THE DAY. Remember you can come from the point of helplessness (Rats' Den) or from the point of power (Palace). Take back your own power and choose the positive aspect or the 'havingness of what you want', rather than choosing the negative aspect or *lack* of what you want. Embrace new language patterning so that speaking positively becomes normal for you. Praise and encourage yourself.

6) PROTECT YOURSELF FROM OTHER PEOPLES NEGATIVITY. You are not responsible for other people's thoughts or opinions. What they think is none of your business. Read the NLP Script on page 41 until you are living it. Put yourself in a protective bubble or forcefield when necessary.

7) FOCUS ON LIVING THE 5 COMPONENTS OF YOUR PALACE MIND UNTIL THIS IS SECOND NATURE:
i. Focus on what you *do* want in any given moment. Choose the thought that makes you feel a bit better rather than a bit worse. Tell things from the most positive perspective.
ii. *Feel* the new 'desired' scenario *as if it were real*. Your mind cannot tell the difference between real and imaginary. By adding the 'weight' of the matching feeling to your desired scenario you tune into that authentically. Until you are aligned to *receive* something, it is just a wish.
iii. Use speech that supports these thoughts and feelings.
iv. Work on your Worthiness and Deservability
v. Learn to Love Yourself exactly as you are. (More coming up on this).

8) TRUST YOURSELF AND THE PROCESS OF LIFE. Your work is to be aligned and only put in action effort when it feels right. Trust the timing, how your blessings are delivered and enjoy the journey.

9) LEARN AND USE THE POINTS TO 'STAY IN YOUR PALACE' (previous chapter). When they become habitual you will live them effortlessly.

10) PRACTISE THE VISUALISATIONS IN THIS BOOK (others are suggested on the Recommended Listening list). Become confident with 'The Swish' etc. Regularly fill yourself with 'White Light' or 'Love Your Body and the Planet', or nourish yourself with 'The Tree'.

Beat Your Depression For Good

11) WORK ON YOUR GROWTH DAILY. Work with the pages in the Cut-Out section of this book, including carrying around with you the duplication of this page, to assimilate your positive changes. Enjoy creating the life and feelings you want. Do the exercises in this book. Read this book over and over. Familiarise yourself with all the tools and techniques so they become automatic. Read other similar material. Living these ways will become easier and easier and your life will change dramatically for the better.

12) EACH NIGHT, get into bed, offer appreciation for all the good in the day (even if it's the lesser part of the day, or only your lunch that was good, remembering that for many people in the world, having food would make it a *very* good day!) **Run through the next day in your mind for a few minutes, as a mental rehearsal, seeing everything going well, with you feeling in control, strong, confident, self-assured etc.** Listen to the 'Relaxation for Sleep' track on the free audio download, every night, for at least a few months and allow it to send you to sleep. Then use it periodically when you feel the need.

Embrace, use and LIVE all of the above to the very best of your ability, making it all as daily a routine as brushing your teeth. You're worthy of all good so give yourself the very best, starting with allowing yourself to live well in this way.

Chapter Eleven
Relationships

When the relationship we have with ourselves is the best it can be and we feel good about ourselves inevitably all our relationships fare better. In addition, there are other factors that can be very helpful to understand in order to create and maintain the best relationships we can. I certainly wished I'd known the following information 30+ years ago! My life would have been hugely different.

Love Languages

There are 5 ways of communicating love in all our relationships. These are through:

Gifts
Acts of Service
Quality Time
Meaningful Touch
Verbal Appreciation

Gifts: these people demonstrate their love through giving gifts and feel loved by receiving them. For example, a mum might not tell her daughter she loves her but instead buys her things. If they 'fall out' she'll buy her something to make up. Equally, that mother will feel most loved by those around her giving *her* gifts.

Acts of Service: these people show love through doing things for someone, for example, a man might not often hug his wife but will bring her cups of tea or clean her car or clear the snow off her windscreen. He will feel most loved and appreciated by someone doing things for him.

Quality Time: these people really like company, to share experiences or just hang out together. Watching a beautiful sunset alone would feel hollow compared to watching it with another. They show love through giving time to others with undivided attention. They feel most loved and appreciated when others want to be this way with them.

Meaningful Touch: these are people who are very tactile and readily hug and cuddle others and for whom hugs and cuddles and physical touch make *them* feel wanted and loved. A touch on the arm, a stroke of a foot against a leg, an intentional brush against when passing by, are all ways they give and feel love.

Verbal Appreciation: these are people who vocalise their thoughts and feelings, offering verbal communication of love, praise or just sharing random or specific thoughts. They feel most loved by *hearing* such things in verbal communication from others or by reading beautiful words in a card they've been sent. They are often very talkative and can express themselves well.

Whilst we are often *all* of these to some degree, there are two that we communicate and receive love through most readily. *Which are your top two?* You may have to dwell on this for some time to really find your true Love Languages. How do *you* feel most loved and valued?

Sometimes it can be a little puzzling because, for example, you might enjoy *giving* gifts yet find it less rewarding to *receive* them. This might mean that you *are* a 'gifts' person and need to work on your Worthiness and Deservability to receive. Or it might mean you are generous yet *not* actually a 'gifts' person and that there are two other Love Languages with which you can relate more.

When you are clear on the two Love Languages that most resonate for yourself, reflect on other relationships you currently have. You may get a very clear understanding of why you connect with some individuals easily, or perhaps struggle with others. Which Love Languages do your parents have; your partner; your children; your friends?

It may also shed some light on past relationships and why they didn't work. It certainly explains why I felt so rejected by my partners in the past when we were each coming from different Love Languages! I didn't appreciate their ways of communication and they didn't connect with mine. What Love Languages do your ex-partners have?

Here are some examples of problems that arise in relationships with differing Love Languages:

Verbal appreciation/meaningful touch mum picks up her *acts of service/quality time* daughter in the car. The daughter feels loved because she's been picked up *(act of service)* and is sitting close to mum *(quality time)* and is content to play on her ipod in the car. Mum wants to have a hug *(meaningful touch)* and a quality chat *(verbal appreciation)* and feels frustrated and unappreciated by her daughter not wanting to communicate. The daughter feels the negative vibe but can't understand her mother's frustration.

Verbal appreciation/quality time woman goes on a trip with her son. On her return she wants to sit down and tell her husband all about it *(verbal appreciation)* and show him the photos *(quality time)*. *Acts Of Service/Gifts* husband has spent all day cleaning the oven *(act of service)* and has bought a big bouquet of flowers to welcome her home *(gifts)*. Five minutes of hearing about the trip is enough for him, leaving her feeling unheard and rejected. She is agitated because she can clean the oven herself and feels 'easily bought' with the flowers. She feels unloved whilst he's left thinking "What can I do to please her?"

Meaningful touch/gifts dad feels rejected when his *quality time/verbal appreciation* 9 year old daughter isn't interested in his affection *(meaningful touch)* and isn't even overly enthusiastic when he comes home with presents for her *(gifts)*. He feels drained when she constantly wants to have him spend time with her *(quality time)* and listen to her endless chatter *(verbal appreciation)* when he'd rather be watching football. She is vaguely aware he finds spending time with her uncomfortable and feels unimportant and even unwanted or unloved.

The best we can do in non-similar relationships is to identify the love languages of the other person. At least we know how to meet their needs when we want, which is applicable in all our different relationships. If we can explain Love Languages to them, especially to a partner and family members, and get them to appreciate what meets *our* needs they may be willing to make an effort too. If not, we can still be aware when they are trying to express love to us even though it's not reaching us in our preferred way. This in itself can be valuable. To realise that your 'acts or service' partner emptying the dishwasher is the equivalent of "I love you" if you're a 'verbal appreciation' person, or the equivalent of spending time together if you're a 'quality time' person can save much misunderstanding and feelings of rejection. We can't expect others to change to suit us any more than we can authentically change to suit them, yet we can pave a way for harmony.

Without knowing about Love Languages we can sometimes really go out of our way to find someone different to a parent or previous partner yet end up in a relationship with exactly the same problems. We find we have the same feelings of rejection or of not being understood or loved. Equally, our partner wont feel truly loved with this misalignment. This can lead to a great deal of pain and negative beliefs about our selves, even causing depression reliving the same unwanted patterns. We need to work on ourselves to feel worthy and deserving of all our good, embrace our Love Languages and only give our heart to someone who can truly meet us in this convivial space.

Best relationships clearly always stem from having common Love Languages (or at least one of them). There is a natural ease and rapport. Harmonious parent/child relationships are much easier with the same Love Languages. Our best friends are usually our best friends *because* they speak our Love Languages and we feel comfortable with them. Successful intimate relationships are invariably based on the same Love Languages, or at least *one* the same. Good work relationships will be based on common Love Languages; there will be a natural affinity even if they are not shown quite so demonstratively in the work place.

Knowing your Love Languages is another way of getting to know yourself and coming home to the 'real you'. Embrace them lovingly and enjoy the new experiences this knowledge allows you to have.

Personality Traits

There are many studies that have been undertaken regarding our personalities and different traits. The renowned family therapist Virginia Satir noted we have an innate tendency to be one of the following:

Blamer - someone who is a fault-finder, blaming others or wanting to know who is accountable for something. A blamer will tend to speak in terms of 'you always do...' or 'they never do....' often without even meaning any blame yet it is in their language patterning. This can inadvertently alienate others or crush them with the constant fault- finding.

Placater - a people pleaser, never disagreeing, apologetic, overly responsible and approval seeking. Placaters tend to have very apologetic language patterning. This loses them respect and does nothing for their own self-respect or self-worth.

Computer/super reasonable - someone who is very calm and reasonable, sounds intelligent and in command yet is completely disconnected emotionally. They come across as unfeeling even if they care greatly. This leaves others feeling disengaged, uninspired and often unheard.

Distractor/irrelevant - someone who avoids things, sweeps them under the carpet, buries their head in the sand, says irrelevant things in conversation. Distractors tend to keep very busy and keep conversations short. This makes it difficult to fully engage with life and can be challenging for others to deal with, leaving them feeling uninvolved or unsupported.

Whichever of these your parents or guardians are (or were) will have had a great deal of influence in your 'blueprint'. You will have first subconsciously and then more consciously witnessed and experienced these behaviours being lived out and will have learned things about yourself and your world as a result, affecting your life and relationships in many ways.

Whichever one *you* are predominantly will also show up in the unhelpful negative ways shown above. You can't change or 'delete' these as such, but you *can* 'turn the volume down'. It is clearly very helpful to do this for everyone's benefit, including your own.

Besides the obvious effect on your children, in an intimate relationship for example, if you are a 'blamer' and your partner is a 'distractor/irrelevant' that is bound to set you up for some angst. If you are trying to discover who is responsible for something and your partner is burying their head in the sand it's likely to cause some frustration at least!

Or if you're a 'placater' and your partner is a 'computer/super reasonable', the chances are you will be wanting to help someone or fit in with someone else's plans and then feel disapproval and feel unappreciated when your super reasonable partner questions why you do these things, pointing out the disadvantages.

To reduce these unhelpful traits you can write out and repeat "I used to…….. I now realise…….. I now choose to……..." (as you did for the Dissolving Resistance script). Or you could ask "Is this an act of loving myself" as you catch yourself 'in the act' and make an appropriate adjustment, or use any number of other tools in this book. Your Palace mind knows how to be much more level about such things and respond effectively when you're on the receiving end of one of them!

A Personality Profile

This profile may also give you some clues as to why you are the way you are and why your relationships show up in the way they do. We can be predominantly one of these, or a mix of two or all three. Many clients feel relieved to discover they are 'allowed' to be the way they are because they can readily see themselves in these profiles. It makes accepting themselves, as well as their partners as *they* are, much easier. Having always felt 'wrong' for who I am this was a huge discovery for me to be able to accept myself more. It also gives us information to know what areas to perhaps work on to lessen our negatives and improve our strengths.

Warriors: These people are intellectually oriented rather than emotionally driven. They are logical and analytical, questioning and sometimes difficult. Everything has to make sense to them. They are forceful, tenacious and perceptive. They are very controlling, often having fears based on control issues. They have a reputation for firmness and will take charge without worrying too much what others think. When things are not going their way, they can be intimidating and/or intolerant, possessive and cynical. They do not suffer fools gladly. They have difficulty seeing other people's points of view. They can also be very charming, particularly when things *are* going their way and will often be high achievers.

Settlers: These people are intuitive, responsive, emotionally oriented and very much in touch with their emotions. They are very tactful and caring with other people's feelings and hate upsetting people. They are easy to deal with, being willing to fit in and come across as nice, pleasant people. They will be adaptable and cheerful even when feeling anxious or depressed. When confident they are excellent talkers and communicators. When fighting for their rights or the rights of others they can be very strong. Negatively they can be needy and suffer from mood swings. They have a tendency toward low self-confidence or an inferiority complex. Their sensitivity can work against them, creating a lack of self-belief.

Nomads: These people have a charismatic personality. They delight in being centre of attention and tend to be lively and noisy, being natural actors. They have a low boredom threshold and like something to be happening all the time. What you see is what you get. They are determined to enjoy life to the full although they sometimes overdo it. Whilst tending to be 'over emotional' they are good at acting the part to buy into the drama. They are often successful and can be inspiring. They make good teachers when they act in a responsible way. Negatively they can be 'drama queens', excessively exuberant and excitable. They will have a temper like a child and have a tendency to act first and think afterwards. They are often untidy or slob like.

Knowing these can also help with all our relationships, including family and colleagues. Instead of thinking "She is so loud all the time!" we can just know she is a 'nomad' and be much less judgmental and more accepting, which of course helps us on so many levels to be more in our Palace, with all the benefits. Instead of feeling 'bruised' by a comment and just using the techniques for handling criticism explained in chapter four, we can realise that person is a 'warrior' type and acting out accordingly. Or instead of having misguided expectations of someone, we can appreciate they're a sensitive 'settler' and can work within their comfort zone to get the best from them.

Seeing people from this viewpoint gives another angle to help us stop judging others and accept them as they are, enabling us to find life much more comfortable and pleasant, have much less in our stress bucket and have much more inner peace and joy.

Intimate relationships

Intimate relationships can be the most satisfying of all when with your true soulmate. There are many happy couples experiencing this joy and it is wonderful to see the fulfillment it brings them. For others, including myself, it can be a rocky road. The most important self-care we can take is to *always be true to our own integrity*. This is something I have neglected to do in the past and have paid the price dearly. We owe it to ourselves to choose to take back our own power and be faithful to ourselves in our heart and soul.

Besides misaligned Love Languages there can be many other challenges to face within our intimate relationships, which may seem diverse and complex. Yet the solution is always the same. When we align the 5 Palace Components, especially Loving Ourselves, we become our very best and create fulfilling life experiences in all areas of life, including our intimate relationships. The work is always needed on ourselves. If you find any of the scenarios below resonate with you, know that you already have all the resources you need within you to change things and find true happiness in an intimate relationship.

We can be lovely, kind, wonderful people and just want a warm, kind, decent partner, which, in our heads, seems perfectly reasonable. If we only attract unfulfilling relationships or none at all, it means that on our deepest levels we believe something negative. Perhaps we don't really feel worthy and deserving of a wholesome relationship, or believe we were 'born to suffer' or some other underlying falsehood, or perhaps we have no positive template for love in our 'blueprint'. Fear is often a root cause too. These, of course, are all Rats' Den thoughts and emotions.

We can fall into the trap of making excuses for a partner's bad behaviour, even abuse (mental, emotional and physical), because we convince ourselves that we 'really love them' or 'they really love us'. Perhaps you find excuses such as 'I can't leave due to the financial situation I would be in' or 'I can't leave because of the kids' or whatever else you hide behind. Realise this is kidding yourself and is not being true to your own integrity.

We can have unreasonable needs. I remember saying many years ago "How can I feel secure if my boyfriend doesn't make me feel secure?" That was before I learned that I needed to feel secure enough *in myself* to not need someone else to make me feel secure. I was giving all my power away being dependent on someone else in this way. If he had 'made me feel secure' I'd have needed reassuring again the next day, the next week, the next month etc. What a burden for him! He'd have had to live his life around making me feel secure - and I no doubt would have kept shifting the goal posts. This sort of needy, dependent relationship is negative for both partners. As I learned to love myself and feel more worthy and secure in myself, I automatically attracted relationships that reflected this and in which I felt more secure. I then stopped being such a burden on a partner, which inevitably made my relationships flow better, albeit not lasting for other reasons.

If you want your partner to change, that is a subtle form of manipulation or even self-righteousness, thinking that you are right and they are wrong. Even if you are well-intentioned because you want them to be happier, or to work less hours for their own good, or exercise more to improve their health, deciding what's best for them is not your prerogative, will not change things, or help them. It may even cause resentment in your partner, feeling obliged to do what *you* want. Some well-chosen Miracle Questions to encourage them to explore these things for themselves is one thing, yet ultimately their life is their accountability; you are accountable for yours. Work on yourself to create a life that is the best possible for you, whether that means you handle their choices with integrity or indeed, decide to leave them and find someone more amenable with your life choices.

I find too that many people dwell on the frustration of what their partner says or does when it completely contradicts their own sense of reason or rationale. I had a client who was incensed that her partner had run up debts behind her back. That's just it. Sometimes people in our lives (not just partners) don't match *our* sense of reason and rationale. Being stuck in the angst or bitterness of 'what they've done' doesn't help us. Even if they *have* made a poor choice or *are* seeing things from a distorted point of view, because of their own issues or pain or quest for avoidance, that's *their prerogative*. Rather than give away your power by giving them and the problem your attention, thoroughly release the negative emotions with the techniques in chapters three and four and Switch or Miracle Question yourself forward. *Accept* that's how it is/they are being and start mentally painting the pictures of what you do want within your own accountability. Take back your own power and choose to live in your Palace mind where you can handle things and make positive choices for yourself.

It's how we deal with a challenge that counts. I remember asking a Miracle Question to a client; "If there was a miracle what would be different in your relationship?" She answered "My husband wouldn't be such a bastard'. This was again giving away her power. She soon realised she would have to look to herself and either learn to handle her husband being a bastard or work on her self-worth to be able to leave him. He wasn't going to change because she wanted him to.

Another woman had been stuck in a negative relationship for years. She had nearly ended the relationship several times but gave in at the last minute on the strength of a few 'promises' from her husband. Her children were difficult much of the time, just acting out the unhappy home environment. She only focused on 'the problems': "If we break up he'll go and live at his mother's. His mother would be quite happy to have him and the children live with her and for me to not exist any longer. We've been to Relate but it's too expensive to afford so we've got the books they recommended - I've read 4 of them and he's still on the first. After we agreed to 'try again' after our last 'almost break up' I feel I've made my choice and I've got 3 kids to think about."

She too was giving away all her power and essentially blaming everyone and everything else for her misery. The problem was *her* not taking accountability for her own life. Nothing could change for her until she took back her own power, focused 100% on what she *did* want and stopped blocking *herself* from achieving it.

Let's *accept* this can be hard. All I wanted when my life was turned upside down, being told by my partner the day before our baby was due to be born that he was leaving me, was to turn back the clock and not have that happen! As that was impossible, I had to get to the point where I could paint the pictures in my mind of life with just my daughter and me together. Then I could move on. Of course it was difficult and abject pain and misery for a time and I didn't even want to go there. But once I started to take back my own power and focus on living for me and my baby, things started to turn round and from the day I moved into my new 'little - big' house I've never been happier.

We don't have to know and indeed can't possibly know, how things will work out or what challenges lie ahead during difficult times. We just need to keep the focus so our neural gangs (Palace mentors) can go to work on solutions, putting our energy into the 5 Components of Palace living. We can trust 'everything is working for our highest good' (or whatever resonates with you to hold that trust). We can tune into our inner self for guidance on each step along the journey to freedom and happiness. "Feel the fear and do it anyway" may be a good mantra and a good book to help.

The key to attracting a wholesome relationship is to have a wholesome relationship with your self. We'll explore this more in the next chapter. I am now happy enough in myself to no longer 'need' a relationship to be happy and I know I will only let in to my life someone who 'ticks all my boxes' and that, if and when he comes along, I will 'tick all his boxes' too. As I said before, if I want a '10' man, I need to be a '10' myself to be attractive to him. It feels empowering when you know you are helping yourself to be all that you can be and because that is an act of Loving Yourself, every day becomes richer as you feel more complete.

Demi Schneider

An Ideal Relationship

Dependent Relationships: This describes one partner relying heavily on the other. Besides being a burden for their partner, what happens if they die or leave? The 'leaner', whether male or female, 'falls over'.

This can be especially hard to pick oneself up from. One client I had actually believed that it was her husband's *duty* to make her happy! How would she have felt the other way around I wonder? Enhancing each other's happiness in mutual joy is one thing, unhealthy dependency is quite another. (Co-dependency is two people leaning on each other, which is fraught with double the trouble)!

Independent Relationships: This describes two partners leading completely separate lives. Even if they share the same bed, their interests are different and they each live their own lives, just teaming up for such things as social occasions or funerals. Whilst this ostensibly may 'work' for them, they are closed off to a more meaningful, loving, fulfilling relationship.

Interdependent Relationships: This is the ideal relationship, when each partner is strong enough to stand on their own two feet, being their 'own person' yet walking hand in hand through life together. If they speak the same

Love Languages and share the same visions and values they will have the most rewarding relationship.

An interdependent relationship is what I would have described as wanting right from my teens. However, with no template for this in my 'blueprint', no inner belief that I was worthy of this (even though my conscious mind thought I was) and an extensive set of negative beliefs about myself and men, it's no wonder that after the first flush of romance after meeting someone I've never experienced this. I realise now I could only live out the misguided place I was coming from. I've had to work on myself a great deal to make the necessary changes. You may need to do this too. Just know that you are not alone and are more than capable of creating the space deep within to attract, cultivate and maintain an interdependent relationship.

Finding A New Wholesome Relationship

Being in a wholesome relationship allows us to experience the fullness of ourselves and is wonderful. Loving and feeling loved makes us feel good.

There is nothing wrong with wanting to be loved. The question is whether we are wanting to be loved from a place of deservability, or from neediness. A deeply honed belief about being deserving of wholesome love will bring that to you. Being needy only creates unsuccessful relationships. If having an intimate relationship is essential to you, what are you setting yourself up for?

Whilst many people meet their soulmate through dating agencies and other 'look for' ways, we need to come from the 'having' aspect of this rather than the '*absence* of having' aspect to achieve a positive outcome. If we're feeling good about ourselves and feel good about patiently waiting for our beloved to come, we can have fun with the dating agency experience and be in our Palace mind. If we're online or anywhere else, looking for our match with any sense of anxiety or doubt about it happening, or feeling desperation, longing, unhappiness or other negative emotion, we're back with the Rats. It is very unlikely we will attract a wholesome relationship from this space.

You might consider what is blocking you from having a wholesome relationship. Do you have unreasonable expectations? Are you really open to receiving your soulmate or is it just a hope? Do you mistrust your soulmate is out there? Do you feel too old, too fat, too skinny, too busy, too independent, too self-sufficient etc? Are you letting impatience get in the way? Are you too 'desperate'? Are you able to let love in? Do you in fact, Love Yourself?

Our capacity to love and be loved comes from Loving Ourselves, which we'll explore more in chapter twelve. When we love ourselves we become the magnet to draw to us our beloved (and all our good).

Consider what qualities you really want in a partner. Make a list. Besides 'kind', 'caring', 'trustworthy', or whatever is important to you, know that there are certain factors that are especially relevant to having a rewarding relationship. Being emotionally available, i.e. free of past emotional 'baggage', willing and able to fully engage in and commit to a relationship, is of paramount importance for a stable, happy experience. Similarly, to share visions and values is more sustaining long term than just having some common interests. Ensure someone you are interested in also shares your Love Languages. You can just explain these and ask which ones they feel they are. You'll be doing them a favour by sharing this for their benefit too. If they don't match yours you might be able to have a friendship with them but save your heart for someone who can truly receive and reciprocate your love in ways that are going to be meaningful for you.

An exercise you can do is to write the details of how you would feel with your ideal partner (in the present tense of course); "With my partner I feel wanted, appreciated, valued, etc). This is tremendously powerful to attract this and may show you where you need to grow to allow this in. When you can align the 5 Components of Palace living, with no negative counter thoughts or feelings, you are in the right place to attract a wonderful relationship.

You could put these written pieces on your vision board along with appropriate pictures to really hone into the focus, feeling and speech patterning of what you want to allow yourself to manifest. Finish off with "I am worthy and deserving of this or even better".

Work on the relationship with yourself and be open for your beloved to come to you in the perfect time and space. Trust that your perfect partner is out there looking for you - and in the meantime enjoy working on yourself to be the best that you can be in readiness for when you meet them and to enjoy your life journey now, engaging in things that are less likely to happen once a partner is on the scene.

As you can't know when your soulmate will come along, keep your focus on creating a great life for yourself now. Even *if* you never meet that special someone, you will still have a fulfilling life! To put your life on hold whilst waiting for Mr/Ms Right contradicts the very essence of living well. Be happy enough in yourself to not need a relationship to be happy.

Existing Relationships

If you are in a healthy fulfilling relationship, congratulate yourself! You obviously have the 'blueprint' or have made the necessary changes to feel worthy and deserving of having that experience or are just blessed with this, maybe because you have been given other areas of challenge in your life. In a healthy relationship, allow your partner to be all they want to be. Focus on all their positive aspects. What we focus on grows!

Ultimately, we need to Love Ourselves to be able to authentically give and receive love. If your partner doesn't love themselves, they will not be able to truly receive your love. If they are insecure, or frustrated, or jealous, or self-loathing or resentful they will not know how to accept your love because these negatives are in the way. Equally, they can never be good enough for you if you are any of these.

If you are in a relationship that has worn out or things have changed, allow yourself to move on for both your sakes. I've known people say "I couldn't leave my spouse; they wouldn't manage without me". How self-important does this sound? Even if it's 'true' realise you are not responsible for their happiness. You are only responsible for your own life and how you live it. Setting *them* free may be just what they need to be able to move on themselves, but whatever happens and however they react it's their choice. You deserve a good life for you!

If we choose to stay in an uncomfortable relationship, it begs the question *why?* What are the pay offs? As Susan Jeffers says 'there is always a pay off in everything we do otherwise we wouldn't do it.' This includes staying where we are because it's easier than facing the rocky road ahead. Clinging onto a worn out relationship just to avoid the pain of parting is not respecting or Loving Yourself.

However hard and challenging it may seem, *always choose alignment with your own integrity over a fear of being on your own or upsetting other people.* If you don't know whether you want to stay in the relationship or not, because your thoughts are having a tennis match in your head, write down a list of reasons to stay and a list of the reasons to go. Add to it over a couple of days. You can stop the tennis match because it's all on the paper so you no longer need to carry it in your head and it will allow you clarity. When you feel it's all written down look at how many things come from your negative Rats' Den space, such as fear or other people's opinions, and how many come from your Palace mind, such as being an act of Loving Yourself. When you have noted this you will readily see which list is more about underlying positives or underlying negatives. With this in mind, close your eyes and tune into your feelings and ask yourself if you were really prioritising your own needs (which is actually the *selfless* act, as explained in chapter twelve), what would be the act of Loving *Yourself*? You now have your direction. However tough it seems, know your Palace mind has all your answers and solutions and aligning the 5 Components will enable you to follow through on whatever you need to do. Just being true to your own integrity will be a major step forward into that Palace.

Of course there are always things that make breaking up difficult: the finances, the children, the fear of what's ahead, even just leaving the familiarity - the list goes on and on. With my track record I've faced quite a few! I now realise that all those experiences, however painful at the time, are all part of the rich tapestry of my life and have shaped who I am today, feeling happy and purposeful. Know you deserve this too.

Ending A Relationship

Many years ago when I was in a dire situation I remember sitting in an Italian restaurant with a good friend literally plotting how to get rid of the man I was with! He had made himself unemployed, was living off me and treated me very badly but if I somehow made him leave he would be homeless. Every solicitor I approached said I would have a 'duty of care' for him and he could 'take me to the cleaners' financially. I was determined not to lose any more money, not to him or to a solicitor!

At that time I had discovered Louise Hay's book "Life!" By then I had learned enough to trust her words so just followed what it said. I kept repeating "I bless you with love and I release you. I set you free and I set myself free". I surrendered to this completely, which is the key to laying down any counter attachments and genuinely connecting with the feeling of our words. The book said I would be amazed at how my relationship dissolved so easily. I just trusted and surrendered to that. For a couple of weeks nothing changed for the good and some things got worse. Then the Universe brought some incredible things together and within three months I'd moved out, he'd moved out of my house of his own accord and the rest was plain sailing to the end of a quick conclusion.

Do not underestimate the power of blessing with love. If you want to end your relationship I recommend you repeat and surrender to those words right now: "I bless you with love and I release you. I set you free and I set myself free". Then focus on being in your Palace mind, making each day as best you can, Staying in the Moment and following the Cut-Out section at the end of this book.

When the relationship is over, look at what lessons you can learn from the experience. Be thankful for the good times and if necessary, release negative feelings either with the Letting Go exercises (pages 27–29) or do an anger letter and the Balancing the Power visualisation until you are clear and can forgive where appropriate.

You will never be truly free to connect with a new relationship if there's unfinished emotional business with an ex. Take the time you need and focus on being in your Palace. If there are children involved that is even more reason to align the 5 Components of Palace living. In that space with those high frequency vibrations you will find many problems just disappear and you can more easily handle the others. Remember to give your power to living your own life well rather than to the challenges that occur.

Know you are worthy and deserving of *all* your good. Reconnect with yourself and Love Yourself, cultivating the space for a new relationship to come to you that is truly loving and fulfilling.

When Your Partner Ends The Relationship

This can be a very difficult and sad time and can leave a lot of pain and hardship. The truth is we can still handle things from either our Rats' Den point of helplessness or our Palace point of power, even if that power seems somewhat diminished at the time. Choose to Stay in the Moment and ask moment by moment 'what would be an act of loving myself right now?' to guide you positively and support you. Be gentle with yourself and reach out for support where you can.

If you're 'dumped' it's not because there's anything wrong with you, despite what your partner may tell you. It's because on one level or another the relationship no longer worked for the other person. You've had your experiences together and have benefitted, learned, or grown from them. Sometimes it takes a while to realise but there's always something better to move onto if you work on yourself to grow and let it in. Even if you feel you were in a great relationship, when you've allowed yourself to move on you may look back and see many flaws, including misaligned Love Languages. Working on yourself to improve your self-feelings enables you to see things from a different perspective. The more self-loving and self-approving you become the richer the relationships you will allow yourself to have in future. The work is always on our selves.

If your Rats' Den emotions are running high from your partner ending things, use the Letting Go exercises or write an anger letter and do the Balancing the Power visualisation. Release that negativity; it's only doing *you* harm! Allow yourself to reach the point of forgiving them (and yourself if needs be) because that's what sets *you* free to be able to move on. You must dissolve any negativity toward that relationship (or any of your past relationships) if you are to be emotionally available for a new partner.

If the relationship didn't work because you know you messed up, trust that you needed that lesson in order to learn and grow to be different. Work on letting go of any self-beating and focus on forgiving yourself for 'all you have and haven't done'. Examine your core 'blueprint' beliefs about love, relationships and yourself and clear negatives that come up. What's blocking you from having a healthy relationship? Use the tools in this book to dissolve and reprogramme those old beliefs and patterns that do not serve you. Work on Loving Yourself so you can be different next time, from an authentic space.

Discover new ways to be with yourself; create a new and exciting Life Grid; Love Yourself and your Inner Child. Focus on the new adventure ahead. Know you are worthy and deserving of being your very best to enjoy your life to the full. Then you are really back in your Palace where you can accept all your experiences without judgment and move forward. This is Loving Yourself! It can feel a whole lot better than what you were gaining from your relationship and creates wholesome space to attract your true soulmate.

Chapter Twelve
The Way To Lasting Happiness

What is the secret to lasting happiness? What is the formula to create a sense of purpose and fulfillment that feels an innate part of us? We all know the most 'successful' people can feel hollow, the most loving person doesn't necessarily have good relationships, those in satisfying jobs can still feel lonely, wealthy people can still be miserable, so clearly none of these things are the answer. What is it that gives us lasting and meaningful happiness?

For most of us, the list of what we wish to have is much the same:

Self-Worth	Good Health
Self-Esteem	Satisfying Job/Career
Self-Belief	Purpose
Self-Confidence	Fulfillment
Self-Respect	Wealth
Deservability	Great Relationships
Inner peace	Good Friends
Joy	Fun
Love	Wonderful Experiences
Happiness	Opportunities to Have and Be and Do What We Want

We can think if we achieve the list on the right (maybe through 'luck', working hard or struggling for it) we will then *feel* the things on the list on the left and be happy.

This is the complete opposite of the truth. This is looking for external things to make us feel good which is never truly satisfying, or at best, only temporarily. We can think 'if only' we had the right house/job/relationship/etc life would be fine and we'd be happy. Then even if we get them, before very long the same feelings of emptiness and hollowness return. Even if life is seemingly perfect it doesn't necessarily mean we'll be happy. This is why people with ostensibly *wonderful* lives can still feel depressed.

The truth is we need to connect with the *feelings on the left*, on our deepest layers, in order to be able to allow ourselves to manifest the list on the right and feel the appreciation and joy of living these.

How can we have the job or fulfillment or wonderful experiences etc on the right without the self-worth, the deservability, the confidence, the self-belief etc on the left to allow them in? We either won't allow ourselves to have them in the first place or sabotage them in some way if they do come to us. Or, sometimes people can have the 'perfect life' but come from a space of false programming or emotional neglect or manipulation so have nothing in their 'blueprint' to enable them to embrace it and enjoy it.

The way to lasting happiness and feeling good every day is to come home to your true self in your source and soul, where you absolutely believe in who you are, live in full acceptance and joy of being you, embracing the precious gift that is your life. You feel good just because you are alive! From this space you can ride on the crest of life's wave feeling the full joy of living.

So, how do we do this? I repeat it is *not* the external things that can produce this on-going sense of inner peace and joy. It has to come from within. The answer is in four words: **Learn to Love Yourself.**

Why? Because Love is the greatest emotional power we have. Let's understand I am not talking about arrogance in "I love myself". Arrogance is a disguise for not feeling good enough. I am talking about truly acknowledging and valuing the magnificence of who you are.

You can Love Yourself just because you exist. Realise the truth that you *are* a miraculous expression of life. Appreciate the miracle that you are! Is there any baby born, anywhere in the world, who isn't lovable, worthy and deserving of a good life and good enough exactly as they are? No. They may very soon *learn* differently but the truth remains: being born was all it took to be lovable, worthy, deserving and good enough. You were a baby once too. That's your birthright too. Your choice now is whether to give your power to your birthright space or to give your power to the false negatives you've learned since.

If on a scale of 1 - 10 you feel '2' out of 10 worthy or lovable you'll find it difficult to allow yourself to move to your Palace even if you can see it's logical and beneficial because it doesn't match the "I'm *un*worthy/*un*lovable" '2' belief you have. You'll need to change this belief in order to come up the scale and allow yourself to live in your Palace.

If you need external approval to feel good enough, even if someone gives it to you this week you will need it again next week and the next. It will never satisfy you and you will move the goal posts. Even if someone approves of you '10' out of 10, if you only believe you're a '2', you wont be able to let it in and believe them. You'll find yourself saying "He can't really mean that" or "Oh, she's only saying that to be nice". You need to approve of *yourself* '10' out of 10 so you can *receive* on that level. Equally, if you have a '2' out of 10 self-approval level, that's essentially all the level of approval you give out, because it is all you can authentically identify with.

If you feel you can only accept yourself '2' out of 10 (deep inside, not what your head might tell you), it means that is all you can receive, or indeed, authentically give.

If you only Love Yourself '2' out of 10, no matter how loving a person you may believe yourself to be, the truth is that all you can give authentically is '2' out of 10 because you cannot give what doesn't 'pattern match' within. And conversely of course, you can only authentically let *in* a '2' level of love.

This also applies to religious people; how can you receive *God's* love if you don't feel worthy of being loved? How can you feel worthy of being loved if you don't Love Yourself enough to be able to receive it in? It's the same with all relationships. No one can love *you* enough if you don't know how to receive their love and you can never love someone else enough if they don't know how to receive *your* love.

The wonderful thing about Loving Ourselves is that it turns all these around! For example, if you have deservability issues about being lovable or loved, when you Love Yourself you are proving you are deserving of love. And when you Love Yourself you can *receive* love! You don't have to be perfect to be lovable. Who is? And who decides what's 'good enough' or 'perfect' anyway? You could choose to say "It doesn't matter whether I believe I am deserving of love - I allow myself to love myself anyway" because being loved is your birthright! In addition, by Loving Yourself you will have increased the level of love in the world. Everyone gains when you Love Yourself.

The four aspects of Love are*:* acceptance, allowing, appreciation, and approval. When we resist our own good we 'freeze' these four aspects and block our way forward. Connecting and flowing with these paves the way to self-love, freedom and joy. These have been covered in previous chapters so let's just recap on our learning with regard to this context:

1) Acceptance: If life seems to have been a disappointment it is because you judge everything in the light of what is good or bad - what went right or what went wrong. When you are busy judging like this there is no place to cultivate inner peace. Accept things as they are because that's how they are. When you are busy judging others you cannot authentically be accepting of yourself. When you accept everyone is responsible for them selves and that their choices are their concern you can let in self-acceptance. It doesn't mean you have to condone behaviour in others that doesn't match your standards and values. It just means you stop exhausting yourself judging it. Once you stop judging and start accepting, you lay down your resistance, which is the pathway to inner peace and happiness.

2) Allowing: When you allow others to be as they are you can authentically allow yourself to be as *you* are, knowing you can always choose to make positive changes for your good. Getting hot and bothered because others don't fit with your ideals achieves nothing. Allowing others to be as they are and then making the relevant positive choices for yourself accordingly, allows you to move forward. What we attract in life is really about what we allow ourselves to have. When we block our good we prevent ourselves from living well. In the Palace we can allow ourselves to experience ourselves at our best and receive all our good.

3) Appreciation: When you appreciate yourself just for being you, focusing on all those qualities you like about yourself and building them to that list of 50 (page 84), you can't help but feel good. Know you are worth appreciating. Start appreciating everything about yourself. The more deeply you appreciate yourself for who you really are, the more you will let in deep appreciation from others.

4) Approval: All the years you've found fault and disapproved of yourself hasn't changed you in any positive way. You have to be with your Rats to beat yourself up like this. When you come from the Palace space of "I approve of myself" and let this become your mantra as you climb up the scale, you'll start to see the results you've previously been striving for. If you approve of yourself '10' out of 10, firstly it makes it very hard for you to do things you disapprove of and secondly, if you are radiating all that self-approval from your very core, you're far more likely to attract it as well as be able to receive it!

Remember to add to and read your list of qualities you like about yourself (page 84) and to create and maintain your Life Grid as acts of Loving Yourself too (pages 86–88).

If you Love Yourself you feel good *every day* regardless of what is going on around you and you can handle life's challenges with clarity and confidence. You will attract the people and experiences that reflect that love!

As Louise Hay says, don't wait until you've lost weight, found a new job, finished your project or whatever other excuse might arise. You'll be waiting forever; you'll just move the goalpost again. Love Yourself now, exactly as you are. Accept yourself now, exactly as you are. Approve of yourself now exactly as you are. Feel those feelings. The more you Love Yourself the more you align with the core of the real 'you' and come home to yourself. It is a beautiful space in which to be.

Beat Your Depression For Good

Loving Ourselves allows us to take our place on our throne in our Palace, as King or Queen of our own Life!

So, how do we get from where we've been, living in our Rats' Den in a state of depression, to the Palace experience of Loving Ourselves? Let's start with looking at where we're off track.

EXERCISE:

On the following list tick each line that applies to you:

Acts Of NOT Loving Yourself

Beating yourself up

Being stuck in negative thinking

Being stuck in negative feelings

Not feeling good enough

Putting everyone else first

Being kinder to others than yourself

Letting other peoples opinions affect you

Shutting life out

Not allowing yourself to be the best you can be/have the best life you can

Denying your own good

Creating pain and illness in your body, including anxiety and depression

Living in disorder

Creating debt or other burdens

Attracting lovers/mates that are wrong for you or who abuse you

Demi Schneider

Staying in unhealthy relationships

Feeling helpless or a 'victim of circumstance'

Procrastinating on things that would benefit you

Abusing yourself with cigarettes, or drugs, or too much alcohol, or over-spending, or self-harming, or over-eating, or other negative behaviours

Having a fixed agenda on how life should be

Fearing life's challenges

Having unreasonable expectations of yourself and others

Having the burden of self-importance through low self-worth

Needing control

Believing you're not worthy of true love

How else do you show lack of self-love? Write them here:

Did you score quite highly on this list and/or add other things? This is the wrong list to be doing well on! No wonder you feel depressed. This is not what living well and being happy is about.

Let's look now at the difference *Loving Yourself* makes:

Benefits Of Loving Yourself

Feeling worthy and deserving, full of self esteem and self respect

Accepting yourself and others exactly as you/they are

Approving of yourself, and letting approval come back to you, knowing how to receive it

Revering this 'temple' that you live in - appreciating all your body does for you

Knowing you're good enough just because you exist

Knowing you're doing the best you can and are constantly growing

Coping better with life's challenges

Trusting you can handle things

Knowing you're free to bend and sway like the willow tree in the wind (no longer rigid)

Believing in yourself

Staying in the Moment - enjoying each moment of your precious life

Having a desire to embrace life

Having a desire to rush to get up every morning to be part of life

Feeling motivated and confident

Knowing you're worth loving

Having harmonious relationships with everyone

Attracting an intimate relationship that's worthy of the real you

Having the courage to let go of relationships that no longer serve you

Vibrating your love, joy, inner peace and wellbeing so that you give authentically and you can receive authentically

Being excited at being 100% accountable for your thoughts and vibrations: "if it is to be it's up to me!"

Knowing you're worthy of the best job, great relationships, success, etc

Being the best you can be - having the wherewithal to 'step up to the plate'

Making positive choices for yourself in life

Being a 'magnet' for all your good

Making yourself the priority and flowing from there

Creating a balanced life grid of what's important to you

Smiling!

Never knowing depression again, being aligned with your inner infinite well of love to bring you joy, inner peace, wisdom, abundance, health, wealth and happiness forever! Or, as one client put it, "Feeling so great every single day feels like you're standing in a garden of flowers on a warm sunny day".

Learning to truly value and Love Yourself is the antidote to all your negatives and the way to lasting happiness. It's something we can all do because it's an emotion we all have and are all capable of giving. We just need to channel it in our own direction. For those who say "I don't know what love is" you really mean you haven't connected with that emotion within yourself yet - it doesn't mean it's not there. You'll find it if you *live* all that I'm sharing with you here.

I want to explain more about 'putting everyone else first' in the first list above and 'making yourself a priority and flowing from there' in the second. I find so often clients have a huge block around the concept of 'taking care of their own needs' as being honourable.

In the situation of putting your own oxygen mask on first before helping others, this is easily seen as the preferable option because you're then much more use to others rather than running out of air and needing help yourself.

Now imagine a young man walking along a path in Africa, with a small child and an elderly woman, in blazing heat, all needing a drink with the nearest watering hole three miles away. Would it be best for the young man to carry the child, help the old lady as best he can and all stagger to the water hole, hoping they can make it in time before one of them collapses? Or would it be best for him to leave them there, (find shade if he can) and run as fast as he can to the water hole. Then, on arrival, even though they are back there suffering, drink his own fill to be at his optimum best, to then bring back the water for them, being fit and fully able to care for them?

The point is when we keep giving and giving without being nourished ourselves we become more and more depleted and eventually end up little use to anyone, let alone ourselves. That's when we end up well and truly in our Rats' Den.

When we prioritise our own needs first and foremost we become the best we can be and feel empowered. When we are functioning at our best we can live well which is to everyone's advantage. We are also an inspiration to others who see how self-sustaining we've become thus helping them to recognise these positive qualities within themselves. And of course, when we are at our best, we have so much more to give others when we choose. Prioritising our own needs is actually the selfless thing to do! By meeting our own needs we even discover the needs of those around us actually begin to change and our world begins to change for the better.

The balance between being selfless and selfish in what we choose to give or not give can be found by asking yourself "What would be an act of loving myself" and tuning into your feelings. If you have any sense of resentment or negativity about doing something *that's the time to prioritise your own needs.* Go with what feels better and true to your integrity. Sometimes it might mean saying "no". It is so important, and an act of Loving Yourself, to be clear about your own personal boundaries. When you erect or resurrect clear personal boundaries and maintain them you take back your own power. It then becomes much easier to connect with that part of you which is able to stand firm, to be decisive and confident and feel comfortable with saying "no" when you need to. And you can be sure you will be loved no less for it; in fact you may well be pleasantly surprised at how those around you adjust accordingly. When we take back our own power others have to respect our decisions and our boundaries and in time adjustments are made and everyone is the better for them.

Let your benchmark between selflessness and selfishness be choosing to prioritise your own needs when that is the act of Loving Yourself.

Demi Schneider

How To Love Yourself

EXERCISE:

You can't go anywhere without a destination. Let's first create a 'template' for your changes. Go back over all the points you ticked on the 'Acts of Not Loving Myself' list. Write down the positive opposite, for example, instead of 'beating myself up' you could write 'I am now kind and gentle to myself'.

Here is a list of examples of 'opposite positive alternatives' to the original list you could choose instead for any points that were applicable to you. You can use my words or be creative with your own. The importance is in wording everything in terms of what you want to cultivate and in the present tense.

Acts Of Loving Myself
(the same list as before, just turned around)

I am kind and gentle with myself and exercise patience

I praise and support myself

I choose thoughts that make me feel a little bit better rather than a little bit worse

I focus on the feelings I want and choose appropriate thoughts

I know I am good enough just as I am

I am happy to prioritise my own needs first and foremost to be the best I can be for everyone's sake

I remember "Love thy neighbour as thyself" means I get to love myself too! I count too

I am only responsible for myself; what others think and feel about me is none of my business

I embrace life

I allow myself to be and do and have the very best for I am worthy and deserving

I lay down my resistance and let my good in

I focus on the health and vitality I do want

I create the best environment I can as an outer show of the new way I feel about myself

I focus on prosperity, enjoying the freedom this brings in all areas of my life

I only allow lovers/partners into my life who reflect my true integrity, leaving neediness behind, knowing I am worthy and deserving of a truly loving relationship. I work on myself to become a whole and complete person to allow in another whole and complete person

I have the courage to let go of all relationships that do not serve me

I take back my own power and choose to move forward rather than stagnating in my Rats' Den

I choose to Stay in the Moment and use Miracle Questioning to deal with any task efficiently and swiftly

I choose to respect and value my body, giving it nourishing foods and beverages. I remember I need my body to live in, so treat it with the utmost care

I flow with life and accept it exactly as it unfolds, giving my attention to all that's good at any given time

I choose to come from a point of power (Palace) rather than helplessness (Rats' Den), knowing I *can* actually handle whatever comes my way

I do the best I can at any given point and accept others as they are

I feel secure in who I am just as I am, relaxed, comfortable and self-assured

I am worthy and deserving of true love, starting with feeling the love from myself

I am willing to Love Myself just as I am!

Doesn't this feel a whole lot better than the original list? However far off it might seem at this present moment, know that each step you take on this self-honouring path helps you feel better and if you keep making those steps you will get to the point you can truly Love Yourself. Imagine how easy it would be to leave depression behind for good if you allowed yourself to live this way!

With the revised list above, or your own version, your brain now has a template of the new choices you want to make to move forward to. Focus on them with all your might so that your anterior cingulate gyrus can come on board to help you live them. Carry your script with you and check in with it often to keep it fresh in your mind until you find you have assimilated this way of being. If you read it enough you will learn it off by heart and can then focus on applying it even more. If you catch yourself slipping back into your Rats' Den just ask yourself "What would be an act of loving myself right now?" or use one of the exercises already learned to release the negative and take back your power again.

This is fun! This is your ticket to feeling great about yourself and your life every day! Baby steps are good and often best; just go at the pace that feels right for *you*. Of course you may fall off the new path quite a bit to start with, and there may be times you feel you'll never be able to fully Love Yourself. Just realise this is all part of the process, just as Olympic champions have their injuries and set backs along the way. It's not rocket science; it's just acknowledging you are worth loving and demonstrating that to yourself. *How can anyone else see your inner beauty if you can't see it yourself?*

If you really feel a huge gap between where you are now and the reality of Loving Yourself and have any doubt about closing that gap, realise you are choosing to hold onto the falsehoods that you've learned rather than embrace the truth of your birthright; you were born loving and lovable. Spend time with your Inner Child, give them permission to embrace this, give them all the love they could ever have wanted so you fill yourself up with this nutrition. Look over the new patterns in the list of 'Acts of Loving Yourself' above and be willing to live them. Or sit quietly, relaxing and tuning into that deep inner part of you to intuitively feel what your blocks are. You may find it's because you feel you 'can't have' or are 'too unworthy' or 'too worthless' or 'feel too inadequate' or 'are bad'. Remember none of these are true and you have the tools in this book to clear these falsehoods so you *can* turn your great capacity to love in towards yourself. You *are* lovable, just as you are!

You can also use The Two Islands visualisation (page 111 and on the free audio download or purchasable CD) to help set yourself free of *these* old patterns as well as your other old Beliefs and Resistances. Whilst some people are naturally more 'visual' (seeing) or 'audio' (hearing) or 'kinesthetic' (feeling) I generally find people who perceive visualising difficult are much more capable than they think they are. Usually any lack of confidence is because people aren't sure if what they're doing is right. It is ok to hear and feel the experiences too. Even if you don't feel you're very good at visualising you will still benefit. Enjoy it!

You may feel you have never known love (or meaningful love) to even know what it is to now be able to receive it. Start by feeling love for another, even it's just your pet – or someone else's! How do you feel being with them, tending to their needs, feeling protective of them, knowing they deserve good treatment and are absolutely worthy of love? Connect with that feeling and realise you are feeling love! Then turn those same feelings towards yourself! You are definitely worth as much as a beloved pet, or other, so start from there. The better you acknowledge your needs and desires and the better the way you treat yourself, the more your self-respect and self-esteem will grow and you will value yourself. If you haven't yet done so, go to the list of 'Acts of Not Loving Yourself' and tick all the relevant ones to you and add others if applicable. Turn them around, as per the example. As you focus on these and apply them you will identify more and more with the feelings of love.

I Love Myself

You will know how you are progressing because you will experience the manifestation of your new space each time that shifts. The more wonderful your life grows will be the evidence of the new level of connection and alignment you have with that core of who you really are.

You will automatically be in the Palace part of your brain, with all its benefits, producing lots of serotonin, feeling the full joy of living, knowing you are worthy and deserving, and having so much more to give when you choose.

I give my clients a copy of Louise Hay's beautiful script called 'I Love Myself Therefore...' so they have a measure of what a 10 out of 10 Loving Themselves looks like. As with the 'Deservability Treatment', when you reach 10 that feeling just expands and becomes bigger and bigger and more and more wonderful.

I feel honoured, privileged and very blessed to have been given permission to include it here:

I Love Myself Therefore.........

Deep at the centre of my being there is an infinite well of love.
I now allow this love to flow to the surface.
It fills my heart, my body, my mind, my consciousness, my very being, and radiates out from me in all directions

Demi Schneider

*and returns to me multiplied.
The more love I use and give, the more I have to give.
The supply is endless!
The use of love makes me feel good. It is
an expression of my inner joy.
I love myself therefore I take loving care of my body.
I lovingly feed it nourishing foods and beverages.
I lovingly groom and dress it. My body lovingly
responds to me with vibrant health and energy.
I love myself therefore I provide for myself a comfortable
home, one that fills all my needs and is a pleasure to be in.
I fill the rooms with the vibration of love so that all who enter,
myself included, will feel this love and be nourished by it.
I love myself therefore I work at a job I
truly enjoy doing, one that uses my
creative talents and abilities,
working with and for people that I love and
that love me, and earning a good income.
I love myself therefore I behave and think in a loving
way to all people for I know that that which I give
returns to me multiplied. I only attract loving people
into my world for they are a mirror of what I am.
I love myself therefore I forgive and totally release the past and
all past experiences and I am free.
I love myself therefore I live totally in the now,
experiencing each moment as good and knowing
that my future is bright and joyous and secure for I
am a beloved child of the Universe and the Universe
lovingly takes care of me now and forever more.*

And So It Is

*By Kind Permission of Hay House Inc. Carlsbad, CA
copyright 1984, 1987, 2004 by Louise L Hay*

Coming Home To Yourself

However much 'head work' you do, it is imperative to *feel* this connection with Loving Yourself deep within to truly feel at peace and comfortable in your own skin; to be at one with yourself.

We can assist this by practising simply sitting in silence and just 'being'. It is when we sit in silence and go within that we connect with our true source and soul from where flows our inner wisdom. Our soul is our life giving force, our peace, our playfulness, our energy and sparkle, our happiness.

This concept is often a turn-off because we are so used to the rushed and noisy world we live in it seems unnatural or alien to us or even scary to sit in silence and connect with our true self. Yet the truth is it's the rush and noise of modern day living that is unnatural and alien and the detachment from our true selves that causes the sense of emptiness and hopelessness! It is a truly wonderful, simple thing we can do for ourselves to nurture our soul. With a little practise you will find the rewards immeasurable.

Deepak Chopra says that 15 minutes a day meditation is the greatest gift we can give to ourselves. Having resisted this for many years myself, preferring to stay in 'head space', (thinking I needed to put in lots of *action* effort to achieve the goals I yearned for so I could be happy) and now having spent quite a few years connecting with my inner being, (to be happy from within, to live well and achieve through my *'vibrational'* effort instead), I can appreciate completely the wisdom of Deepak Chopra's words.

EXERCISE:

If you are new to meditating try this simple exercise to begin with. Start with just a couple of minutes and slowly build up to 15 minutes or more (or do a few minutes 2 or 3 times a day). Do this every day for a month and notice the difference:

Sit comfortably in silence with yourself, eyes closed, just concentrating on your breathing. Breathe in through your nose, tummy pushing forward; breathe out through your mouth, tummy relaxing back. Follow the gentle 'in' and 'out' of your breath, allowing each breath to become slower. If you find you need something to occupy your mind to still the constant flow of thoughts, breathe in "I am" and breathe out "at peace" allowing any other thoughts to just float on by. Let each breath become slower and deeper.

When it feels right come back to awareness of your room, your time, your space. As you progress and allow yourself to sink deeper you may be surprised at how much time has gone by! With a little practise you will feel wonderfully relaxed and peaceful afterwards, your anxiety levels generally will reduce and you will feel calmer and more in command.

Demi Schneider

EXERCISE:

Besides practising longer and deeper meditations, you could choose to spend 20 seconds every hour during your day deeply breathing in "I open myself to receive my true source and soul" or "I allow myself to connect with my true self" or something similar that resonates with you, really connecting with your words and feeling them. When you do it right it feels great! Just practise, with the willingness to get to that space.

For those of you who are more spiritually inclined, know you can achieve deeper and deeper connection with your true source and soul. Trust that you will be shown the way and that everything you need to know will be revealed to you in its right time and space. I learned this from Louise Hay a long time ago, yet it took the connection with myself on this soul level to really appreciate this wisdom, when I could look back and see how my journey had unfolded. You only need to trust the process of life and stay attuned to your own intuitive guidance as to which paths to follow. When the student is ready, the teacher appears. Reach out to other mentors and guides with whom you feel resonance. Use your learnings to further explore your true self. You are the only one on your journey and ultimately are the only one who can truly connect with your own true source and soul. Enjoy the thrilling journey of connecting with the magnificence of you!

With practise you will be able to access your answers and guidance from within. I remember a particular occasion I sat in silence and focused completely on listening to my intuitive self for enlightenment. Being experienced, I was able to sit for a long time and many things of great value on many levels were revealed to me. I gained wonderful clarity on several aspects of my life and what I needed to bring myself back on track in some areas or move forward in others. More importantly, I also realised how, in my busy schedule, I was *neglecting to nurture my soul.* When we don't nurture our soul space it shrivels and leads us to feel hollow and undervalued and disconnected. To feel good we need to come back home to that sacred space within, to feel valued, connected with who we are, content and at peace. From this space of oneness with our true source and soul and the infinite well of love within we feel wonderful!

And, as the Barbra Streisand song from "Yentle" says, "There are certain things that once you have no man can take away, no wind can blow away, no wave can wash away - and now they're about to be mine!" This will be true for *you* when you learn to connect with yourself in this way. Every step you take will help you feel better.

Having pledged to give myself sacred time everyday to sit in silence, I continue to do so at least 6 days out of 7 and I feel fabulous - more focused, in command and beautifully at peace.

I encourage you now to do the same and really focus on connecting within so you understand more and more the meaning *and feeling* of Loving Yourself, allowing your chakras to open and your energy to sink into those deeper spaces to be aligned with your true self.

To help fill yourself with Love the following visualisation is a pleasant reminder to appreciate every part of your incredible being and spread that good feeling to all.

VISUALISATION:
LOVING YOUR BODY & THE PLANET

Sitting or lying comfortably, arms and legs uncrossed, close your eyes and just focus on your breathing, relaxing completely. Turn your attention to your toes and realise how wonderful it is to have toes; without them you couldn't bend your foot to walk! Love them! And your feet; all the standing around they've done for you or perhaps you've squashed them into uncomfortable shoes – or just moaned when they've ached. Appreciate them; the ability to stand on your own two feet, love them. Your ankles and the wonderful flexibility they give to make moving so much easier, appreciate them and love them. Where would you be without your legs? The ease with which they allow you to move from A – B, that you probably take for granted. Acknowledge and thank your legs; love them. Become aware of the miracle of all your internal organs and how they work without any conscious direction! Your liver has over 500 functions! See it plump and healthy and thank it for doing such a wonderful job. Appreciate your digestive system that allows you to take in nourishment to sustain you, to assimilate it and then eliminate the waste. Appreciate all your other organs, muscles, tissues, nerve endings and every piece of skin. Just revere and love and choose to cherish the temple that you live in. Acknowledge and thank your lungs. Without another breath you wouldn't last more than a few minutes; something else we take for granted – that our next breath will be there. Appreciate them and see them as plump and healthy, revitalised – and relaxing back as you exhale, giving you the joy of life. Shoulders are meant to carry joy yet look at all the burdens put on them so often. Thank them and love them. Thank your arms and all they do, your hands and fingers and thumbs. Appreciate and value every part of them. See every vertebrae of your spine perfectly aligned, strong and supported. Say "Backbone be strong". Put Love into your spine. Now turn your attention to your neck and the wonderful flexibility it gives your head, being able to turn from side to side. Appreciate that gift. Love your neck. Love and value your mouth through which you take in nourishment and communicate! Appreciate your nose and the ability to take in life. Love your ears and the ability to hear – laughter, sounds of nature, a loved one's voice, beautiful music. And your eyes and the phenomenal ability to see! Appreciate all these gifts and love and value every part of you. Then there's your control centre – your wonderful brain, the most complex known thing in the Universe. Thank your brain for all it does and feel love for it.

Now bring your attention to your own heart centre and tap into the infinite well of love deep within. Feel this spreading through your body and then radiate out from you filling the whole room. Let this love spread out across your town, all across your country and up and out and all around the world. See the people well fed, clothed, educated, with access to fresh running water. Envelop the whole planet with your love, knowing this is a precious gift you are giving in this moment. The more you Love Yourself, the more the level of love in the world rises!

Staying with this sense of connection with your own pure love heart centre space, anchor this into your belly and bring it up through your body to the forefront of your mind and hold this beautiful space all the rest of this day.

In The Face Of Challenges

When the Universe 'bashes us over the head' with a challenge (or challenges), it is always telling us something; maybe something specific, or indicating that we're just off course, or is giving us an opportunity for growth (for example when we get made redundant but then, having nothing to lose, go on to greater things). When we 'go within' we can access our inner guidance and intuitively find the route forward that feels right, to better utilise the immense resource of our Palace mind.

When we are challenged the key is to hold the faith and trust our ability to handle things and to trust the process of life. Things do work out; we can just either feel the ease of going with events or the discomfort of resisting them. As I've said, my favourite mantra in times of challenge is "Everything is working for my highest good", especially if I can't possibly see how. Or I might say "Ok Universe – I leave it to you to sort this out" and send my problem out with trust the Universe will indeed handle it much better than me. Stressing about things only ever creates Rats' Den scenarios. It's holding faith and trust that keeps us in the Palace mind and enables us to weather the storm. When we stop judging our experiences as 'good' or 'bad' and just accept them as experiences, we don't give unnecessary power to what we don't want and inadvertently nurture our Rats.

Of course if any resistance comes up, we can use any of the four ways to handle this: Stop It, Switch It, a Letting Go exercise, or Miracle Questioning ourselves out of it. It's all life experience and without challenges there would be no growth. It's much more helpful to look at "What can I learn from this?" or "What would an act of loving myself be?" rather than lament things aren't the way we want.

Then we can focus on "What's good about this" and work on aligning the 5 Components of the Palace mind, including Loving Ourselves and taking time to be in sacred space, to feel inner peace and innate happiness because we are connecting to our true self at our source.

Loving Ourselves enough to trust ourselves, as well as the process of life, is the essence of faith. "I love myself exactly as I am." "I trust myself to give myself the very best I can, knowing I am worthy and deserving of all my good". "I trust the process of life and know I am supported by the Higher Consciousness in the Universe."

When I was updating my vision board one day and typing out some new words to accompany my pictures, a wonderful thing happened. When I was typing "I am sacred" "I give myself sacred time every day" I found I'd mistyped the word 'sacred' and put the 'a' and 'c' the wrong way round. It spells the word 'scared'! Oh what enlightenment! *All the years I was 'scared' to really embrace myself - which meant I could never really embrace others - or life!*

What a wonderful mantra to have: *'don't be scared; be sacred'* and bring all your attention to the pit of your belly to anchor it there and *feel* it there for all time.

Learn to Love All of Yourself And Come Home To Feeling The Joy of the Magnificence That You Are.

You will never know anxiety or depression ever again!

Chapter Thirteen
My Life Ambition

Imagine if you had been taught the essence of this book in school, if you had learned 'How to Live Well' as a subject from the age of five. What difference do you think it might have made to you in your life if:

~ You'd learned 'how your mind works' so you understood all the implications and knew you were in charge of your thoughts and could use the power of your mind to live to your full potential?

~ You'd been able to programme or replace your 'blueprint' with positive beliefs for all areas of your life, regardless of your home background?

~ You'd learned about your worthiness and deservability from the age of five and how much more you might have consequently allowed yourself to have throughout your life?

~ You'd learned all those years ago how to release negative thoughts instead of being overwhelmed by them?

~ You'd learned how to use Miracle Questioning as a matter of general language and been living all its benefits ever since?

~ You'd learned how to handle fear to have helped cope better at school, with exams, with peers, a home situation etc and the difference going on into adult life and your life today if fear hadn't held/didn't hold you back so much?

~ You'd learned to make use of your intellectual (Palace) mind to dissipate anger and react to triggers from a sensible perspective, to cease all criticism, including that of yourself and to not let other people's opinions hurt you or hamper you; if you'd learned way back then to address guilt in the moment rather than carry the pain?

~ You'd learned the value of forgiveness and how to forgive, non-judgmentalism and acceptance, how to create inner peace and how to live in joy?

~ You'd learned to believe in yourself and go beyond the limitations of parents?

~ You'd learned how to live authentically in your intellectual (Palace) mind, thinking, feeling and speaking in positive ways as a matter of course?

~ You'd learned about love languages to have more rewarding relationships?

~ You were living now from the space of being comfortable in your own skin, able to create and embrace your good?

~ You'd learned to love your self and value and appreciate the magnificent being you truly are?

Do you think your life might have been easier and more joyful?

Do you think if this was taught as a subject in schools we might have some happier, more fulfilled people? Do you think young girls might gain enough self-worth and self-esteem to outgrow teenage pregnancies? Or that it suddenly might not be so 'cool' for kids to smoke behind the gym or take drugs if that was an advertisement to the world that they were in their Rats' Den? Do you imagine it might help avoid frustrated teenagers acting out in anti-social behaviour if they understood how to nurture themselves and handle anger constructively? Might it give abused children an earlier opportunity to heal and help them go beyond the limitations of their background more easily? Would it help encourage children to be the best they could be if they *learned* how to live well? Do you suppose it would help their future relationships fare better? Do you think it would create a friendlier, safer, more enjoyable society in which to live?

We have this incredible brain, the most complex known phenomenon in the Universe, of which we use approximately 5%. The potential for our positive growth is immeasurable!

Yet we are seeing modern gang warfare where power, territory and tribal allegiance count for everything, hunting for status and prestige through the strength and conquest of arms, exhibiting behaviour not seen since the passing of the Stone Age. Many young offenders don't know any other way to live than the template they have in their 'blueprint' from their influences and environment. They are living what 'life has caused them to become' rather than from their true core being. With change to their understanding and 'blueprint' they could have an authentic alternative to ending up back in prison. At heart many of them just want to feel loved and valued.

Children with no positive template use their mobile phones for bullying which can cause the recipient immense psychological damage. A study in Britain found that at least half of suicides among young people are related to bullying. In some areas, *60 - 70%* of police time is taken up in dealing with issues of abuse and harassment on Facebook, email and texting, or being called to essentially trivial family issues of bickering and accusations. These can blow up out of all proportion, sometimes leaving one member isolated and vulnerable. Often these people feel they have no alternative way to express their anger or to feel heard other than to call the police, who, whilst trying to establish if anything criminal has occurred, are obliged to effectively act as untrained social workers trying to deal with deep seated issues that ultimately are not within their remit.

These people started out as beautiful babies. They all have that phenomenal intellectual (Palace) mind! Yet all they know is how to live in their Rats' Den, sometimes with little more than caveman morals and life styles, coming from where they've come from.

They have all *learned* to be entrenched in their Rats' Den. What chance do children stand with these influences? If I told you about a war torn place in the world where the average child would witness 150 murders before the age of 10 how would you feel? This is in fact true of the UK! With all the violent video games, TV, films and so on, *as the brain cannot tell the difference between real and imaginary,* the effect is the same. Research has shown the de-sensitisation to another's needs after just 20 minutes of playing a violent video game. Watching or playing negative things teaches the brain that this is 'normal' so our responses change, even if they don't directly turn us into killers. This is not Living Well! To be exposed to Rats' Den influences can only put us in the Rats' Den with all the consequences.

To be this disconnected from our true source and soul within can never lead to peace and harmony within our selves, or therefore, the planet.

Now that we know how our minds work, doesn't it make sense to teach this in school? We understand the importance of education globally, be it literacy and numeracy or health and welfare. If a new subject of 'How To Live Well', incorporating How Your Mind Works, and How to Feel Good About Yourself with Self-Respect, Self-Esteem and Self-Love was taught in schools, wouldn't we be giving children the opportunity to realise their full potential for positive change for the future? The opportunity which if *you'd* had back then, may have saved you from being trapped in your Rats' Den today? And have all the other benefits listed above? Does it not make sense to allow children to have a greater opportunity to live well, for the greater good of all?

If you agree, please do go to **www.learntolivewell.co.uk** and register your support for the essence of this book to be taught in schools. It will take

Demi Schneider

just a couple of minutes and help to change lives and society. Particularly if you have any influence in schools please do get involved. Also, if you have a personal story to share as to how learning this information earlier would have helped you, perhaps to have dealt with bullying or to have handled nerves or to have allowed yourself to live better in some way, please do write it in the space provided on my website **www.learntolivewell.co.uk** and know I am extremely grateful.

It doesn't take much of a shift to create a huge change. For example, just 1% of the population in an area meditating has been proven to make a noticeable improvement in social conditions such as crime etc. Many things start as One Voice and grow to be Global.

This is *my* life ambition.

N.B. Look out for my next book "The Essential Teenage Guide to Having a Good Life". Follow me on Facebook and Twitter for updates or visit www.demischneider.com

Chapter Fourteen
Time For Action

To put all this information into practise, the following Cut-Out pages are all you'll need to guide you to and keep you living in your Palace, loving yourself. Keep them to hand and choose to work with them and turn the words in this book into something meaningful for yourself, to enable you to change your life for good. If it seems a big task, take heart. Tiny steps will still get you to your destination of lasting happiness.

Know that you do have all the ability and capability you need and that you *can* close the gap from where you have been living, in your Rats' Den, to a joyous life ahead, starting from now. It just takes willingness and a little commitment. Choose to enjoy the journey!

It is imperative you **LIVE** these new ways to make a difference. Reading this book in itself won't make change happen. You'll need to learn off by heart the pages indicated so your brain has the templates for positive change. You can't get somewhere without a destination. You'll need to put into action the straightforward things laid out in the other Cut-Out pages. With this focus your anterior cingulate gyrus and neural gangs (Palace mentors) will help you achieve this. When you go there in the mind you go there in the body.

One word of caution: sometimes clients embrace everything and become really happy but then don't bother, or 'forget', or just stop doing these things. As soon as something challenging happens or else gradually over a period of time, they find themselves back on the slippery slope. The point is you have the choice of being in your Palace or your Rats' Den *every day of your life*, so to stay 'tuned in' to your Palace you need to *permanently live* these new ways. It's so much nicer than being in Rats' Den misery!

If you get fit and healthy you have to maintain some physical exercise to stay that way. It's the same with your mind. Those clients who keep up The Palace Regime (page 127), which after all is straightforward and pleasant to do, stay there. This is automatically an act of loving themselves too. They are the ones who update me now and then with wonderful stories of their continued progress and exciting manifestations.

It is natural to move forward and then plateau, or even come back a bit, especially when you experience life challenges. It is at these times it's so important to go back to the basics that you first worked on to see what needs deepening, or to seek some support. I'm always available for any clients in these situations and generally a phone session or two is all they need to get back on track. Always remember the choice is to come from helplessness (your Rats' Den) or from power (your Palace). Giving extra focus to Loving Yourself supports you and keeps you connected to your true self.

The key is to accept all your experiences in life without judgment, as part of your life's rich tapestry. I have learned to see challenges as opportunities for growth, so even when something catches me off balance it's not long before I'm able to take back my own power, handle it and give all my attention again to the 5 Components for living in my Palace and I'm soon sitting back on my throne, queen of my life again.

I have to smile as I write this. If you knew the complete screwball I used to be, bless me, living out to the full every negative thing in my 'blueprint', *no one*, least of all me, would ever have expected me to be who I am and where I am today in emotional stability, inner peace, acceptance, joy and happiness, just as I am.

It took me some 20 years of self-help, studying, training and experience to know and live what I do today. I have shared much of this with you in this book to help make your journey very much quicker. If you faithfully apply the simple process in the following Cut-Out pages, you will live well too - for good!

With my fondest love and blessings,

Demi

Cut-out Plan For Action
Step by step guide to Palace Living

Your Brain. Learn off by heart really well the **7 aspects of the Palace mind** as shown so they are part of you without thinking. Use them as a basis for Miracle Questioning as and when appropriate.

Staying In Your Palace. Learn off by heart really well all the points listed so they are part of you without thinking. Use them all day every day.

The Palace Regime. Carry this round with you and follow it all day, every day, until it is second nature. To start with you could just focus on point 1. Then the next day focus on points 1 and 2 and so on till you've gradually built up to be living all of the points. Some things may take a while to totally assimilate and incorporate into your life yet with focus and willingness you will master them. You are more than capable. Start every day with appreciation thoughts to be in your Palace mind, with all the benefits. End every day with the bedtime routine. You will soon experience the rewarding difference.

Your Life Grid. Fill in the boxes as per page 86. Create a life grid that looks interesting to live! Know when you will be allocating time for each box, particularly Personal Growth time. Work to make each box a '10'. Take command of your life.

7 Rotational Daily Reading Pages. Read these pages one each day, in rotation, every day as early as possible. Then give attention all day to what you've read to *live* the content, appreciating and acknowledging yourself for making your changes, however small, to 'wear in those new grooves' in your brain so the old patterns are replaced. You might choose to work on one or two things specifically rather than all the points on each page in one go. Go at a pace that feels right for you. Every step on your new path is bringing you closer to your Palace.

Ongoing Personal Development Time. This page offers suggestions for you to make the most of your allocated Personal Development time each week. Let your Personal Development time become your favourite time of the week. It's an act of Loving Yourself and acknowledging your deservability to spend time on developing *you!*

   I recommend reading a page or two of this book every night in bed (before following the bedtime routine on The Palace Regime page). When you've read it, start again - and again. It will only take around five minutes and be a constant drip feed of all you need to know to be in your Palace mind and nurture your true being to feel good.
   If you embrace the above you will be back on your own self-honouring path, walking more and more easily and confidently through richer and more vibrant landscapes unfolding before you, enjoying your journey through your precious life.

This is what LIVING WELL is all about!

Your Brain

Familiarise yourself with how your mind works from this drawing and learn off by heart really well the 7 aspects of your Palace (Intellectual) mind. Go through your day focusing on these. Use them to Miracle Question yourself: "If I was being more positive what would I be thinking?" "If I was making a sensible assessment here what would it be?" Etc.

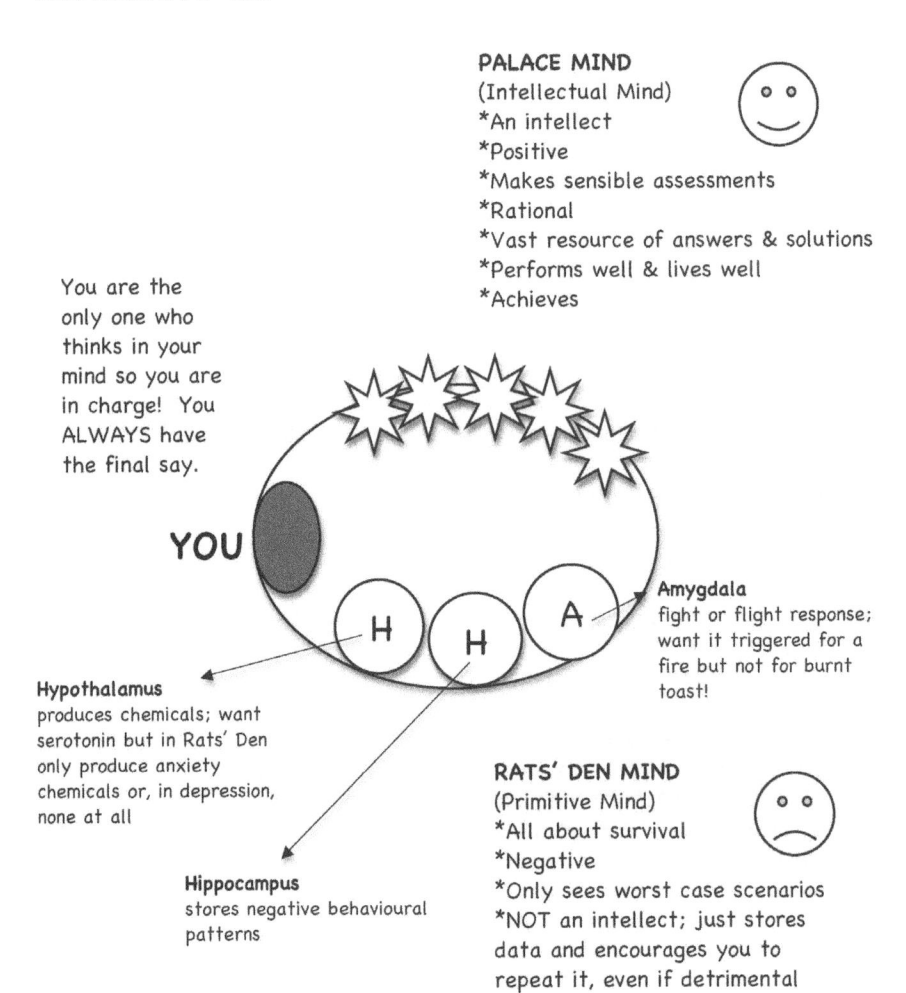

PALACE MIND
(Intellectual Mind)
*An intellect
*Positive
*Makes sensible assessments
*Rational
*Vast resource of answers & solutions
*Performs well & lives well
*Achieves

You are the only one who thinks in your mind so you are in charge! You ALWAYS have the final say.

YOU

H   H   A

Amygdala
fight or flight response; want it triggered for a fire but not for burnt toast!

Hypothalamus
produces chemicals; want serotonin but in Rats' Den only produce anxiety chemicals or, in depression, none at all

Hippocampus
stores negative behavioural patterns

RATS' DEN MIND
(Primitive Mind)
*All about survival
*Negative
*Only sees worst case scenarios
*NOT an intellect; just stores data and encourages you to repeat it, even if detrimental
*Either 'throws tantrums' to get its own way or seeks comfort in negative ways

Staying In Your Palace

Learn the questions and concepts **in bold** off by heart really well and use them throughout your day, every day, allowing them to become second nature in your thoughts and actions.

1) What part of my brain am I in? You can't catch 60 - 90,000 thoughts but you can tune into your emotions. If you're not feeling good you've not been having 'good' thoughts - you're in your Rats' Den. Immediately Switch to a thought that brings you back to your Palace; something funny, beautiful, a happy song, or your anchor thought (your 'guaranteed to put a smile on your face' thought) or perhaps an appreciation thought. Choose a thought that makes you feel a little bit better rather than a little bit worse. You are in charge and always have the final say on what goes on in your mind. When you change a thought to a positive one, you're in your Palace, you're producing serotonin, and you've saved the negative thought going in your stress bucket! Win, win, win!

2) How do I want to feel right now? If you're feeling stressed and you want to feel calm, choose calming thoughts and images to focus on and buy into the feeling of them. Say "I am calm" 10 times (the 'strong arm' effect on page 45) or imagine cool waterfalls or strolling along a beach in a beautiful sunset. If you want to feel safe or in command or whatever else, choose thoughts and images which 'paint the picture' of how you want to feel, buy into the feeling, and then choose your next thought from this space, perhaps using a Miracle Question if appropriate.

3) What's good about this? Whatever has happened or is happening, find something, however small, that's *good* about it. Focus on that. Grow the positives from there. It keeps you in your Palace and you will find solutions and the way forward. If there really is nothing good about a situation, *turn* it into something good. (See page 71).

4) "This is the activity I get to do now". Acceptance saves so much stress! (See page 71).

5) Is this an act of Loving Myself? What would be an act of Loving Myself right now? Follow through on your answers. When you are moving toward Loving Yourself, you are moving toward the essence of who you really are, to be at one with yourself, which is where your true happiness lies.

6) For what purpose? This question gives clarity and can be inspiring and motivational. Use it often. See page 124 for different applications.

7) Catch negative thoughts and eliminate them. Use the Letting Go exercises (pages 27–29) or Switch the thought (page 29) or simply Stop It (Page 25).

8) Use the Miracle Questioning technique. "If I was a '10' how would I handle this?" "If I was being positive what would be different?" "If I was more confident what's the first thing I would notice?" "If I was being more assertive/efficient/tolerant how would this show?" Build on your answers. Refer to the chapter on page 30 and practise to perfect the art so that it becomes part of your normal vocabulary without thinking. The dividends will be well worth the effort expended in doing this.

9) Accept things as they are because that's how they are. Trying to change things from a space of judgmentalism and self-righteousness, however well intentioned, focuses

on 'what's wrong' and keeps giving the energy to 'what's wrong'. This feeds it even more and will only keep you in the primitive part of your mind nurturing the Rats. *Acceptance neutralises the negative energy and allows the authentic space for change;* whether that is *accepting* there are people in the world with a different view point to yourself (so you no longer give 'what you don't agree with' the energy), or whether it is *accepting* a loved one has died so you can lay down the angst and allow yourself to grieve and let the pain go.

10) Accept people as they are. It is not your prerogative to decide how anyone else should act or behave or to decide what they should want or do etc. *Accept* everyone is on their own journey, doing the best they can coming from where they've come from. If you'd had their influences you may be that way too. It is only *your* job to be accountable for yourself. How can *you* best handle things you don't like? How/what can *you* change to alter the situation. It is amazing when we change *our* perspective how other people change too. Accept others as they are; you don't have to agree with their beliefs or standards or behaviours or have them as part of your life - just accept they are the way they are and it's not your prerogative to judge. *Work on yourself.* Wanting others to change never works.

11) Choose, write down and use mantras: for example "I am worthy and deserving of all my good", "I approve of myself", "I love myself".

12) Love Yourself – every moment of every day. Embrace the 'Acts of Loving Yourself' list and live it. Nurture your Inner Child to fill him/her with what you lacked as a child. You are effectively feeding yourself all this nutritional emotional support. Spend quality time with yourself. Sit for 2 or 3 minutes breathing in through your nose, tummy pushing forward, saying "I am" and out through your mouth, tummy relaxing back, saying "at peace". Build up to 15 minutes a day if you can. Allow yourself this time in silence, 'being' instead of 'doing'. The rewards will be well worth this commitment. Allow yourself to reconnect with the core of your real self. Come home to yourself. It is the way to great health, great relationships, great experiences, great self-feelings, and a great life! And you are automatically in your Palace mind!

The Palace Regime

Carry this page around with you as a checklist until you are living all of these as second nature. You'll then need to revisit this from time to time for reinforcement.

1) Start each and every day with gratitude *whilst you are first waking up. Feel* the appreciation of the things you are saying. Be thankful for the comfortable bed that you've slept in; appreciate your eyes that *see*, ears that *hear*, legs that *walk*; that you have fresh running water without walking miles; that you can read and write (2 billion people in the world can't); that you live in a country of free speech; a country of plenty; or feel the appreciation of the beauty of the daffodils welcoming in the spring; etc. There are plenty of people out there who would gladly swap places with you. Appreciate your very existence. Feel the appreciation in every cell of your body.

2) Go through your day Staying in the Moment. There is no past and future – there is only now. The Universe only works in the now. You can only receive your blessings in the now. When thinking about the past or future, bring your attention back to *now* by looking at the clothes you're wearing, the decor of the room you're in, the view out of the window. Practise giving 100% attention to the task/ experience in hand, be it showering, working, being in the gym, spending time with your family etc. Appreciate *this* precious moment of your life - before that too becomes the past. Then move to your next task/experience. You will get lots more done and feel good in the process. Living in the moment is the key to so many benefits: more efficiency, more joy and peace, more awareness, and *living!* (See page 45).

3) Go through your day smiling at people, even if you don't feel like it. Notice and appreciate the smiles you get back!

4) Look for all the positives in a day. Look for what's good about things, how the old patterns are changing, how your increased sense of Worthiness and Deservability is showing etc. What you focus on grows.

5) Choose constant, positive, supportive self-talk all through the day. Remember you can come from the point of helplessness (Rats' Den) or from the point of power (Palace). Take back your own power and choose the positive aspect or the 'havingness of what you want', rather than the negative aspect or the *lack* of what you want. Embrace new language patterning so that speaking positively becomes normal for you. Praise and encourage yourself.

6) Protect yourself from other people's negativity. You are not responsible for other people's thoughts or opinions. What they think is none of your business.

Read the NLP Script on page 41 until you are living it. Put yourself in a protective bubble or forcefield when necessary.

7) Focus on living the 5 Components of your Palace mind until this is second nature:
i. Focus on what you DO want in any given moment. Choose the thought that makes you feel a bit better rather than worse. Tell things from the most positive perspective.
ii. *Feel* the new 'desired' scenario *as if it were real*. Your mind cannot tell the difference between real and imaginary. By adding the 'weight' of the matching feeling to your desired scenario you tune into that authentically. Until you are aligned to *receive* something, it is just a wish.
iii. Use speech that supports these thoughts and feelings.
iv. Work on your Worthiness and Deservability
v. Learn to Love Yourself exactly as you are.

8) Trust yourself and the process of life. Your work is to be aligned and only put in action effort when it feels right. Trust the timing, how your blessings are delivered and enjoy the journey.

9) Learn and use the points to Stay In Your Palace. (Page 175 in this Cut-Out section). When they become habitual you will be living those ways effortlessly.

10) Practise the visualisations in this book. (Others are suggested on the Recommended Listening list). Become confident with 'The Swish' etc. Regularly fill yourself with 'White Light' or 'Love Your Body and the Planet', or nourish yourself with 'The Tree'.

11) Work on your growth daily Enjoy creating the life and feelings you want. Do the exercises in this book. Read this book over and over. Familiarise yourself with all the tools and techniques so they become automatic. Read other similar material. Living these ways will become easier and easier and your life will change dramatically for the better.

12) Each night, get into bed, offer appreciation for all the good in the day (even if it's the lesser part of the day, or even only lunch - only focus on the *good*). **Run through the next day in your mind for a few minutes, as a mental rehearsal, seeing everything going well, with you feeling in control, strong, confident, self-assured etc.** Listen to the 'Relaxation for Sleep' track on the free audio download, every night, for at least a few months and allow it to send you to sleep. (Then periodically when you feel the need).

Embrace, use and LIVE all of the above to the very best of your ability, making it all as daily a routine as brushing your teeth. You're worthy of all good so give yourself the very best, starting with allowing yourself to live well in this way.

Your Life Grid

Fill your grid to show a life you feel excited to live and which motivates you to wake up and be enthusiastic about your life. It's your life. Start with boxes reflecting what is currently in your life and add others you'd like to create. (Remember "I don't know" is never true. You always do know, even if you have to write out what you don't want and turn it around). Work on each of your boxes so they are as close to '10' as possible, using the tools in this book.

LIFE GRID

	PERSONAL GROWTH	

TIMETABLE

Spend a few minutes, perhaps on a Sunday evening, sketching out a timetable like the example below, for your following week so you allocate specific time to comfortably fit each box into your life. This is a great way to take command of your life. *When* will you be working, or going to the gym, or doing that job you've wanted to do for ages, or spending quality time with your kids, or having 'you' time – or whatever is appropriate for you? (See page 88). Know when you'll allocate time to your personal growth box in particular, to continue to enhance your life.

7.00 8.00 9.00 10.00 11.00 12.00 1.00 2.00 3.00 4.00 5.00 6.00 7.00 8.00 9.00 10.00 11.00

Monday

Tuesday

Wed'day

Thursday

Friday

Saturday

Sunday

Rotational Daily Reading:
Your New Beliefs

This is your opportunity to create the 'blueprint' of beliefs you wished you'd had installed when you were little, to now retrain your brain with to serve you better. Refer to the list on pages 107/108 or create your own. It doesn't matter how far away they are from where you are now; as you wear in these new choices with enough attention they will become true for you.

Depression -

Yourself -

Men -

Women -

Friends -

Love -

Work -

Money -

Success -

Failure -

Read this weekly, in rotation with the other Rotational Daily Reading pages, as early as possible in your day. Give attention to these new beliefs (or maybe one or two at a time) ALL DAY to LIVE them and look for any evidence that demonstrates them, however small, to 'wear those new grooves' into your brain so the old patterns are replaced.

Rotational Daily Reading:
Dissolving Resistance Script

Using the guide on page 96 create your own script to change the Resistance you underlined on pages 14–16 to the opposite positives. It is a very effective way to reprogramme your mind. You can also do this for any Core Beliefs you identified or anything else you want to change.

Read this weekly, in rotation with the other Rotational Daily Reading pages, as early as possible in your day. Give attention to your new choices (or maybe one or two at a time) ALL DAY to LIVE them and look for any evidence that demonstrates them, however small, to 'wear those new grooves' into your brain so the old patterns are replaced.

Rotational Daily Reading:
Acts of Loving Myself

Using the list of 'Acts of Not Loving Yourself' on pages 151/152 note all the statements that are relevant to you, or add your own. Switch them to the opposite (see pages 156/157) or write a Dissolving Resistance script with "I used to........" "I now realise........" and "I now choose to........" to pave the way for change. You can use the space below.

Give all your attention to the ways of behaving that *are* acts of Loving Yourself. You might choose to start working on one or two and build up from there until you are fully living life from the space of Loving Yourself. You will feel better and better as you assimilate each one.

I am proud of myself for making these positive changes!

Rotational Daily Reading:
NLP Script for Taking Control of One's Feelings

I used to believe that other people can make me feel bad. I believed that because there was a time when I felt hurt by what someone else said. I realise now that we build fortresses around our weaknesses and I was protecting and guarding something that I believed about myself and that they pointed out. I realise now that anytime I am inclined to feel hurt by what someone else has said it is always me that is in agreement with what they said or it would not have hurt my feelings. I realise now that it isn't always that I agree with them, it's just that it hits a nerve in me or resonates with an issue charged with lots of energy. So it is my responsibility to analyse why. No one out there can make me feel anything. I choose to feel everything that I feel. I realise now that as I am convinced of this I will no longer think that I am responsible for how other people feel towards me. Other people's opinion of me is none of my business. I salute the divinity within all people including myself. I treat all people, including myself, with respect. Therefore I am free. I love myself and I love others. Thank you Self for realising this now. I forgive you Self for having held on to my old patterns of thinking for so long.

I am free and I love myself

IT IS DONE.

Read this weekly, in rotation with the other Rotational Daily Reading pages, as early as possible in your day. Give attention to living this out ALL DAY, taking back your own power. Notice the impact, however small, to 'wear those new grooves' into your brain so the old patterns are replaced.

Rotational Daily Reading:
Deservability Treatment

*I am deserving. I deserve all good. Not some,
not a little bit, but ALL good.
I now move past all negative, restricting thoughts.
I release and let go of the limitations of my parents.
I can love them yet go beyond them. I am not their
negative opinions, nor their limiting beliefs.
I am not bound by any fears or prejudices
of the current society I live in.
I no longer identify with limitations of any kind.*

*In my mind, I have total freedom.
I now move into a new space of consciousness
where I am willing to see myself differently.
I am willing to create new thoughts about myself and my life.
My new thinking becomes new experiences.
I am willing to forgive all those who have harmed me in the past.
I am willing to set myself free.
I am willing to love and approve of myself, exactly as I am now.
I accept myself as I am now. I am a magnificent expression of life.
I am worthy. I am willing to receive the very best.*

*I now know and affirm that I am at one with
the Prospering Power of the Universe. As such,
I now prosper in a number of ways.
The totality of possibilities lies before me. I deserve life, a good life.
I deserve love, an abundance of love. I deserve good health.
I deserve to live comfortably and to prosper. I
deserve joy and happiness. I deserve freedom to be
all that I can be. I deserve more than that.
I deserve all good.*

*The Universe is more than willing to manifest my new beliefs.
And I accept this abundant life with joy, pleasure, and gratitude.
For I am deserving. I accept it. I know it to be true.*

And so it is.

*Louise Hay
"You Can Heal Your Life"
By Kind Permission of Hay House Inc. Carlsbad, CA
copyright 1984, 1987, 2004 by Louise L Hay*

Read this weekly, in rotation with the other Rotational Daily Reading pages, as early as possible in your day. Give attention to your worthiness and deservability ALL DAY and look for any evidence to support your growth, however small, to 'wear those new grooves' into your brain so the old patterns are replaced.

Rotational Daily Reading:
50 Qualities I Like About Myself

See page 84 for inspiration and write below as many positive qualities about yourself as you can. Add to them until you have 50! It will help boost your self-worth and esteem. Looking at 50 good things about yourself has to help you feel good!

Read this weekly, in rotation with the other Rotational Daily Reading pages, as early as possible in your day. Pay special attention to all your good qualities ALL DAY to LIVE them to the full. Notice the difference it makes, however small, to build your self-esteem and self-worth.

Rotational Daily Reading:
I Love Myself Therefore.........

Deep at the centre of my being there is an infinite well of love.
I now allow this love to flow to the surface.
It fills my heart, my body, my mind, my consciousness, my
very being, and radiates out from me in all directions
and returns to me multiplied.
The more love I use and give, the more I have to give.
The supply is endless!
The use of love makes me feel good. It is
an expression of my inner joy.
I love myself therefore I take loving care of my body.
I lovingly feed it nourishing foods and beverages.
I lovingly groom and dress it. My body lovingly
responds to me with vibrant health and energy.
I love myself therefore I provide for myself a comfortable
home, one that fills all my needs and is a pleasure to be in.
I fill the rooms with the vibration of love so that all who enter,
myself included, will feel this love and be nourished by it.
I love myself therefore I work at a job I truly enjoy doing,
one that uses my creative talents and abilities,
working with and for people that I love and that
love me, and earning a good income.
I love myself therefore I behave and think in a loving
way to all people for I know that that which I give
returns to me multiplied. I only attract loving people
into my world for they are a mirror of what I am.
I love myself therefore I forgive and totally release the past and
all past experiences and I am free.
I love myself therefore I live totally in the now, experiencing
each moment as good and knowing that my future is bright and
joyous and secure for I am a beloved child of the Universe and
the Universe lovingly takes care of me now and forever more.

And So It Is

Louise Hay
"You Can Heal Your Life"
By Kind Permission of Hay House Inc. Carlsbad, CA
copyright 1984, 1987, 2004 by Louise L Hay

Read this weekly, in rotation with the other Rotational Daily Reading pages, as early as possible in your day. Embrace these ways of loving yourself (or one or two at a time) ALL DAY and look for any evidence to show yourself, however small, that your self-love is growing.

Ongoing Weekly Personal Growth Time

Suggestions for valuable things to do to continue Living Well:

1) Read this book often, especially any chapters particularly relevant to any given situation. Make sure you are aligning the 5 Components to live in your Palace mind (chapter six) and brushing up on the finer details in 'Palace Protocol and Etiquette' (chapter seven). Love yourself.

2) Work on your goals or set new ones. They can be immediate small goals such as tidying up the garden or bigger ones such as decorating a room or finding a new job or buying your dream house or car. Whatever it is, align the 5 Components to be in the Palace mind and then Miracle Question yourself to move forward, always remembering to ask "For what purpose?"

3) Make or update your vision board (page 74). Have fun! Put anything and everything you want to have feature in your life, including some positive things you have already, such as pictures of your family or your dog or a trophy. Holidays, short term goals, longer term goals, a new relationship, more friends, a new sofa, more money, you at your ideal weight, images of joy, contentment, laughter etc. It is so easy now we can google 'images of.....' and find anything we want! Write the details using positive language such as "I love my new sofa!"....." or "It feels so wonderful now that....." keeping it *present* tense and stick those on too.

4) Work on your Worthiness and Deservability to let these in, using all the information in this book or perhaps writing out what's good in your life now and celebrating your success in letting that much in. Feel the appreciation. What we focus on grows!

5) Test yourself regularly to make sure you still know off by heart the aspects of the Palace mind from the illustration, the Staying in the Palace page and are living The Palace Regime.

6) Update your Dissolving Resistance script as you uncover more things that don't serve you and write what you do want to choose instead.

7) Review your Life Grid to make sure you are still living a life you are pleased with and are incorporating all your boxes in a fulfilling way, working on them to be the best they can be.

8) Write affirmations to support your new choices and have as mantras to embed them into your mind.

9) Spend quiet time, sitting comfortably, eyes closed, listening to any of the visualisations on the accompanying free audio downloads/purchased CD (or doing them on your own when you are familiar enough with them). Or purchase one of the hypnotherapy downloads/CDs on the Recommended Listening page at the back of this book.

10) Spend time in visualisation with your Inner Child. If you are aware of an old pattern that is still hampering you, ask your Inner Child if they are willing to let go of it. Feel the answer from them and follow through accordingly. How can you help them let it go or feel safe or happy? Have fun being with them for a while or just tell them how much you love them and give them all the other things they want to receive to build their self-worth and esteem. *You* will gain the benefit.

11) Go to my Facebook page or follow me on Pinterest or Twitter or read my blogs for ongoing support. Register your email address on my website www.demischneider.com to receive supportive information.

12) Read the books on the Recommended Reading list and others that you feel drawn to.

Download some free positive mental attitude apps. Louise Hay has some wonderful messages and affirmations! We have so much available to us now online – and free! Have fun exploring and embracing the marvellous world of enlightened people who have such gifts to share.

13) Learn to meditate. There are plenty of books on the subject or perhaps join a class near you. Working with others can be very empowering.

14) Learn about chakras. When your chakras are open you allow your energy to sink down to feel peace.

15) Practise Loving Yourself in all the different ways that allow you to Come Home to Yourself. Create a life full of JOY and Love Yourself enough to embrace it and FEEL the joy every day!

FEEL GOOD!
You deserve it.

NOTES

NOTES

NOTES

NOTES

Chapter Fifteen
Real Life Scenarios

I have found that sometimes reading or hearing about other people's situations and their ways forward is helpful to understand more fully how to apply new learning.

To this end here is a selection of some of the issues that have arisen with clients. I have formulated them into questions or statements for simplicity and have contrived the answers from the conversations and emails involved. I trust they are helpful.

How can I feel more confident?

Realise a lack of confidence stems from fear of not being able to handle something and/or of not being good enough. Often we seek outside validation to reassure us yet this can only help temporarily at best.

To turn this around your focus needs to be solely on how you want things to be - giving no power to any negatives whatsoever. Repeat "I can handle this" in any given moment and use Miracle Questioning; "If I did feel confident/good enough what would be different?" Thank the negatives for wanting to protect you, release them and then paint those pictures in your mind very clearly of how you want to be in all the situations at work and in life and imagine all the good feelings that go with those thoughts. Use the language that matches, for example, "It feels so good to be making these positive changes" "My confidence is growing daily". Stop, Let Go or Switch any contradictory thoughts immediately. Re-focus on the positive image.

Remember, when you go there in the mind you go there in the body. Keep your mind focused on positive images and remember you always have the final say, either to take back your own power and feel strong in your Palace or to give in to your Rats and nurture the fear.

Staying in the Moment prevents overwhelm. Live each moment of your life as it happens. You can visualise the 'positive future scenarios' you want whilst still being aware of what's around you and this precious moment of your life. That is very different to getting caught up in the angst of the future, which takes you out of awareness of this moment and puts you in your Rats' Den with all that negativity going in your stress bucket.

Also remember to work on Loving Yourself. Self-worth and self-confidence improves along with all the other benefits that Loving Yourself brings. It is the short cut to *all* your good. Do the breathing exercise to feel calm and centred. (See page 161).

I put various things I've learned into practise yet in a meeting at work I lost my positive focus and felt the anxiety again.

What's happened is that because you're assimilating new ways of thinking and being, your Rats are 'upping the ante' (throwing a tantrum) to get their own way and to get you back to the familiar data stored that says you need to feel anxiety in these situations to survive.

We have to keep firm with a child over and over till they've got the message we wont budge and then they give up the tantrums because they know there's no point. If we give in we're doomed because they know they only have to throw a bigger tantrum and they'll get their own way.

That's effectively what you did here. You were in your meeting, so the anxiety popped up as the pattern for your survival. Those Rats 'upped the ante' more because you've been choosing strange new positive ways they don't recognise and consequently fear will stop you surviving. (Foolish of course, but remember this part of your brain isn't an intellect). Then, when you gave attention to those anxiety Rats, giving in to their tantrum, you metaphorically threw your hands up in helplessness, gave those negative feelings all your power and ended up in the old place again. The key is to Splat those 'anxiety thought' Rats, or use another Letting Go exercise. Stay in the Moment saying "I can handle this" over and over (till you get the 'strong arm' effect described on page 45). Think of your 'anchor' thought and keep asking "If I were a 10 how would I be handling this?" or "What's good about this?" and other Palace mind thoughts. You will then be taking back your own power and stay in your Palace, starting to create this new behaviour as your new pattern.

Be gentle with yourself - it takes time to assimilate new things and have them become second nature. Praise yourself for being on this new path and accept you'll hit little bumps in the process. Learn from this and use to your advantage, for example, how would you handle things differently next time? Paint the pictures in readiness. You could even do a Swish. You've had the opportunity to experience this and can now grow further. Think like a 10, feel like a 10, act like a 10 and you will be!

I've been doing so well yet I was so annoyed with myself for messing up today and really blushing in front of my boss.

Please let that annoyance go! Stop berating yourself. Only *you* can put yourself in your Rats' Den like this, beating up your Inner Child and giving power to the problem. Instead, release the negative feelings with a Letting Go exercise and just hug yourself, bless yourself with love and encourage yourself, understanding that you're doing the best you can, that Rome wasn't built in a day and that you'll overcome this. Treat yourself as you would others - or your children. Would you get annoyed with them or would you be gentle and supportive? Which would give the best result? In your Palace mind how would you deal with this? If you were making a sensible assessment how would it look? If you were Loving Yourself what would be different? Stay in the Moment! Embrace the positive changes you are making and know the more you practise them the more 'second nature' they'll become. Live in your Palace, love yourself and blushing will be a thing of the past.

No matter how hard I try, even small steps seem too much. I struggle to remember the things to learn off by heart and feel despondent and useless. I've tried to hurl thoughts in the river but they're not gone. Staying in the Moment and other coping mechanisms don't make me feel better and I fear next week could be worse and I'm not meant to do that. I feel in a black hole. How can I love myself or feel worthy when I feel like this?

You are focusing on all the problems here! Rats' Den thoughts with Rats' Den feelings and Rats' Den misery.

You're looking at what you can't do or haven't done or how impossible it all is. At best you are coming from a point of half-heartedness and 'when I get the result I want I'll believe it' rather than focusing on lining up the 5 Palace Components and being authentic. Hurling thoughts in the river *won't* help if you're not buying into the feeling of what you're doing.

On page 13 I talk about 'willfully stuck people' who can only see the negatives in everything. You are giving away all your power, over and over. Remember the 'arm exercise' on page 45. This would be very floppy arm time! And look at all the negative vibrations you are tuning into (Rats' Den) to create your tomorrows with this same negativity!

Instead, if you've learnt even *one* point off by heart *praise yourself for that!* See how many times you can use it during the day! You will have a taken a small, yet hugely valuable step forward! This would be an act of Loving Yourself! If you choose to, you *can* do it. Staying in the Moment allows you complete command of what thought and feeling you choose to have. It is not a coping mechanism; it is a beneficial way to live!

If you don't want to be in the black hole, what would the opposite be? What do you want? (Yes, you do know!) Spell it out in detail and line up the 5 Palace Components. That way you can get out of your black hole. Give your power to creating what you *do* want. That's energy well spent. Tell yourself you *can* do it and buy into that feeling! (Strong arm). It's your mind and you *are* in charge.

Let your mantra be "I choose to reconnect with the power I was born with", however much that might have been robbed from you early in life. Allow yourself to turn self-criticism into self-praise. Your self-love will grow automatically.

I've read a lot about 'Loving Myself' but it still feels silly.

This shows huge resistance to your own good. Such reluctance to connect with your true self will only manifest in frustration and neediness for life to give you exactly what you want so you can be happy. Other people may then find you demanding or self-obsessed or get fed up with you always complaining things aren't how you want them. Others may even, in time, feel burdened by the weight of your needs, or find you defensive, or difficult and draining to be with.

When you Love Yourself you have self-acceptance and can connect with others more readily. You have an innate sense of calm and knowing about who you are. You feel inner peace and are in your Palace mind where you live well. You can give and receive love authentically. Other people feel good around you and you can be an inspiration to them just by 'being'. Take a look at all the benefits of Loving Yourself on pages 153/154. Does that look silly? Loving Yourself is the guaranteed way to lasting happiness.

Be willing to work through your blocks and lay down your resistance. You are only denying yourself your good.

How will 'loving myself' change the fact that we committed to this extension for the family and are struggling financially? I can only buy food with what I have each month and my husband has nothing left for himself after bills.

Loving Yourself enables you to feel good about yourself first and foremost. From this space you are empowered and in your Palace mind. Choose to focus on creating financial expansion as an *act* of Loving Yourself. Focusing on 'lack' puts you with the Rats, stuck in a rut and miserable. That's certainly not Loving Yourself. Line up the 5 Components of the Palace mind and allow yourself to move forward. You can change or handle this situation. Your Palace mind has the answers! Loving Yourself and automatically feeling good, automatically puts you in your Palace mind to be able to utilise its incredible ability.

Beat Your Depression For Good

How can I love myself when I'm going through life challenges? I was stuck home all last week with sick kids.

What does 'staying at home all week with sick kids' have to do with you Loving Yourself? Loving Yourself is what enables you to handle life challenges more easily!

Your kids are ill. What's good about it? You are blessed to be able to stay at home and take care of them when they need you most. You could make this a really fun, memorable time with bed picnics or reading to them or playing a game with them. What else? I'll wager you can find other good things too, if you choose to.

Say "I am loving and lovable", enjoy loving your kids and open yourself to receiving their love and appreciation. Use Miracle Questions, for example "If I was loving myself and projecting love to my kids, where would I start?" "What's the first little thing that would show me I was being more loving to myself?" "How would this change things if I let it?" "If I was to think about how much I love my children, what difference would that make?" Follow through on your answers, with more questions if needs be to move forward.

Read the 'I Love Myself Therefore...' script on page 159 and allow yourself to align with every point. Everyone will gain.

I can't see how some things in the Deservability Treatment will ever apply to me or indeed other people. It seems to suggest 'being deserving' implies one must be perfect to deserve all in life that's good. It's not reality. What makes us all deserve good things - love, worthiness, support, happiness etc? It's not authentic to believe.

As described on page 20, in a line of little children which one would *not* deserve a good life? (Including all those things mentioned in the Deservability Treatment). The answer is 'none of them'. They all deserve a good life with abundance and happiness! Now put yourself as a little kid in that line - and realise that means **you** deserve a good life with abundance and happiness too!

What makes us *all* deserve all good things - love, worthiness, support, happiness etc? *We were born!* That is the only qualification we need. It is our birthright. There is no baby born that isn't lovable or deserving or good enough exactly as they are.

Everyone *deserves* to be and feel everything on that Deservability Treatment. Where does 'needing to be perfect' come into it? We all deserve all our good - the Universe doesn't have a measure of 'who gets what' depending on how 'perfect' we are! It is really about *us* and what we allow ourselves to have.

Remember that deservability is something *we* measure. The Universe doesn't do that. If someone is comfortable having money they will get it regardless of whether they are a 'good' person or a 'bad' person! Some of the richest people in the world aren't necessarily the sweetest. There are plenty of successful 'stars' who have nowhere near the talent of others less successful. It's not about what they deserve - it's *what they allow themselves to have* from their deepest levels. Choose to get off the *'I have to be good enough to deserve'* merry-go-round and accept that if you allow yourself to have something it doesn't matter whether you deserved it or not. Now you've got 'it' embrace it and know the more good you attract the more positive the vibration is that you are contributing to the planet! Everyone gains!

What would you allow yourself to have in your life right now if you simply took deservability out of the equation? Would you allow yourself to have lots of wonderful things and experiences? Or would you need to be honest with yourself and realise 'I don't deserve' is an excuse to hide behind? If you believed you deserved more, might you have to be more accountable for creating a positive life? Does that feel uncomfortable or scary? If this resonates with you, realise it is fear that is holding you back.

The Deservability Treatment is an authentic depiction of what feeling a 10 looks like. We all deserve that and for many of us it is already a reality. For others, they are on their way up the scale. For still others, they prefer to look at why they can't possibly feel deserving. Which choice best serves your wellbeing?

I can see that as I line up as that child we all deserve a good and happy life. However, since having my kids and suffering depression I have not worked. Meanwhile my husband has worked hard in his career, kept us afloat financially, looked after the kids when I've not been able to cope and not left me. My husband is far more worthy and deserving than me!

The fact you've been feeling 'less than' has got nothing to do with your Worthiness and Deservability! It doesn't follow that when you've 'been good or contributed' you are worthy and deserving and when you've been 'less than' you are *not* worthy and deserving! This is misunderstanding deservability.

It isn't that you're not worthy and deserving – you are - it's the false beliefs you have to the contrary that are the problem. The truth is it is your birthright to be able to read the 'Deservability Treatment' and have every word feel true. Anything less you feel just demonstrates the amount you are pulled off from this truth by your false programming. The Treatment isn't 'wrong' - your false beliefs to the contrary are.

Choose to say "I was born worthy and deserving" "I am willing to reconnect with this truth and allow myself to recognise this in how I live". Watch out all day for the little ways this shows when you embrace your deservability. If you do this with full commitment you will 'move up the scale' and let more good in!

Besides "I am willing" to feel more deserving or to love myself, what can I say to add more impetus?

When we're wanting to move from our existing space to somewhere that seems 'far off' from where we are now, or to encourage and support ourselves 'getting there', a perfect 'bridge' is to affirm *"I am in the process of.........."* It helps us keep the focus and feel empowered.

"I am in the process of improving my Worthiness and Deservability"
"I am in the process of learning to Love Myself"
"I am in the process of assimilating all this new information"
"I am in the process of allowing myself to have a wonderful new job/home/relationship"

I am fed up on my own and really want to have a relationship.

Wanting to be close to someone and feel loved is very natural. The crux is whether you want to be loved from healthy space or needy space. Also, if you're feeling "I want a relationship or my life will be disappointing", you are setting yourself up for all sorts of pain. Equally, feeling the *absence* of what you want (a relationship) rather than the *havingness* of one, will keep the gap between where you are and what you want, because that is what you are observing and thus giving your attention and vibrations to.

Remember the work is always on our selves. What patterns or unhelpful beliefs do you need to release? How worthy and deserving do you feel, not just of having a relationship, but attracting your true soulmate with whom you can really experience all the glorious detail of what you're wanting from having a relationship. Are you really emotionally available to receive your soulmate? Whilst you're working on these, align the 5 Components of the Palace and enjoy making a vision board with wonderful pictures and written pieces about what you really want and how it makes you feel being in this relationship. "Close the gap' by buying into this as if it had already happened. Work on Loving Yourself to open up the space within to receive.

Make a Life Grid (page 86) that is fulfilling now and live happily, trusting your soulmate is out there wanting to be with you too. Then just trust the process of life and that everything will work out in its perfect time and space, letting go of any attachment to the outcome, (otherwise you'll be tuning into fear and doubt about it not happening, i.e. the negativity again and prevent it from manifesting).

See the chapter on Relationships and particularly about 'Finding a New Wholesome Relationship' for more support.

Can you please explain again about shifting power to move forward in my relationship scenario?
Your bad experiences with men mean you must have negative or unhelpful data somewhere in your 'blueprint'. For example, I unknowingly attracted men with the same love languages as my dad, (which are different from mine) and felt the continued pain of my emotional needs not being met. Blueprint = experience. When we know something is in our 'blueprint' that we need to change yet *still have emotional connection to our bad experiences (which still gives the power to the bad experiences),* we stay powerless and can't move forward. The antidote to shift the power is to forgive the men and experiences, recognising we attracted them from our 'blueprint' space and can now identify what we need to change. Accept the experiences and understand they have caused us to become who we are today searching for answers to go on our new and better path. We need to be free of baggage and emotionally available in order to cultivate a new wholesome relationship. Forgiveness sets us free to change our 'blueprint' and move forward.

My family know I'm unhappy in my relationship but keep warning me that I would be worse off without him and that I should be grateful he provides and has put up with me whilst I've been depressed. "Don't think the grass is greener on the other side because it never is".
Why are you giving your power to your family? It's just their perspective. The answer to them is "I accept all that you say about him and you are right, yet *am I happy?* The answer is *no!* The grass *will* be greener the other side because I will have empowered myself to take control of my life and whatever challenge that brings I have the freedom and power to handle it. There is no price not worth paying to be true to myself at last. This is *my* life. I trust you want the best for me. On my deathbed I want to know I've lived my life for *me* and not for anyone else's approval."
Be true to your own integrity. Erect and maintain your personal boundaries that align with your integrity. Love Yourself enough to allow yourself to live your own life. You deserve it.

I really want a divorce but my kids keep begging me not to leave their dad. The guilt and fear of damaging them or not handling their reactions if I do end it keeps me trapped here!
Of course children invariably want mum and dad to be together and everything to be happy. It is also a valuable part of their learning curve to

realise 'how they want it' doesn't always happen in life and allow them to see the positives the 'other side'. Of course they can't envisage 'the other side' now - even less than you - they're children! That's why you need to stay strong to set an example of how to handle difficult situations so they can do this for themselves when they are adults and face their life challenges in whatever form they come. They will adjust and be able to see the benefits. The key is to make sure they feel loved, nurtured, heard, reassured, safe etc and any of the words you wrote on your own Inner Child picture. Use Miracle Questioning to help them rationalise things rather than 'telling them' things. Keep your focus and strength to do what's best for *you* on track by constantly asking yourself "What would be an act of loving myself" and remember prioritising your own needs is ultimately the selfless thing to do.

I feel so jealous that my ex has moved on even though we're still constantly in touch.

Your jealousy is about you not trusting and believing you are worthy of a wonderful relationship yourself. The needing of constant calls to feel you were, and still are, 'important' to him just perpetuates this sense of unworthiness. Being this needy is not an attractive quality. Work on your own self-feelings and Loving Yourself to recognise your true deservability and self-worth. The more you work on yourself to feel self-confident and self-assured and give attention to becoming a 10, (to also be attractive to a '10' partner) the easier it will be to handle things with your ex. If you feel your ex *is* a 10 you may then even be attractive to him again as a 10 yourself and this time be able to maintain a healthy interdependent relationship. (See page 140). If not, you'll be a 10 anyway and attract someone else maybe even more wonderful. If you're a 10 it's win win for you in every way. Shifting the focus to working on yourself with the tools and techniques in this book will also occupy your mind and allow you to be in your Palace instead of nurturing the Rats of jealousy and neediness in your Den, with all the attached misery. "If you were to move toward Loving Yourself this very minute what would you do?" Staying in the Moment will help you too.

I've had a big fall out with my family. I keep going over it yet I genuinely feel my sibling is in the wrong.

When you give power to the annoyance and run through who said what and whose feelings were hurt you are re-running the pain and it's all going in your stress bucket. If you re-run this scenario 50 times in your mind, you'll essentially have 50 fall outs, as your brain can't tell the difference between real and imaginary. For what purpose?

This is being reactive and giving your power to the problem. Instead use a Letting Go exercise for all your negative thoughts and feelings, or write an anger letter if you need to. Do a Balancing the Power visualisation if you really need to. (See page 53). Then fill yourself up with the healing 'White Light Treatment' on the free audio download or purchasable CD that accompanies this book (it is imperative to restore balance once you've done releasing work) or do the breathing exercise "I am at peace". (See page 161).

Now choose to make a sensible assessment and use Miracle Questions to arrive at the best possible scenario which aligns with your own integrity and that you feel comfortable with. Does it really matter who is right or wrong? Write forgiveness letters and dissolve the negative energy for your own sake.

Focus on what you do want and cultivate that situation, in line with your integrity. Let your decisions come from your inner guidance, feeling what would be the act of Loving Yourself. If you were Loving Yourself first and foremost how would you deal with this? Stay in the Moment to live this precious moment of your life and *trust* your Palace mind to come up with the solutions. Have a mantra running through your mind to the effect that "The perfect solution presents itself" or "I trust everything is working for my highest good". Know you can handle this and experience an even better relationship with your family than you had before.

My daughter has really upset me. She exaggerated about her health condition, even lying about possible consequences and what had been said to her. She told me I had been unsupportive and uncaring which is completely untrue. What should I do?

I am suspecting that she has some deep (fear or anger type) issues, which rightly or wrongly she is directing at you. I don't know how much might be directly related to issues with you, from *her* perspective, (I understand you've always done the best you could) or whether she's just taking it out on you as her closest loved one. Either way, clearly she is unhappy with herself on those deep down levels.

This is a time to absolutely be in your solution focused Palace mind and not give power to the problem. When she was berating you that was an ideal time to put yourself in your pink bubble (or a Star Trek force field if you prefer). This is why we need to practise these things so we can turn to them in an instant. In your pink bubble you would not have felt the criticism so intently, which took you into *your* Rats' Den mind and went into *your* stress bucket. (For what purpose?)

Use Miracle Questioning on yourself and with her to get things on an even keel. If you were to accept each other's point of view what would be different? If you have different love languages, how can you meet each other's way of communicating love and receiving love for mutual benefit? If she was willing to lay down her angst and focus on empowering herself to feel better about herself and life, what might she focus on first? (You don't always need answers to such questions; sowing the seed can be enough).

Meantime, focus on an image of the two of you happy and smiling together, without any sense of manipulation. If you have a photo like this of the two of you, stick it on your vision board and write underneath something like "I am in the process of creating a harmonious relationship with my daughter" or "I welcome in a wonderful relationship with my daughter" and be open to how *you* need to change for this to happen (in line with your own integrity of course). Practise Miracle Questioning so you are expert for when you are in contact with her again.

Remember to be gentle and Love Yourself too. Love is the great healer yet if your love for her takes you away from your own integrity that is not Loving Yourself. 'People pleasing' never gets us respect or self-respect and can even rob the other person of the opportunity to do something for themselves. The more you love your self the more you will always handle things well.

I am in the process of losing my excess weight. How can I best help myself?

Good for you! If you've got excess weight to lose *Love Yourself as you are* and watch the weight drop off, no longer needing that outer protection. If you say "When I've lost the weight I'll love myself" you'll be blocking your own good and find it much harder. Loving Yourself means accepting all the things you would like to change too. Enjoy the feelings of self-acceptance *now*. Loving Yourself feels good to help keep up your morale and focus. Loving Yourself will also enable you to automatically be in your Palace mind where you can make positive choices for yourself, including what food and beverages you consume.

Choose to reflect on how much weight you have lost already and praise yourself. Picture the scales showing the next few pounds down. If doubt comes up, use the 'Swish' visualisation until you can clearly see yourself with a big smile on your face saying "Yes!" because you've achieved this target. When you go there in the mind you go there in the body. Put a picture on a vision board of a gorgeous outfit that you want to buy when you've reached your goal weight, along with a picture of scales reading that weight. Write some sentences such as "I feel so great wearing this outfit" or "I am so thrilled to feel this slim again". Praise and encourage yourself all the way. You may find some fun exercise helps tone you up and speed up the process too and it is an excellent serotonin booster.

I never feel relaxed and able to enjoy a social occasion, especially with family, unless I know they are all happy and having a good time.

Why make other people responsible for your happiness? What would happen if other people were waiting for *you* to be relaxed and happy before they could be? If everyone was waiting for everyone else to be happy first it might well be a very subdued occasion!

Be your own person. Lead the way with feeling relaxed and happy *because you choose to* regardless of the venue or occasion or other people. This way you inspire others to do the same. Use Miracle Questions to paint the pictures in your mind; "If I was feeling relaxed and enjoying this, what would be the first thing I'd notice or be enjoying?" Etc. If someone else doesn't have a good time that is their prerogative and their responsibility. You are only accountable for yourself.

I have been working on 'letting in' more money yet am not seeing this manifest.

This very much sounds as if you're coming from the space of "I'm focusing on having more money and *when it comes* I'll believe it". That means what you're really doing is *hoping* this positive focus comes true for you but have a doubt or fear it will actually happen. That means your Rats' Den doubt and fear is what you're tuned in to rather than the 'havingness' of the money. The antidote is to work on your deservability generally and focus on *the experiences you want to have with that money*. This way you help shift the direct connection with money and the fear surrounding 'not having it'. If you are really 'desperate' for money, for example to pay off bills, you need even more to be in your Palace mind to use your resources for answers and solutions. Focus on the 5 Components and use Miracle Questioning to expand your prosperity consciousness. Spend a little time each day to visualise prosperity and tap into your resourcefulness to get there, whilst Loving Yourself to keep grounded.

Going to the gym is good for me but when I go I think 'I don't know why I'm here, I'm not very good at this'. I feel I need reassurance.

Looking for reassurance from others is the same as looking for approval or acceptance from others in order to validate yourself. It is not their responsibility to reassure you; it's your responsibility to build your self up to where you no longer need it. Even if you received reassurance this week you'd need it again next week, just like the approval or acceptance. You would continue to move the goal posts. You cannot 'let in' more than you have the template for. (See pages 148/149). Choose instead to say "I allow myself to do my best and enjoy being here, focusing on the benefits". This is the difference between looking at the negative side or the positive side. Switch negative thoughts to the opposite positive and focus on the positive images. You could do a 'Swish' visualisation. Align the 5 Components for living in your Palace mind. Enjoy the journey too, appreciating every little improvement in how you *feel* as well as your prowess in the gym! Alternatively, if going to the gym really isn't your preferred way to exercise, Love Yourself and quit! There are many other forms of exercise you could embrace with joy, which will then be much more beneficial just for that reason.

I am taking a course to lead to a job I really want to do but I am finding it really arduous and joyless.
The question to ask yourself is "How important is it for me to achieve this qualification to do what I love and know I'm good at?"

If your desire for the end result is solid you can then choose to accept all the experiences that go with the journey and realise putting the rest of your life on hold is not forever - just a temporary choice. Once you've qualified you can make different choices.

I was in a similar situation with some of my studying yet I absolutely wanted the qualification and letters after my name. With that overriding desire my perspective shifted and it seemed a whole lot more manageable and enjoyable.

No one is making you do this course - remember it is a choice and embrace it. Focus on 'what's good about it?' Use a Miracle Question: "If I were being more positive here how would this look?" "If I were using my vast resource of answers and solutions how would I be handling this/what would I be doing?"

Take those few minutes a day to nurture your soul to keep energised and when you do have a break from the studying, *make it fun!*

Selling my business was a huge mistake.
Your business was your identity for many years so now you are faced with "*Who am I* without my business?" Furthermore it has exposed other areas in your life that are not working well and you have nowhere to 'hide'.

The key here is not to lament and want your old life back (Rats' Den). The key is to realise selling your business has given you the opportunity to address the other areas in your life that need attention so that you can live a richer, more rounded, fulfilling life to the point where you no longer have your self-worth tied up in your status and earning potential. You can rediscover the real 'you' and live life to the full. How exciting! What changes in your current life would serve you? What would you like to create now? What new interests could you explore? Choose to "Feel the Fear and Do it Anyway"! (Read the book of this title to help if needs be). In five years time you may well look back and decide selling your business was the best thing you've ever done! (And who knows, if you hadn't sold it you might have had a heart attack 6 months later from all the ongoing stress!)

Choose to create a great life with an exciting Life Grid and focus on Loving Yourself to feel good. Live for now. Cultivate the courage to let go of what doesn't serve you and embrace new things that can make your life far more rewarding than just a career.

Despite my good life I find myself depressed.

What old belief or pattern is it that stops you embracing what you have? Guilt? A belief you're still not good enough? Fear that it might not last? Bitterness from the past? You're not allowed to feel good? You've lived life from an agenda, relying on external things or other people to make you feel good? Sit quietly with your eyes closed, focus on your breathing until you feel calm and centered, and ask yourself "What is in my way?" The answer may come immediately, or the next morning when you awake, or in some random conversation with someone. When you know, you can use the appropriate method in this book to dissolve it.

Work on coming home to yourself, where true happiness resides. Work on truly Loving Yourself and nurturing your Inner Child. You may find the 'Severance From Negative Feelings' track on the CD 'Free To Be' helpful to identify and release deep-seated emotional blocks. Explore meditation and chakra work to open yourself to let love sink down to connect you with who you really are. Become an expert at the breathing exercise on page 161 and allow yourself to just enjoy 'being'.

Choose to take back your own power and embrace your good, praising yourself for having achieved all you have. Choose to take accountability for your feelings and work to dissolve any resistance in the way of feeling good.

I feel inspired by these new ways but I feel it is going to take a while for me to recover, having been depressed for so long.

There is a difference between 'burning up' and 'burning out'. For a long time you were 'burning *up*' firing on all cylinders, being that high achiever etc. Because of your background underlying beliefs of 'having to be perfect to be good enough' and similar, you continued to push yourself, giving out more and more, to be the way you perceived you needed to be in order to be as good as your peers (even though you were way up there anyway). This relentless pushing yourself, without any self-support, self-nurturing, self-recognition, or releasing of old outmoded patterns and beliefs etc, then caused you to become 'burnt *out*'.

From the space of being as 'burnt out' as you were, it is going to take time to replenish, re-energise and rejuvenate yourself to be on top of everything again. Choose to be gentle with yourself and focus most on nourishing your soul, coming home to yourself and being *whole*. From this space you will balance life so you neither burn up or burn out - but live in harmony in mind, body and soul - feeling strong and capable to meet all your challenges.

To this end I strongly recommend you nurture your Inner Child, listen to the White Light Treatment on the audio download often, do things that make you happy, treat yourself as you would treat someone else you loved. Do the breathing exercise on page 161. Reach out to others for support.

When you're ready, gently release all the old false beliefs from your 'blueprint', both mental and emotional. Allow yourself to embrace the new truthful data you want to install instead. Release your guilt, fear, anguish etc as described in chapter four and then move to chapter five, Forgiveness. Work on *truly* forgiving the past and all past experiences, forgiving anyone who has ever wronged you or been less than you'd have liked, and forgiving yourself for all you have and haven't done. Set yourself free and fill yourself up with love and light.

Read your list of 50 qualities you like about yourself to remind you of your worth. Know you are worthy and deserving of living well and feeling good about yourself, your achievements, your future etc and are 100% good enough exactly as you are. Gently take back your own power and allow yourself to step into the fullness of embracing the full joy of yourself and your life.

I can understand what you're saying about it being my choice to stay miserable in my Rats' Den or move into my Palace and I am really putting the new ways into practise, but I really feel blocked from really engaging with them. I don't know why it's so hard for me when I truly want to live well.

It may well be that your block comes from negative inner core beliefs that keep pulling you back when you're trying to move forward. This is a time to sit quietly, relax as deeply as you can and ask yourself *what it is you need to know*. If you come from a core belief that says you're worthless or inferior or can't have, that belief will always keep you fundamentally stuck. Similarly, how can you allow yourself to move into your Palace if you feel unworthy of living there, or don't feel it's safe to move from where you are, or that you don't matter?

Observe what's happening in your life and ponder the deeper underlying reason. For example, if you find it difficult being in a group scenario, what is at the core of that? Maybe you feel other people don't like you because essentially you believe you 'don't belong' or are 'too much' or 'not good enough'. Or if you are incredibly loving and giving to others but find it's not reciprocated, or feel profoundly sad at your inability to thrive in life, it may be you essentially feel you're not loved and then keep on attracting situations that reflect that, no matter how hard you try. As you discover such things you can write a Dissolving Resistance script, or use The Two Islands visualisation to shift from the old falsehood to the new truth. I'd also recommend the 'Severance from Negative Feelings' visualisation on my CD 'Free To Be'.

The main focus however still needs to be on what you do want! Mending the broken path you're on isn't the answer. Ask a Miracle question "If I was going to get past all my blocks, what's the first thing that would be different?" "What would I allow myself to have or be or do?" Maybe your answer would be that you'd allow yourself to spend just a bit more time in your Palace today than yesterday! You always have the final say; choose thoughts that make you feel a little bit better rather than a little bit worse. If a block comes up, tune into it and lovingly release it.

Look at the bigger picture of what you want, accept 'core beliefs' have stopped you having it up till now and work on Loving Yourself. You were born lovable, worthy and perfectly good enough so choose to hone into your birthright and live from that space. Imagine you have every good belief you could possibly have and live as though that were true. Then guess what? It will become true!

Create some mantras to have revolving around your mind all day every day. For example, "I go beyond my false conditioning" "I joyfully create my own new set of beliefs about myself and my life that I do want" "Life supports me and I flow with the River of Life". With enough attention these will replace old false beliefs.

I really believe I've worked on myself well and for a long time and though I feel so much better I still don't seem to be able to 'let in' the life I want. I have a relationship but not my ideal one, I'm earning but not comfortably, I have friends but not the social circle I'd like etc. How can I address this?

I appreciate there are times we can think "Universe – give me a break!"

It is possible you too have very deep 'blueprint' beliefs that are holding you back and limiting the good you allow yourself to have. Sit quietly and tune into your inner wise self and examine what beliefs and patterns you have that are in your way. Beliefs such as "Life is hard" "Life doesn't support me" "Life is sad and lonely" "I'm not allowed to have/don't have" "I'm not loved" etc are immensely damaging blocks to thriving in life. These core beliefs keep us apart from what we want. For example, if you believe 'life is hard' then no matter how much effort you put in to make life good, you will experience a hard life because that is the core vibrational space you are coming from. Relax into your inner self, focus on something you want and then gently ask "Why can't I have this?" and see what answer comes up. This will be your block.

Work on releasing negative beliefs by writing a Dissolving Resistance script (see pages 96/99), using The Two Islands visualisation (page 111). You could also use the 'Severance of Negative Feelings' track on the CD 'Free To Be' (see Recommended Listening) to talk with your Inner Child in depth at all ages from about 2 or 3 upwards and feel what beliefs they are carrying which prevent you receiving all your good. Release those unwanted beliefs and focus on the beliefs you do want to adopt instead.

Your question is very much focused on what is missing from your life. Remember that feeling the *absence* of what you want rather than the *havingness* of what you want, will keep the distance between where you are and what you want, because the absence is what you are observing and is therefore where your vibrational energy is flowing from – your Rats' Den rather than your Palace. Impatience, or a fear of these things not manifesting, puts you back with the Rats too and need releasing and Switching.

It may be that you are not making way for what you really want to have come to you. How can you let in a new relationship if you are staying in an unsatisfying one? What if you were honest with your partner and let her go so that she can find a relationship with her true match too. If you're earning but not comfortably, what could change that scenario? Maybe you need to get a different job. How can you let in new friends if you keep mixing with the same ones? Start to see them less and go places or join groups where like-minded people are likely to be. Open up the space for the Universe to deliver what you truly want!

Know what you want clearly and specifically. A vision board can be an enormous benefit here to help you expand your consciousness and 'vibration' to higher frequencies which in turn allows more good in. Know *why* you want what you want; ask yourself "For what purpose" to help you get clarity. Find pictures to encapsulate your desires. Add sentences, worded in such a way as if they had already manifested (e.g. 'I love being with my true soulmate who......... and with whom I feel so alive') and put the relevant words with each picture. As you look at the images and read the words, feel them like they're real now and feel trust and believe these are coming to you in the perfect time and space.

Focus on your Life Grid to expand your life quality. Keep aligning the 5 Palace Components and enjoying your journey. Accept life as it is, embrace it and work on Loving Yourself to automatically create an evermore exciting and rewarding pathway ahead, aligned with your own integrity, enjoying every minute as you move forward. Loving Yourself feels good regardless of what has manifested for you at any given time and connects you with those highest frequencies to allow in more of your good. Win win! Have your main goal be to feel *joy* each and every day just because you're alive!

THIS IS YOUR LIFE!

Recommended Resources

Demi Schneider
Depression Busting Courses
www.depressionbustingcourses.com

Louise Hay
www.louisehay.com
www.healyourlife.com/daily-affimations

Deepak Chopra
www.deepakchopra.com

Neale Donald Walsch
www.nealedonaldwalsch.com

Katherine Woodward Thomas
Calling In The One: 7 week online course
www.callingintheone.com
(There is a very helpful Identity Matrix in session
3 to identify and address core negatives)

Dr. Ritamarie Loscalzo – MS DC CCN DACBN
The Women's Fatigue and
Vibrant Health Mentor
www.drritamarie.com

Recommended Listening

Demi Schneider
Free To Be
Available through www.demischneider.com

These 4 tracks are the perfect addition to the free audio download/CDs that accompany "Beat Your Depression For Good". Offering deeper disconnection from the past and re-connection with your true self now, they inspire you to move forward confidently.

Severance from Negative Self Feelings 23:08
This specially designed visualisation enables you to safely, powerfully and beautifully free yourself from negatives that you learned and experienced in earlier years.

The Vase 6:52
Expand your consciousness to receive your good with this short, easily remembered imagery, which you can hold in your mind all day as an attracting force.

The Village 10:26
Allow yourself a few minutes to take time out, relax and listen to a story to stimulate your inner resources and regain positive focus.

Relaxation 19:18
A day time visualisation to feel relaxed, rejuvenated and revitalised through visiting your own special 'happy place', connecting with that space of peace within, enhancing your wellbeing and good feelings.

Demi Schneider
White Light and Relaxation
Available through www.demischneider.com

This CD offers the beautiful background music from 2 of the tracks on the "Beat Your Depression For Good" free audio download/CD's, to allow you to do the visualisations without guidance or to do your own visualisations and meditations.

White Light Treatment Music **34:00**

Relaxation for Sleep Music **34:00**

Demi Schneider
Stress Relief and Self Recognition
Available through www.demischneider.com

These beautiful and powerful tracks enable you to relax and experience peace and calm whilst reinforcing positive messages into your mind on a deeper level to support positive change and positive self-feelings.

Stress Relief **25:06**
Feel yourself in a space of peace and tranquility being guided to drift in a boat on a beautiful lake, surrounded by mountains, becoming at one with yourself and life, resting in gentle music that helps clear your mind and calm emotions.

Self Recognition **32:36**
Release unwanted feelings and move into a space of empowerment and strength, whilst sinking into the deeply relaxing music that can help lift your spirit and open you to a feeling of joy and expansion.

Demi Schneider
Self Feelings and New Direction
Available through www.demischneider.com

These powerful and effective tracks enable you to relax whilst introducing positive messages into your mind to access your own intuition and inner guidance toward positive change.

Self Feelings 28:47
Experience reconnection to your own innate strength from which to grow more positive self-feelings to empower you, expanding your consciousness with the long sustained harmonies that lift you increasingly higher.

New Direction 27:57
Sink into the wisdom and be enveloped with positive messages to access your own ability and resourcefulness to move forward with clarity, with expressive music to enhance your wellbeing.

Louise Hay
Forgiveness/Inner Child

Inner Child
Meet your Inner Child, i.e. 'you' at your younger ages, and love them! How can we be whole when we are rejecting any part of ourselves?

Forgiveness
This beautiful imagery enables you to rid yourself of all past negative experiences and forgive all those who have harmed you, safely and completely.

Relaxation Music for your own Meditations:

Relaxation For Sleep and
White Light Treatment
(see Recommended Listening)

The Fairy Ring - Mike Rowland

Music for Healing - Stephen Rhodes

Music by Thaddeus - www.orindaben.com

Recommended Reading

You Can Heal Your Life
Louise Hay

Life!
Louise Hay

Heal Your Body
Louise Hay

Feel the Fear and Do It Anyway
Susan Jeffers

Stand Up For Your Life
Cheryl Richardson

Cutting the Ties That Bind
Phyllis Krystal

The Soulmate Secret
Arielle Ford

Lightning Source UK Ltd.
Milton Keynes UK
UKHW042252261021
392864UK00013B/50